Labour Laws in India

Labour Laws in India

A New Perspective

R.K.A. Subrahmanya

SHIPRA

Rs. 850.00 US $ 42.50

ISBN: 978-81-7541-695-6

First Published in India in 2013

Labour Laws in India : A New Perspective

Published by:
SHIPRA PUBLICATIONS
H.O.: LG 18-19, Pankaj Central Market, Patparganj,
Delhi-110092, Tel: 91-11-2223 5152, 2223 6152
Br.Off.: 4617/18, Ansari Road, Darya Ganj,
New Delhi-110002, Tel: 9650028065, 9810522367
E-mail: info@shiprapublications.com
www.shiprapublications.com

Foreword

Octogenarian, Mr. R.K.A. Subrahmanya, has done a great favour by distilling his experience of nearly three and a half decades to compile his essays and lectures on various Labour Issues which are of interest to all the social partners.

India has a plethora of Labour Laws. In fact we are a country with too many laws and the subject of labour is no exception. Many of our Labour Laws have drawn inspiration from the International Conventions of the ILO. Even our Constitution has a large number of Articles and it has been amended with regular periodicity. Labour being a concurrent subject, the Centre as well as the States have been legislating on the subject with regular frequency. It has become difficult even to a diligent student of the subject to fathom the complexities of these laws. Hence, there is an urgent need for simplification, rationalization and codification of Labour Laws. Accordingly, sincere efforts were made in this direction culminating in the formation of the Indian Labour Code in 1994. The second National Labour Commission in its report had also highlighted the urgency for simplifying our laws. But it is easier said than done, as it requires a fair amount of consensus amongst the tripartite partners, viz., government, labour and the employers.

Mr. Subrahmanya has painstakingly covered the issues relating to Industrial Relations, Trade Unions and Worker Participation in Management. He has specialized in the field of wages, wage policy and labour welfare. He has been the Secretary General of the Social Security Association of India for long. The chapters on wage policy, minimum wages, labour welfare and legislation for unorganised workers give us an insight into the depth of knowledge which he has in these fields. I have tried to touch upon only a few subjects which he has covered. There is hardly any subject connected to the field of labour which Mr. Subrahmanya has not covered.

I read this book with great interest. It is written in a simple lucid language bereft of technical jargons. Reading Mr. Subrahmanya's book has been an educative and enjoyable experience for me. I am persuaded that a wide readership would replicate my experience. The book is useful to the labour administrators, labour law practitioners, trade unions, workers and also to the employers.

New Delhi
17.01.2013

Dr. P.D. Shenoy
Former Secretary to Govt. of India
Ministry of Labour and Employment

Preface

I joined the Union Ministry of Labour in the year 1979 on deputation from the Indian Audit Department. Since then I have developed interest in labour laws. While in the Ministry I was associated with several proposals for enactment of new laws as well as amendment of existing laws. Post retirement I initiated a research project called Simplification, Rationalisation and Consolidation of Labour Laws under the auspices of the National Labour Law Association for which I was appointed Coordinator. The Project gave me the opportunity to review all the labour laws under the expert direction of a Committee headed by Justice D.A. Desai. Eventually it ended with the production of a book called Indian Labour Code, (draft) 1994. Subsequently I was invited to contribute two volumes to the Halsbury's Laws of India on Law of Employment. With this kind of experience I have been writing papers and giving lectures on various aspects of labour laws. As I am getting old it occurred to me to compile these papers and to have them published for the benefit of the public. I have therefore decided to release them in the form of this book. I hope that the book will be received by the Public with goodwill.

Srimathi Vasantha Radhakrishnan prepared material for publication. I am thankful to her.

R.KA. Subrahmanya
Bangalore

Contents

I
Labour Laws in India

The term labour law is a generic expression. It is synonymous with the law of employment in so far as it seeks to regulate employment, conditions of service including wages, conditions of work, health, safety, work environment, welfare, social security, settlement of disputes and other related matters. It confers certain rights on the workers and certain obligations on the employers and to a certain extent, on the Governments as well.

There are a large number of labour laws in India and there is a feeling that they are much too large in number and that labour is over protected and pampered at the expense of the industry.

There is no doubt that the number of laws is quite large. Under the Indian Constitution labour is a concurrent subject. The Central government as well as the State governments can legislate on the subject. Accordingly the Governments at all levels have enacted laws concerning labour.

It cannot however be stated that these laws provide excessive protection to workers because : firstly, the scope of these laws is vey much limited to specified industries, employment and or classes of establishments of specified size and are applicable mainly to the working class. Although the scope of these laws has gradually been extended to more and more industries, classes of establishments and activities, including agriculture, cottage and village industries, the self employed as well as the administrative and supervisory staff, the labour laws in India are still in an early stage of development as compared to those in the developed industrialised countries where the bodies of law originally intended for the protection of the working class have gradually been transformed into broader welfare legislation and with the gradual extension of the laws to the self employed, the scope of the laws has gone beyond employment relationship and covers a much wider ground aimed at improving the living and working conditions of all disadvantaged groups who need protection. Secondly, the laws and practices in India also fall short of the various international standards set by the International Labour Organisation and the United Nations so much so that the Government have not been able to ratify most of the International Conventions and Recommendations.

The labour laws seek to regulate employment, conditions of service including wages, conditions of work, safety, health and work environment, social security and welfare, labour relations and other related matters. They are called as labour laws or as industrial laws but are essentially laws relating to employment. Employment may be in Government or outside Government. Services under the Union and the States are regulated by law or rules framed under Art. 309 of the Constitution. Employment of labour and other classes of personnel outside Government are regulated by laws framed under other the relevant entries in the Seventh schedule of the Constitution of India.

The origin and growth of labour legislation in India is ascribed to the development of organized industry where considerable number of men women and children are employed under conditions detrimental to their health, safety and welfare and it has become a duty of the State to enact measures to control the working, and in some cases even their living, conditions of the workers and to mediate or arbitrate in their relations with employers whenever necessary.

The first labour laws were enacted more in the interests of the employers than the workers to regulate employment of labour under the indenture system and penal sanctions. These were the Bengal Regulation of 1806 and the Indian Emigrant Act of 1837. The Bengal Regulation which legalized forced labour and made breach of contract a criminal offence was eventually abolished. The Indian Emigrant Act 1837 which provided for recruitment of Indian labour for employment in British Colonies for replacement of slave labour under the indenture system was replaced by the Indian Emigration Act, 1922. The origin of labour legislation as a measure to protect labour is traced back to 1881 when the first Factories Act was passed to regulate employment of labour under civil contract. Since then many more laws have been enacted.

Many of the labour laws have been enacted by Parliament but the State Legislatures have carried out local amendments to those laws for application within their respective territories. There are also some State laws such as the Bombay Industrial Relations Act, 1946 (Bombay Act No XI of 1947), Karnataka Shops and Establishments Act 1961 and the

Tamilnadu Manual Workers (Regulation of Employment and Conditions of Work) Act, 1982.

The laws enacted by Parliament are broadly of two types: those concerning certain specific classes of establishments, industries, employments or workers such as Factories Act,, 1948, Plantations Labour Act, 1951, Mines Act, 1952, Beedi and Cigar Workers (Conditions of Employment) Act, 1966 etc., and those concerning certain aspects of the law which are of general application such as the Minimum Wages Act, 1948.

These laws may also be classified on a different basis into two groups as regulatory and administrative. Regulatory laws are those which lay down the ground rules which the employers are expected to observe in their relationship with their employees or workmen, e.g., Minimum Wages Act, 1948. Administrative laws are those which have been enacted for administration of a welfare or other programme such as the Employees State Insurance Act, 1948. In the former case the responsibility for implementation of the laws rests on the employers and the function of the Government is to enforce the laws. In the latter case the responsibility for implementation of the laws rests on the Government itself or on an agency of the Government created for the purpose which is also responsible for their enforcement.

A major characteristic of the laws is that application of the laws is generally restricted in various ways.

The Minimum Wages Act is applicable to the employments listed in the schedule to the Act. The EPF Act is applicable to the industries and employments listed in the schedule to the Act. The ESI Act is also applicable to certain specified classes of establishments. The WC Act, the Maternity Benefit Act, the Payment of Gratuity Act and the payment of Bonus Act are applicable to those classes of establishments listed in the Schedules thereto.

Some Acts specify certain threshold limits for application of the laws with reference to the number of employees employed. In some cases there is provision for extension of the scope of the Acts to smaller establishments.

There are wage ceilings for application of some of the laws.

The basic reason for the limitation of the application of the laws is the widely varying economic conditions obtaining in the country, reflected in lack of continuity of employment, low rates of income and allied phenomena.

One of the criteria in framing a law or expanding the scope of a law is its enforceability. The question of enforceability has two dimensions :

one is the ability of the target population to honour the requirement of the laws and the other is the capacity of the administrative machinery to enforce the law; there is also a third dimension, that is the respect for law.

Multiplicity of Laws and their Consolidation

There are widespread comments on the multiplicity of the laws and a demand for their consolidation. The question is whether in the circumstances obtaining in the country it is practicable to have uniformity of the laws.

Uniformity can be brought about in two ways. One is to have a comprehensive law in the form of a Labour Code covering every aspect of labour management relations as has been done in countries like the Philippines. The other is to have uniformity in respect of each separate law among the Centre and the States. We could also consider integration or consolidation of several laws which are interrelated, e.g., we could have one law for industrial relations, one law for wages, one for social security, working conditions, health and safety, etc. Or we could aim at uniformity in the administration of, say, the Minimum Wages Act throughout the country; or again we could consolidate all the laws relating to social security into one law; that is, we can put together the ESI Act, the EPF Act, Coal Mines Provident Fund Act, Seamen's PF Act, Assam Tea Plantations Act, the Maternity Benefit Act, the WC Act, the Gratuity Act, etc.

All these ideas are very attractive.

Let us consider the various possibilities in practical terms. What does the comprehensive labour law mean? It means that the terms used will be common, coverage will be common, system of administration will be common, the judiciary will be common. In other words the law would have to be applicable to all types of economic activity or certain types of activity will have to be excluded from the protection of all types of law which they are now enjoying. For example, the arrangements for settlement of disputes, the system of collective bargaining and the laws relating to bonus, etc. would have to be extended to agriculture, or some of these activities will have to be excluded totally from the purview of the law or the law will have to have a series of schedules indicating what provisions will be applicable to which activities. Would such a uniformity be possible in a Federal State like India ? If such a uniformity were to be achieved either there should be uniformity on all aspects of labour administration among the Centre and all the States and all sections of people, or labour should be come a central subject. It would seem that in bringing about uniformity of this nature it would be necessary to make structural changes in our constitutional set up. This does not seem to be in the realm of possibility in the near future

Assuming therefore that consolidation of all laws is not practicable, let us consider the second possibility of having uniformity in respect of each separate law between the Centre and the States. The idea of having a Central law on a concurrent subject is to ensure a measure of uniformity in its application. Even so, it may not be possible to have absolute uniformity. While there is a Central law the States are allowed to make modifications therein so long as they are not repugnant to the general principles governing the law. For example, while the Central Government has enacted the Minimum Wages Act, the States are allowed to carry out their own amendments to it in response to local needs In this context the question is whether such variations are desirable or not. Variations exist, firstly, in the list of employments included in the Schedule to the Act, in the methods adopted for fixation or revision of minimum wages, in the rates of wages prescribed and in the arrangements for enforcement of the minimum wages.

The Study Group on Wages Income and Prices headed by Mr Bhootalingam had recommended introduction of a national minimum wage at ₹100 to be raised to Rs 150 eventually. Today the rates of minimum wages for unskilled workers vary widely ranging from ₹ 66 in Tripura to ₹ 322 in Kerala (Annual Report: Union Ministry of Labour.) If we have to introduce a national minimum wage, at what level would it be, at the lowest level of ₹66 or at the highest level of ₹322 or at an intermediate level of, say, ₹160? What would be the consequence of having such a uniform rate of wage? If we have a national minimum wage at ₹ 66, all those having higher wages would have to bring it down to that level or they will have to be allowed to continue the existing rate until the national minimum wage is raised above these levels. If we have a national minimum wage at ₹ 322, all those having lower rates of wages will have to raise them to that level. This makes nonsense of the entire procedure of fixation of minimum wages, the essential ingredient of which is consultation with workers and employers. Would all employers all over the country be willing to pay such a wage?

Let us consider the third possibility of consolidating groups of laws. In the past, several attempts have been made to integrate the various social security measures and it has not been found practicable.

The Second National Commission on Labour had recommended

consolidation of the laws group-wise but these recommendations have also been shelved.

The impediments in the way of integration of the laws are that their coverage has not been uniform and it has not been possible to bring about uniformity in their coverage. For, coverage of the ESI Act is limited by non availability of adequate medical facilities for providing medical care to the insured persons according to prescribed norms. Construction of hospitals and dispensaries has not been keeping pace with the growth of insured population. For example, in Delhi while the medical facilities exist for certain number of insured persons, the number of insured persons within the sectors of employment to which the ESI Scheme has been extended in that territory has increased manifold. The attempts made by the Corporation to put up greater number of hospitals and dispensaries have not been successful so far owing to difficulties in getting land and other requisites. In the circumstances while the EPF Act covers over 60 million workers the ESI covers less 15 million.

It would be seen that the major obstacle to uniformity among the labour laws is the difficulty in bringing about uniformity in coverage. There can be no doubt that workers would welcome the extension of all laws to all types of economic activity without any limitation as to number of persons employed or the wage ceilings. Government would equally be happy to extend them. But would the employers be prepared for such extension? If there cannot be uniformity on the basis of universal coverage what other basis can we evolve acceptable to all sections of the society?

Unfortunately uniformity in labour legislation has another dimension which concerns Centre –State relations. The employers are of the view that the concurrent jurisdiction of Central and States in the field of labour has led to passing of separate legislations by the States Governments creating problems for the management. This view calls for some analysis with reference to specific laws for a better appreciation of the situation.

Labour being a concurrent subject it is certainly true that both the Centre and States can legislate on the subject. The question is whether it has created any major problem for management or labour and if so how the problems can be solved.

As stated earlier, there are different classes of laws: Central laws, State laws, Central laws administered by States wholly or partly. It seems there would be no overlapping of functions in so far as the first two classes of laws are concerned except that in the case of companies having branches or units in different states, different State laws can create difficulties. In the latter case the position of a company would be analogous to that of a multinational company operating in different countries. It is doubtful if such difficulties can ever be resolved so long as India remains a federal state and labour continues to be in the Concurrent list. At the same time it may not be feasible take labour out of the Concurrent List and put in the Union list; that would be contrary to the current trends towards greater devolution of powers to States. The only way to resolve this type of difficulty is to make submission to State authorities at appropriate times through State tripartite advisory bodies, if any, and effective intervention in State legislatures.

As regards those subjects on which there are Central laws and the States who wish to have their own laws the position is slightly different. In such cases, the States cannot enact the laws without the approval of the Central government. Consultations between the Central and State Governments do take place at various stages and very often Presidential assent is withheld or the State Government is required to modify their proposals. In such cases diversity of views may be resolved by discussion, and if the differences persist one may have recourse to the Courts.

Administration of the Laws

So much about enactment of new laws, what about the implementation of the laws?

Administration of labour laws has aspects other than the question of bringing about uniformity. Mainly it involves the question of the form of machinery to be created for administration of the laws, its strength and composition, its competence, its powers and responsibilities. The form of machinery to be created for administration of the laws depends upon the nature of the law. Regulatory laws would require machinery for inspection, settlement of disputes by conciliation, adjudication or arbitration and for imposition of penalties for their contravention. Laws meant to provide certain types of benefits would require a machinery for collection of contributions and administration of benefits to be provided, the rates or scale of benefits to be provided, the rates or scale of contribution to be collected, collection of contributions, dealing with defaults and administration of the benefits, such as, medical benefit, sickness benefit, disability benefit, dependants benefit, etc., under the ESI Act. Laws meant for providing service to the workers would require altogether a different form of administration.

While talking about administration of labour laws, it needs to be mentioned that there are cases where the responsibility for administration of programmes is shared by the Central Government or its agencies and the State governments as in the case of the Medical Benefit under the ESI Scheme. Such division of responsibilities is not conducive to effective administration.

Whatever be the nature of the law, the administrative machinery in India is burdened with the numbers involved. To provide administrative machinery, adequate to provide satisfaction to the growing number of workers covered by the laws, is a major concern of the Governments at the Centre as well as the States. The difficulty is compounded by the tendency on the part of several people to evade or avoid the law by any means, fair or foul.

There is a general feeling that while we have several laws, they are merely on paper. This feeling has been generated by the extensive violation of the laws and inadequacy of the administrative machinery to enforce them. Violation of the laws could be deliberate or due to ignorance; it could also be due to genuine difficulties. In any case, the machinery will have to be extremely alert and forceful. At the same time it has to be imaginative and constructive in its approach. No social law can be administered mechanically. There has to be a human touch. Unfortunately, in the social milieu in which we are working, any softness on the part of the law enforcement machinery is apt to be viewed with suspicion. It calls for the highest degree of integrity and rectitude on the part of the officials to be able to act with courage according to their convictions.

Administration of the social laws, particularly the beneficial laws requires that the administration concerned should be infused with the social purpose. They should realize that before every application for a benefit, there is a human being in dire need of sympathy, understanding and assistance. But it is too much to expect that all the persons engaged in this activity will be imbued with this kind of spirit.

No administrative machinery will ever be found to be adequate to administer the laws as a police operation so as to detect and to punish every single instance of violation and to ensure that every single person who is entitled to the benefit under the law derives that benefit. Implementation of laws depends to a large extent on the goodwill of the employers. In my humble opinion labour laws should be self enforcing. The enforcement machinery should only exercise a random check and when it does so the punishment for infractions of law should be exemplary and highly deterrent. Such an arrangement can succeed only where people are generally law abiding. The organisation of employers can render useful service to its members as well as the society by inculcating among their members the respect for law and adopting measures for self discipline.

On the other hand, the workers also need to be educated to play their due role in society. Workers education therefore plays a crucial part in the system of administration of labour laws. It is important that they should know their rights and their duties, the nature and problem of economic activity they are engaged in, the value of increasing productivity, the means of increasing it and how they can benefit from it; how they will suffer if there is continual increase in the wage cost without corresponding increase in productivity. Much of the labour problems can be attributed to the fact that the trade union movement is generally in the hands of professional trade unionists. It is necessary for the health of the movement that they should in due course be replaced by leaders thrown up from within the industry/ organization who have worked in it and know the strength as well as the weaknesses thereof and are able better to appreciate their problems and negotiate from the position of strength derived from knowledge.

Administration of labour laws has also another aspect relating to manning of the labour department and the organizations working there under and their training. There is a general feeling that the State labour Departments are very weak and are not well staffed. Obviously, the enforcement machinery of the Departments of Labour as well as the adjudication machinery needs to be strengthened. The working conditions of the officers and staff of the Departments of Labour in the States are not comparable with those of Central government staff. These differences can only be resolved if there is a National Wage Policy. The National Tripartite Conference held few years ago recommended that a committee should be appointed to evolve a National Wage Policy and this recommendation has been under consideration of government for long.

The weakness in the Labour Department in the States as well as at the Centre lies in the growing numbers they have to handle. The major problem of labour administration is the problem of numbers. As the strength of the labour force, the number of trade union organizations, the number of members of the Provident Funds, the number of insured persons and other related numbers grow the number of persons employed for the administration of the Department also needs to grow. More important is the training of the staff employed in the Department. They need firstly to know the laws, rules and procedures. Since they will be dealing with men they also need to be acquainted with the behavioural sciences. They should be infused with the sense of service. Training for management of business or industry would be different from the training for management of social services. The training system would need to be suitably oriented.

Some of the staff employed in the Department of Labour will be involved in educational training of workers and in research. Workers education is not everybody's cup of tea. It calls for special training; the methods and techniques of workers education need to be developed. Research in the field of labour also requires special training.

One cannot remain content with the introduction of new programmes for the welfare of workers. We have to build up a monitoring system to see how the programmes are being executed and arrange for periodical evaluation of the programmes.[1]

NOTES

1 Speech delivered at the ILO/CIE Programme for Excecutives of Empolyers Assocations on Oct 28, 1983.

II
Rationale of Labour Laws

India is a developing country embarked on a process of development. The objectives of its development plans are both economic and social; they include growth, modernization, self reliance and social justice.

Social justice is said to be the signature tune of the Indian Constitution. The state is committed to bring about social justice along with economic self reliance. How does one bring about social justice?

India has a large population of which nearly 30 per cent are said to be living below the poverty line. While the country is progressing economically there is an apprehension that the gap between the haves and the have-nots has been growing. It is said that the rich are becoming richer and the poor poorer. Inequality of incomes and wealth is growing. Why is it so?

Such inequalities are inherent in the capitalist mode of production we have adopted. It is to be distinguished from the communist or cooperative mode of production and subsistence mode of production.

In a capitalist mode of production the owner of capital is separate from the worker and their interests are in conflict. The capitalist aims at maximization of profit by minimization of cost. Wages paid to workers are an element of cost. He therefore seeks to minimize it, hence the disparity in income. A State committed to social justice tries to narrow down the difference. This is done partly through fiscal measures and partly through labour laws.

Labour laws seek to ensure to the workers and their families minimum wages, safe and healthy conditions of work, security against various risks and contingencies, namely, sickness, oldage, death of the breadwinner, etc. They protect the workers against exploitation.

Those of us who are in the position of employing labour should realize this. In the interest of getting the work done economically we deny the workers what is rightfully due to them. We blame labour for organizing themselves and making demands and stopping work when the demands are not met. Work stoppage is certainly bad. It should be avoided. But we should not deprive the workers of their rights.

When we talk of workers' rights we are apt to think in terms of "we" and "they". We should not forget that we are not different from them. In a sense we are also workers holding different positions. The workers' rights are also our rights. Viewed in this light we will be able to better appreciate the significance of these rights.

Government employees are assured of their rights without their having to ask for them. One is therefore apt to take them for granted. One realizes the value of these rights only when one is deprived of them (Government employees are now deprived of the right to pension which was till recently regarded as a property).

What are these rights?

First is the freedom of association. Frequently we hear of a strike by the employees of one Government or the other. A strike would not be possible but for the freedom the employees enjoyed to form or to join an Association of their choice. Freedom of Association is regarded as one of the most fundamental rights of man. Although Government servants are not allowed the right to form trade unions they can form associations. The associations cannot function in the same way as trade unions. There is an international convention concerning Freedom of Association which India has not ratified primarily because of the restrictions on the public servants to form trade unions and the Government has come in for criticism on this score.

While there is restriction on the Government servants to form unions there is no such restriction on other workers. Yet the percentage of workers who have formed or joined trade unions is comparatively small. This is because of their ignorance and lack of education. It should be expected that, by and by, more workers will get unionized and it is to be welcomed and not to be despised. The country will gain by solidarity among workers and not by their disparateness.

When a person has a grievance he first makes a representation or a complaint. When it is not heeded he resorts to strike. Right to strike is said to be inherent in the right to freedom of association and is regarded as a basic right of trade unions. (Supreme Court has since ruled that the workers have no such right).

All government servants have job security. There is no danger of their services being terminated before they attain the age of superannuation in the normal course. If you have to terminate the services of a Government servant for misconduct or otherwise you have to follow an elabourate procedure designed for protecting employment. Such protection is lacking among other workers. Witness the closure of a large number of textile mills which threw out of employment over 50,000 workers. Is such a thing possible in government? Has any public enterprise closed down in living memory? What happens when a person is thrown out of employment. He starves to death unless there is some alternative arrangement to provide him the means of livelihood. Many countries have unemployment insurance scheme. We do not have one. There is a demand for introducing such a scheme. But there is provision for payment of retrenchment compensation and gratuity These are meant to help the workers subsist when they have no employment.

What happens when a person falls ill and cannot go to work. A Government servant applies for leave and he is paid leave salary for the period of illness. He is given medical treatment at government expense. What happens to an industrial worker?. There is no provision in the law for leave salary on medical grounds. Instead the employers as well as workers are required to pay contributions to the ESIC which gives them medical benefit and sickness benefit under a social insurance scheme. This is social security. This is again a basic human right.

Like this there are many other rights which go by the name of social rights.

The idea that man has certain rights dates back to Greek history, before Christ. But then human rights meant only civil and political rights. The fact that man has certain social and economic rights came to be recognized much later. that is, only in the 18th century. They were given expression first in the American Declaration of Independence and the French Declaration of the Rights of Man. The French Constitution of 1793 declared that "Public assistance is a sacred duty. Society owes subsistence to unfortunate citizens either by procuring them work or by ensuring those who are unable to work the means of existence". This is the origin of the concept of social security.

All this also happened at the time of the Industrial Revolution which witnessed exploitation of man by man on a large scale. It gave birth to social legislation. Protective measures took shape gradually in one country after the other.

The development of labour laws involved the recognition of social rights. The laws did not confer any benefits but gave expression to the social rights of man and sought to protect and uphold them. In 1917 the constitution of Mexico contained provisions recognizing the economic and social rights and laid down rules to regulate hours of work, wages, safety and health, trade union rights and other matters. Two years later Weimar Republic of Germany also made similar enumeration of economic and social rights. Subsequently many other Constitutions, including the Constitution of India, have followed suit.

Passage of labour legislation imposing strict conditions regarding employment of labour gave rise to fear that the countries having such legislation would lose their comparative advantage in trade if the other countries did not have similar laws. Need was therefore felt for international regulation of labour conditions. The Treaty of Versailles at the conclusion of the First World War contained a workers' clause which provided that the members of the League of Nations would endeavour to secure and maintain fair and humane conditions of labour for men, women and children and for that purpose would establish and maintain an international organization. Accordingly, the International Labour Organization (ILO) came into being. The preamble to the Constitution of the ILO set out the objectives of the Organisation. Subsequently, in 1944, at the International Conference held in Philadelphia, the ILO adopted a declaration of Aims and Objects. The main objective of the ILO was stated to be to set international labour standards. These standards are in the form of Conventions and Recommendations. They are in the nature of international law in the field of labour. All the member countries are expected to follow them Conventions are binding on the ratifying countries. Recommendations are recommendatory as the very term signifies. The ILO has adopted a very large number of Conventions and Recommendations reflecting the social rights of man.

In 1945, the UNO came into being. One of the objects of the UNO is to promote:

(i) higher standards of living, full employment and conditions of economic and social progress and development
(ii) solutions to international economic social and health related problems
(iii) universal respect for and observance of human rights and fundamental freedoms for all without distinction as to race sex etc

An explicit declaration of these rights came three years later in the form of the Universal Declaration of Human Rights.

In the sphere of law a distinction is made between natural law and positive law. The natural law is a moral principle. It is usually an unwritten law said to be inherent in the human or world situation.

We in India believe in *Dharma* which rules the world. It governs the relationship between man and man, between man and the world. Greeks called it natural law. Romans too believed in it. Cicero, the famous writer said, "There is true law, a right reason, in accordance with nature; it applies to all men; it is unalienable and eternal". At one time this law was considered to be the law imposed by the gods. It is now expressed in secular terms as 'Natural Law'. The concept of human rights is derived from the concept of the natural law.

A natural law is expected to be observed by everyone. It is not meant to be enforced. If it is to be enforced it should become a positive law. A natural law becomes a positive law when incorporated in the Constitution or in a law enacted by the legislature. The Universal Declaration of Human Rights was only in the nature an affirmation. It was not enforceable. In order to make the rights enforceable it became necessary to incorporate them in a covenant or a treaty. The UN adopted two such Covenants: the International Covenant of Civic and Political Rights; and the International Covenant of Social Economic and Cultural Rights.

International Covenants and Conventions cannot be enforced within a State unless they are a ratified by the respective legislatures. A State legislature cannot ratify a Covenant or a Convention unless the laws enacted by it conform to its provisions. Being a member of the comity of nations every member country has the obligation to give effect to the commitment it makes in the international organizations while adopting the Convention/Covenants. So every country tries to incorporate the concepts in its own Constitution and enact laws for the purpose.

There are certain articles in the Constitution which give expression to the noble concepts enshrined in the Universal Declaration of Human Rights. All the labour laws have been enacted in pursuance of these constitutional provisions.

Thus the labour laws are derived from the recognition of the social rights of man as expressed in the Universal Declaration of Human Rights, International Labour Standards and the Constitution of India.

I shall try to illustrate this point.

The preamble to the constitution of the ILO says, "Whereas universal and lasting peace can be established only if it is based upon social justice".

Article 38 of the Constitution of India says that the State shall strive to promote the welfare of the people by securing and protecting as effectively as it may a social order in which justice -social economic and political- shall inform all the institutions of the national life. According to the 44th Amendment it is now further provided that in particular the State shall strive to minimize the inequalities of income.

All the labour laws are intended to promote social justice by ensuring equitable remuneration for the work one does, equal pay for equal work, etc., and protecting the workers against exploitation.

The preamble to the Constitution of the ILO says, "And whereas conditions of labour exist involving such injustice hardship and privation to large numbers of people as to produce unrest so great that the peace and harmony of the world are imperiled; and an improvement of the conditions is urgently required; as for example, by the regulation of the hours of work, prevention of unemployment, provision of an adequate living wage, protection against sickness, disease and injury arising out of his employment, protection of children, provision for oldage and injury etc., recognition of the principle of equal remuneration for work of equal value, recognition of the principle of freedom of association etc." These objectives are elaborated in the Philadelphia Declaration concerning the Aims and Objects of the ILO.

Article 22 and 25 of the Universal Declaration expresses these concerns more specifically as follows:

- Every one has the right to social security;
- Every one has the right to work, to free choice of employment, to just and favourable conditions of work and to protection against unemployment;
- Every one has the right to equal pay for equal work;
- Every one has the right to just and favourable remuneration insuring for himself and his family an existence worthy of human dignity;
- Every one has the right to form and to just and favourable remuneration insuring for himself and his family an existence worthy of human dignity;
- Every one has the right to form and to join trade unions for the protection of his interests;
- Every one has the right to rest and leisure including reasonable limitation of working hours and periodic holidays with pay.

These concepts are again reflected in the Indian Constitution and the labour laws.

Article 41 says that the State shall within the limits of its economic capacity and development make effective provision for securing the right to work, to public assistance in cases of unemployment old-age, sickness and disablement The various employment schemes, unemployment relief schemes, the social security laws, are derived from this directive principle contained in the Constitution.

Article 42 says that the State shall make provision for securing just and humane conditions of work and for maternity relief. The Factories Act, the Mines Act, the Maternity Benefit Act can be traced to this Article.

Article 39 says that the State shall direct its policy towards securing equal pay for equal work. The Equal Remuneration Act derives authority from this Article.

Article 43 requires that the State shall endeavour to secure to all workers work, a living wage, conditions of work ensuring a decent standard of life and full enjoyment of leisure and social and cultural opportunities. The Minimum Wages Act is designed with this object in view.

Thus all the labour laws derive inspiration from the Fundamental Rights and the Directive Principles of State Policy contained in the Constitution which in turn derive inspiration from the UN Declaration and other international commitments.

In studying labour laws one should keep this perspective.

Is Labour Over Protected in India

The proposition before us is that over protection is counter-productive. It implies that the protection provided to the workers in India by legislation and Court pronouncements is excessive and it has a negative effect in the sense that it is impeding progress. To verify the validity of the proposition the first thing we have to do is to examine the nature of protection provided and to see whether it is excessive and, if so, by which standard.

Those who aver that labour is over protected in India refer to the provisions of the Industrial Disputes Act, which enables a worker to challenge a management decision regarding discharge, dismissal etc. They also refer to the provision which requires an employer to seek permission of the Government for lay off, retrenchment and closure etc. and the various Court judgments which have widened the scope of the legislative provisions.

In this connection it should be noted that the Indian Constitution under which all the laws and the judiciary operate is based on the bedrock of social justice. This implies justice to the weaker sections of the people as against the stronger sections. The essential ingredient of any system of social justice is to provide employment and to ensure a reasonable standard of living. It follows that a State committed to social justice cannot view with equanimity deprivation of employment for any reason; whether it be a case of discharge of dismissal or a case of lay off, retrenchment or closure.

It has been rightly observed in the background paper that the present system of labour management relations has been evolved out of four parallel strands of thought and action, namely, legislation, voluntarism, collective bargaining and judicial pronouncements. Of these, the idea of over-protection seems to be directed more against legislation and judicial pronouncements. Legislation represents the will of the people and the judicial pronouncements reflect the social consciousness. There is a measure of inevitability about these and there seems to be no possibility of reversing the trend.

Labour-management relationship is an element of the social structure which is continually in a state of flux. V.K.R.V. Rao says "In every living society, there is always some movement from within and some movement from without and therefore there is always some change. The combination of endogenous and exogenous forces released in India during the recent few decades combined with the development of science, technology and communications during the same period have started a chain of social changes in India that is more massive and national than anything that has been witnessed in the past". What we are witnessing today in the field of labour relations is the manifestation of the social changes that is taking place as a result of the dissatisfaction with the existing social structure. It cannot be wiped away. The business system has to adjust itself to the rising aspirations of the working people and also to the fact that power centers are shifting.

The background paper refers to our failure to imbibe 'work ethic' among the workers. It seems to me that the lack of work ethic is inherent in the modern business system. In his preface to the book "Corporate Social Policy" Robert Heilbriner has observed hollowness at the center of the modern business civilization and traces the two aspects of this civilization, namely, the tendency to substitute impersonal pecuniary values for personal non-pecuniary ones and the disregard for the value of work. He says : a business as a civilization regards work as a means to an end in itself. The end is profit, income, consumption, economic or whatever, but the fact that labour itself is regarded as nothing more than an unfortunate necessity to which we must submit to obtain this end.

These aspects have tended to alienate workers from management. It would be futile to try to imbibe the work ethic among the workers unless correspondingly there is a change in the values of the business system itself. It should be realized that material advancement by means of growth of business is not an end in itself. It should be lead to the betterment of man. The good of man is the ultimate goal and fulfillment of all economic activity; and this man is anyone who could be a producer or manager, worker or consumer. We cannot serve one man at the expense of another. The social or business system should be such as will promote the welfare of interests of all.

Business should, therefore, become human. If it does, it will be seen that what legislation or judicial pronouncements are trying to do is to give a human touch to the impersonal business decisions. I would suggest that those who consider that the protection extended by these measures is excessive might place themselves in the position of the persons who are thrown out of employment for any reason and see whether in that position one would feel it really excessive.

These measures may appear to be counter-productive in the short run for business men are apt to look at everything from the immediate point of view of how it affects their production, productivity or profits. It may look differently from a long range point of view.

No doubt, there can be no progress without order and discipline Every game has a set of rules and has to be played according to the rules. One cannot subscribe to the violation of the rules but discipline and respect for law cannot be imposed by force or fear of punishment or withdrawal of protection, for it makes the people desperate. Respect for law has to be inculcated among the workers by education, by involving them in the decision making process and making them feel as one unit. They should be made to realize that their interests and those of the employers are not antithetical and that they have common interest with the employer in the success of the business and that they will not gain anything by its desecration. Every effect should, therefore, be made to educate the workers on these lines.[1]

NOTES

1. Speech delivered at FICCI Seminar at Ahmedabad on 16.9.1983.

III
Reform of Labour Laws

An Over view

Legal improvements in the context of labour can be viewed from several points of view. I propose to view them from the system approach because the labour laws can be viewed as constituting a system; it consists of several elements namely,

(a) The labour laws and the rules proper
(b) The enforcement machinery.
(c) Penalties for their contravention.
(d) Labour judiciary.

The proposition I propose to place before you is that in framing the laws and in implementing the laws the system approach is necessary but it is lacking in India. This is because the laws have been enacted piecemeal in response to the demands of the particular time without a coherent policy objective; they represent a compromise among the conflicting interests. An overall design is lacking. The various elements of the system therefore hang loosely and desperately.

Firstly, there are several gaps in the laws. For example, the field of labour has the following aspects, namely, Employment and Training, Conditions of work, Social Security, Labour Management Relations, etc. There is no general law regarding employment or training. There are however a few laws relating to compulsory notification of vacancies to the employment exchanges and apprenticeship training, industrial employment (standing orders), employment of children etc There are also several laws relating to regulation of employment in certain specific categories of workers, namely, dock workers, cine workers, plantation workers, sales promotion employees, etc.

The major employment and training programs launched by Government are under executive orders; they are not governed by any law. There are ILO conventions concerning Employment Policy, vocational guidance and rehabilitation and Human Resources Development. There is no corresponding law in India.

Besides, there is no single responsible agency in Government for employment. The subject is distributed between Ministry of Labour, Rural Development and Planning Commission. The entire plan is employment oriented but no Ministry seems to be responsible to ensure that the plan programs do actuarially generate the anticipated volume of employment.

The coverage of the various laws is limited in various ways, with regard to the industries covered, number of persons employed in the industrial units, wages drawn, etc. There is no uniformity in these respects either.

For example, the Minimum Wages Act is applicable to employments listed in schedule thereto. The Payment of Wages Act is applicable to Industrial and other establishments as defined therein. The E.P.F. Act is applicable to industries specified in Schedule-I and other classes of establishments listed in Schedule-II thereof. The E.S.I. Act is applicable to all factories and such other establishments to which it may be made applicable.

The payment of Bonus Act and the E.P.F. Act are applicable to establishments employing twenty or more persons. The Contract Labour Act is applicable to establishments employing ten or more persons. The Inter State Migrant Workmen's Act is applicable to establishments employing 5 or more persons.

While most of the Acts contain provision for inspection there is no such provision in the Workmen's Compensation Act.

While the hours of work in factories are prescribed in the Factories Act, there is no such Central Act to regulate the hours of work in offices and other classes of establishments. It is difficult to find the rationale, if any, for the fact that while the Central Government has taken the initiative to frame certain laws like the Minimum Wages Act. Payment of wages Act, etc., it is left to the State Governments to enact laws to regulate employment and conditions of work in Shops and Establishments and each State has enacted its own laws and there is no uniformity among them.

There are a variety of arrangements for providing social security in India, which while overlapping in some respects leave wide gaps in other respects.

Secondly, there are wide variations among the laws in the definition of some of the key terms such as, industry, establishment, employer, workman, wages, child etc. There is also much ambiguity in these expressions with the result that it has given rise to litigation as to whether an establishment or a person is covered by a particular Act or not. A study of the Judgments of the High Courts and the Supreme Court relating to the Industrial Disputes Act, the E.P.F. Act, the E.S.I. Act, the Minimum Wages Act, etc., would indicate that bulk of the litigation concerns this issue. An analysis of the notifications issued by the Government of Gujarat under the Minimum Wages Act shows that there are variations in the rates of minimum wages prescribed for part-time workers, piece rates workers, apprentices and child workers from notification to notification.

Such variations among the laws have made them unnecessarily complex and the function of enforcement has become extremely onerous. The arrangements for enforcement of the laws are equally diverse. The State laws are undoubtedly administered by the respective State agencies. So far as the Central laws are concerned, some laws are administered by the Central Government itself exclusively, the administration of some laws is entrusted to the State Government exclusively; in the other cases the concept of appropriate Government has been introduced under which the Central Government is responsible for the enforcement of the laws in certain respect of certain classes of industries and establishments and the State Government in the others. While there is provision for inspection in most of the Acts there is no such provision in some Acts like the Workmen's Compensation Act.

Many laws provide for registration of establishments for the purpose of these laws, e.g., registration is required under the Factories Act, the Contract Act, the Inter State Migrant Workmen's Act, the E.P.F. Act, the E.S.I. Act, Beedi and Cigar Act, Motor Transport Workers Act, etc.

Every law provides for maintenance of a set of records, e.g., the Factories Act, the Working Journalists Act, Maternity Benefit Act, Contract Labour Act, Inter State Minimum Wages Act, and Payment of Bonus Act.

A brave man is one who can claim to know the subtle differences among the laws and the requirements of each law. Inspection is usually entrusted to low level functionaries without adequate training who are generally left to their own resources with the result that the inspections carried out by them are more often than not very ineffective.

While some laws such as the Payment of Bonus Act are linked to the I.D. Act for adjudication of claims through Labour Courts and Industrial Tribunals, the others are regarded as self-contained codes having their own arrangements for adjudication, e.g. in the Minimum Wages Act where any employee has any claim he may apply to the Authority specified in the Act who issues directions in that regard; the Authority can be a Labour Commissioner or any other officer who may be nominated for the purpose. In the Payment of Gratuity Act also a separate Controlling Authority is constituted for settlement of disputes. The claims under the Workmen's Compensation Act are to be referred to the Commissioners appointed for the purpose under the Act.

The disputes under the E.S.I. Act are required to be referred to the E.S.I. Courts. In the E.P.F. Act the officers of the E.P.F. Organization, namely, the C.P.F.C. and the RPFC. have been invested with the powers to determine the dues from the employers; they thus function in an administrative as well as quasi judicial capacity. There is no special provision in this Act for adjudication of disputes concerning the claims of the subscribers.

All the acts make provision for penalties for contravention of the provisions thereof. The penalty includes fine and/or imprisonment. Fine ranges from ₹500/- to ₹1000/- and imprisonment from 3 months to 6 months. The courts have the power to impose lower penalties. It has been the experience that the Courts invariably let off the offenders with petty fines so much so that employers find it economical to pay the fine instead of honoring their commitment under the law. There is a pressing demand for enhancing the penalties so as to make them deterrent. The Supreme Court has also come down heavily on the courts for awarding minor penalties for offences under the labour laws. It does not seem that there has been much improvement.

While the workers or their nominees can submit their claims to the Court/authority concerned directly the Acts provide that no cognizance shall be taken of an offence under any law save on a complaint made by or under the authority of the appropriate Government or by an Inspector. There is a persistent demand that this power to prosecute an offender should be given to the workers themselves or to the trade unions. This demand has not been accepted.

The I.D. Act says that an arbitrator, Court, Labour Court, Tribunal or national Tribunal shall follow such procedure as the arbitrator or other authority concerned may think fit. They have been given the powers of a Civil Court under the Code of Civil Procedure in certain matters. Every enquiry or investigation by them is deemed to be judicial proceedings within the meaning given to those terms under the Indian Penal Code. The Supreme Court has given several guidelines for the procedures and practices to be followed by Tribunals especially Industrial Tribunals. Similar provisions or guidelines do not seem to exist for the guidance of the special authorities created under the Various Acts.

There is a provision for grant of exemption in many laws, which have had the effect of weakening them. While exemptions may be justified in a few genuine cases, the provisions lend themselves to abuse.

There is a provision for constituting advisory boards in many of the labour laws. e.g., Apprentice Act, Beedi Workers Welfare Fund Act, Bonded Labour Act, Contract Labour Act, Dock Workers Act, Equal Remuneration Act, etc. Separate advisory boards have been set up under each of such laws leading to avoidable multiplicity of institutions. They could all be replaced by one Labour Advisory Board for each State and the Centre.

There is a tendency to multiply the agencies in other respects too. e.g., while the labour courts and Industrial Tribunals deal with disputes generally the Cinc Workers' Act provides for establishing separate Tribunals for the Cine Workers.

The foregoing paragraphs describe the situation of great diversity without a unity of purpose.

A review of the laws indicates that in providing protection to particular classes of workers, the generality of the workers is left without any protection thus creating pockets of privilege among the working classes.

In recent years several countries have consolidated their laws in the form of labour codes or otherwise unifying them and making them applicable to all the workers with provisions for regulating employment, wages, conditions of service, conditions of work, settlement of disputes, etc. This development suggests the need for enacting a general law covering all the workers supplemented by special laws with respect to particular classes of workers concerning their special problems. It seems to me that time has come for us to consider adopting a such a law in India.

Enactment of a Basic Law

The most significant feature of labour laws in India is their multiplicity. The Central Government as well as each of the State Governments have already enacted several laws and more laws are being enacted each year. A few years back, the Central Government brought in a new law for construction workers. Another law for agricultural workers is in the offing. There is demand for separate laws for home-based workers and other workers in the unorganized sector. Besides piecemeal proposals for the welfare of various sections of workers are also floated.

Multiplicity of laws makes the management of industry and business difficult. Enforcement of the laws also poses great difficulty. These difficulties are well known and need not be dilated upon.

The system calls for a major reform in reducing them into one basic law which lays down the general principles and minimum standards to regulate the employment and conditions of service of all categories of establishments and workers with special provisions for such classes of establishments and workers such as mines and factories in hazardous industries which may not be necessary for the general classes of establishments.

Framework of a Basic Law

The general law may lay down the principles and standards with respect to the following matters:

- Employment
- Wages
- Safety and Health
- Industrial Relations
- Social security and Welfare
- Labour Administration

The general principles, which should be applicable to these mattes, are set out below:

Employment

For purposes of employment, jobs may be classified as follows:

(i) Casual,
(ii) Temporary
(iii) Permanent

A person may be employed on a casual basis if the job does not last for more than three months.

A person may be employed on temporary basis if the job does not last longer than one year.

Every person should be appointed on a permanent basis to a post, which lasts longer than one year, initially on probation, eventually to be confirmed.

There is a distinction between the principal function and the ancillary functions of an industry/business. The management should farm out on contract the ancillary/auxiliary functions. No person may be employed for permanent jobs in respect of the principal function of the industry/business through a contractor.

Every establishment should frame a set of standing orders to regulate the conditions of service of its employees, namely:

Minimum age of entry to employment; Age of retirement/ superannuation; Hours of work; Leave and leave salary; Conduct rules; Discipline; Terminal benefits.

The appropriate Government may frame model rules setting out the minimum conditions to which the standing orders should conform. The managements would be free to improve upon them.

Training

The appropriate Government would be responsible for providing pre recruitment technical and vocational education and training and vocational guidance. The Government should associate the representatives of employers and workers through an appropriate institutional framework in planning and programming such education and training.

The employers will however be responsible for providing induction training and continuing education and training while on the job for upgrading skills continually. For this purpose, a Skill Development Fund should be set up which may be administered by a tripartite or bipartite or board or an expert body.

Hours of Work

No one shall be required to work for more for more than 8 hours a day or 48 hours a week. If a worker is required to work beyond the prescribed hours he/she will be entitled to overtime pay which shall not be less than double the ordinary rate.

The management in consultation with the trade union concerned, where it exists, shall fix the hours of work in such a way that no person will be required to work for more than four hours at a stretch before he has had an interval for rest of not less than half an hour in addition to two recesses of shorter duration and that the total period of work inclusive of the intervals for rest and recesses does not exceed 10 hours a day.

Wages

The appropriate Government shall fix a general minimum wage applicable to workers in all employments taking into consideration the relevant criteria, namely, the basic needs of the workers and the level of economic development of the State. The minimum wage shall be adjusted to the rise in the cost of living every six months by attaching a variable dearness formula or otherwise. The minimum wage shall be revised every five years coinciding with the five-year plan periods taking into account the economic growth during the period.

All wages above the minimum level will be fixed employment-wise/ industry-wise through collective bargaining taking into account the level of skills and the capacity of the industry to pay. If there is no agreement between the parties the matter will be decided by an industrial tribunal or wage board or a Labour Relations Commission.

Bonus as a deferred wage shall be paid at 12.5 per cent of the annual wages for meeting the needs of lump-sum expenditure, which may have to be incurred by the employees annually. This shall be taken into account in fixing the monthly wages. Any bonus in excess of this amount shall be related to profits or productivity.

Safety and Health

Every employer shall ensure so far as is reasonably practicable the health, safety and welfare of all employees employed by him while they are at work.

Specifically every employer shall be responsible for-

- The provision and maintenance of plant and systems of work that are safe and without risk to health;
- The arrangements in the workplace for ensuring safety and absence of risk to health in connection with the use, handling, storage and transport of articles and substances;
- The provision of such information, instruction, training and supervision as are necessary to ensure the health and safety of all employees at work;
- The maintenance of all places of work in a condition that is safe and without risk to health and the provision and maintenance of means of access to egress from such place in a condition that is safe and without risk;
- The provision, maintenance and monitoring of such work environment in the workplace which is safe without risk to health of the employees and which has adequate facilities and arrangements for their welfare at work;
- The provision where necessary of adequate protective clothing and protective equipment to prevent risk of accidents or adverse effects of health.

Employees belonging to particularly sensitive risk groups shall be protected against dangers, which specifically affect them.

Where several undertakings share a work place the employers shall be jointly and severally responsible for ensuring the safety and health of their employees and shall cooperate with each other in implementing the safety, health and occupational hygiene provisions and, taking into account the nature of their activities, shall coordinate their actions in matters of protection of their employees and prevention of occupational risks.

Every employer shall take necessary measures for first aid, fire fighting and evacuation of employees adapted to the nature of the activities and the size of the establishment.

Employers shall consult their employees or their representatives and allow them to take part in discussion on all questions relating to safety and health at work.

It shall be the responsibility of each employee to take care, as far as possible, of his own safety and health and that of other persons affected by his acts at work in accordance with the training and the instructions given by his employer.

Industrial Relations

Trade unions may be formed area-wise, industry-wise or establishment-wise. But no trade union shall be registered unless it has a membership of not less than 25 per cent of the total number of employees of the area, industry or establishment as the case may be. In no case shall it be less than 10.

The president, secretary and other office bearers as well as the members of the executive or managing committee of every union shall be appointed by election through secret ballot and no office bearer or member of the executive or managing committee shall hold office for more than three years, but every such person shall be entitled to be reelected. No person who is not an employee in the area, industry or establishment shall be eligible for election as an office bearer or as member of the executive or the managing committee.

Every trade union should have a set of byelaws based on a set of model rules to be framed by the government. The byelaws of the trade union shall lay down inter alia, the procedure for election of the office bearers and the other members of the executive committees, periodicity of the meetings of the executive committee and the general council. The law shall lay down the penalty for failure to hold such meetings.

The byelaws should also lay down the procedure for maintenance and compilation of the accounts of the union, their audit and presentation to the general body periodically. The law should prescribe the liabilities of the office bearers for failure to do so and other cases of misdemeanour.

There shall be one bargaining agent in each establishment to represent the employees of that establishment in collective bargaining, mediation, arbitration or adjudication on matters relating to a collective demand. There shall be a bargaining council for each activity or area to represent the employees in the area or activity in collective bargaining, conciliation, mediation, arbitration or adjudication.

The union having the largest membership in an establishment shall be recognized as the most representative union of that establishment provided it has a minimum of not less than 50 per cent of the total number of employees of the establishment.

The bargaining agents of all the establishments in the area or activity shall constitute the bargaining council for the area or activity.

The membership of the bargaining agent/council shall be determined by secret ballot.

All labour disputes shall be settled by collective bargaining failing which by conciliation, mediation, arbitration or as a last resort adjudication.

The role of the State in labour relations shall be minimal. The requirement that the standing orders and collective agreements should be certified by a government official may be done away with. Conciliation and Mediation may be entrusted to a tripartite body. The requirement of permission of government for retrenchment and closure of establishments may be done away with. The law itself may specify the circumstances under which retrenchment or closure would be permissible. A higher rate of compensation may be prescribed. Any dispute in that regard should, if possible, be settled bilaterally failing which it may be referred to the Labour Relations Commission.

- A collective agreement may be concluded for an establishment, activity or area; but as far as possible the agreement should be concluded on activity/industry basis.
- A collective agreement shall be binding on the entire establishment, industry/activity or area as the case may be and the heirs, successors and assignees of the employers concerned.
- A collective agreement shall be in force for a minimum period of three years.

There shall be a Labour Relations Commission comprising of five members with one representative each of the employers and the employees in the State and three independent members. The Commission shall have the following functions:

(a) Certification of bargaining agents and bargaining councils.
(b) Determination of the level at which collective bargaining should be held.
(c) Conciliation and mediation of disputes failing which adjudication of disputes.

The procedure for adjudication of labour disputes should be simplified so that the cases are disposed of without delay, say, within a maximum period of six months. The system of Lok Adalats may be developed for disposal of the disputes, which do not involve any major legal issue.

There shall be grievance settlement machinery in each establishment for settlement of individual grievances.

There shall be no strike unless a ballot is taken and not less than 60 per cent of the work force in the establishment or activity/industry vote for it and not less than fifteen days notice is given. Any strike without conforming to these requirements shall be illegal. Any loss or damage caused to the establishment by such illegal strike shall be recoverable from the union and/or its office bearers as a permissible deduction from wages.

Industrial actions in the form of *gherao*, go slow, sit in strike, work to rule etc, shall be banned. Any person indulging in such action shall be punishable.

An institutional arrangement should be made in each establishment to involve the employees in the decision making process.

Social Security

There shall be a National Social Security Authority of India. It shall be the function of the authority to advise the Central and State governments generally in the matter of social security administration, to prepare or approve the schemes of social security and to coordinate between the Central and State governments in the matter of implementation of social security and to monitor and to report on the implementation of the schemes. The main schemes of social security are to be framed in consultation with this Authority.

There shall be a Board of Social Security at the Centre and in each State. The Board shall be responsible to formulate supplementary schemes where necessary and to implement all the schemes.

There shall be different schemes for different classes of people, namely:

1. Persons who are in regular wage employment where a well defined employer-employee relationship exists;
2. Persons who are in employment of irregular or discontinuous nature where the relationship between the employer and the employees is tenuous;
3. Persons who are self-employed; and
4. Persons who are not in employment.

There shall be broadly two types of schemes: contributory and non contributory. Contributory schemes will be applicable to persons who are in regular employment or who are self employed for whom contributions can be made by their employers or by the beneficiaries themselves or both. Non contributory schemes would be meant for those who are either not employed or, if employed, there is no continuity of employment or in the employer-employee relations and the wages are very low in respect of whom it would be difficult, if not impossible, to collect contributions. These are essentially social assistance types of programs financed by the public exchequer out of the general revenues or special levies, if any.

Labour Administration

A State Labour Conference shall be held once in three years. It may be organized on the same lines as the Indian Labour Conference. A Standing Labour Committee shall be constituted to deal with the policy matters during the interregnum. No decision should be taken on a labour policy matter without consulting the committee.

All other advisory bodies may be wound up.

There shall be tripartite vigilance committees to keep watch over the enforcement of the laws.

Violation of laws will be visited by exemplary punishment.

No court other than a labour court of a Magistrate of First Class shall try any offence under this law.

There shall be one or more labour court in each district so that all disputes are disposed of speedily. The matters, which will be adjudicated by the labour courts, will be specified. All other matters go to the Labour Relations Commission.

Appeals over the decisions of the labour court shall lie with the Labour Relations Commission.

There shall be a Director of Prosecutions to prosecute persons who have violated the laws.

An All India Labour Judicial Service shall be formed so that expertise may be built on labour jurisprudence which will help to dispose of labour disputes pending in the courts quickly.

Special Laws

With the enactment of the basic law as outlined above the following laws would remain as special laws applicable to select classes of establishment or workers:

- The Factories Act
- The Mines Act
- Plantation Labour Act

In addition, special provisions may be made for particular categories of workers who work under conditions which are not normal or who need special protection such as agricultural workers, bonded labourers, motor transport workers, head-load workers, domestic workers and such others.

Reform of Existing Laws

Adoption of the basic law and the special laws would undoubtedly take much time. In the meantime the existing laws may be suitably amended to adjust them to the changing conditions in the economy marked by globalization and a high order of national and international competition. The following suggestions may be considered:

Apprentices Act

Continual upgradation of skills is of primary necessity to cope with the technical and technological advancement of the economy. The existing arrangements for the purpose do not seem to be adequate. A Skill Development Fund may therefore be established urgently and the training facilities improved.

Beedi Industry

The work in this industry is being done increasingly in the homes of the workers under unhygienic conditions. To improve their productivity it is necessary that their working conditions should be improved. One way to achieve this objective is to set up industrial estates for the industry or to construct work sheds with all the necessary facilities as prescribed in the law so that the workers may work under reasonable comfort. These sheds may be constructed either by the government or by the employers themselves, in either case the cost being financed from the Welfare Fund.

It appears that the benefits of the Welfare Fund are provided only to those who are registered with the welfare commissioners. The number of workers registered is reported to be small. The procedure for registration seems therefore to call for a change.

The Welfare Fund may be converted into a social security fund and it may be required to provide all the social security benefits needed by the workers and their families, particularly, old age benefit, medical benefit, sickness benefit, maternity benefit, accident benefit survivors benefit and unemployment benefit.

The beedi workers may be covered under the health insurance schemes of the ESIC and the premium may be paid out of the welfare fund instead of the existing arrangements to provide the medical care of the workers.

The Beedi Workers may also be covered under the various group insurance schemes of the LIC and the GIC the premia being paid by the Welfare Fund instead of the Fund carrying the risks itself.

Bonded Labour

While the law prohibits bonded labour and there is a scheme for rehabilitation of the labour released from bondage there is no provision for giving assistance to those who are released from bondage for their subsistence until they are rehabilitated with the result that there is a tendency on the part of the released bonded labourers to slip back to bondage. It is therefore necessary that some provision should be made to provide relief to them for a period of six months or one year till the rehabilitation measures start yielding them adequate income for a decent living.

Child Labour

Employment of children below the age of 15 may be prohibited in all cases.

Special conditions of work, relating to hours of work, holidays, wages, dangerous machines, excessive weights, etc., may be prescribed for young persons up to the age of 18.

Cine Workers

The provisions of the Cine Workers Regulation of Employment Act may be brought on par with the other labour laws. For purposes of settlement of labour disputes they may be brought under the Industrial Dispute Act instead of making provision for appointment of separate Officers and Tribunals under the Act.

Cine Workers Welfare Fund

The application of the Fund may be broadened as suggested in the case of the Beedi Welfare Fund.

Employees' Provident Fund Act

Definition of the term 'wages' may be amended to mean basic wages and dearness allowance or any other allowance paid to an employee on account of the rise in the cost of living.

The wage ceiling for application of the Act may be omitted, if necessary, by freezing the rate or amount of contribution by the employer at the level of the contribution payable on a salary of, say, ₹ 10,000.

Huge sums of money are lying unclaimed with the EPF Organization. (According to the Trade Union Record [Vo.71 No 6] a sum of ₹ 22,636 crore was lying unclaimed in the PF Accounts). It seems necessary to investigate why such large amounts have remained unclaimed. It is likely that these amounts belong to the workers who move from one employer to another; the EPFO loses track of the members and the members being uninformed about the procedures do not know how to claim their dues. The EPFO has to devise appropriate procedures to ensure that the workers are not deprived of their hard earned savings in such cases and are not denied the benefit of pension admissible under the Employees' Pension Scheme. Such a measure is particularly necessary in the case of industries like the construction industry. It has been reported that there are over 2 million workers in the construction industry but hardly 200,000 workers are covered under the scheme; there is reluctance on the part of the workers to join the scheme which is understandable because they are not sure that the money they contribute will come back to them. If the EPFO wishes to extend its operation to the unorganized sector it has to carry out some radical changes in the Schemes. One change could be to make the contribution by the workers in specified industries optional or to reduce the rate of compulsory contribution. Another would be to introduce the system of social security numbers, which will remain constant irrespective of where the person works so as to avoid transfer of accounts whenever the person changes his employer.

The associations of employers have also suggested that in order to reduce, if not eliminate, paper work the total contribution under various heads be allowed to be remitted through a single challan with the break up of the amount under the various heads. In this connection it is relevant to recall that the National Commission on Labour had expressed the view that an ideal arrangement would be to gradually work move towards a comprehensive social security collections in a single fund, which different agencies can draw upon for disbursing various benefits according to needs.

There are several suggestions that loans for various purposes such as house building be de-linked from the EPF with access to such facilities being provided through other agencies in the field (e.g. mortgage finance agencies for housing).

The EPF may also cover gratuity payments through an insurance mechanism in replacement of the Payment of Gratuities Act.

The Law Commission is reported to have suggested the establishment of an Ombudsman to look into the grievances of the subscribers. This suggestion should be implemented.

The EPF Act provides for the establishment of State Boards for administration of the Schemes. This provision has not been implemented. Instead Regional Committees have been appointed which function in an advisory capacity. In practice these Committees are found to be ineffective. It is desirable that for more effective decentralization of administration of the Schemes under the Act the State Boards are constituted with full administrative and financial powers.

PF adalats may be constituted to hear and dispose of disputes and complaints expeditiously and also to keep a check on the working of the organization.

There is a view that the Employees Pension Scheme is very complex; there are also doubts about its long-term viability. Yet there are criticisms that the scheme does not yield adequate return on the money put into it.

In this connection it is relevant to refer to the report of Secretary General of the International Social Security Association to the 25th General Assembly where he has stated that pension schemes all over the world are undergoing change. One recurrent element of all such changes is the increasing roles of personal savings and the private sector in the overall context of old age protection. It is said that there is hardly any country which has failed to take steps to lighten the obligation of the basic compulsory scheme by means of new provisions based on personal savings and private management or which are not contemplating that kind of action in the near future. The changes made in pension schemes during recent years have clearly brought about a long-term tendency towards increasing the role of the private sector in old age protection. This tendency which is accompanied by a general move towards greater liberalism in national economies is corroborated by a recent World Bank study "Averting the Old age Crisis: Policies to protect the old and promote growth" (Washington DC, World Bank, 1994) which after a sharply critical analysis of the effectiveness of current pension schemes proposes a model based essentially on personal old age protection (fully funded private insurance schemes) supplemented by benefits for the most needy which might be means tested.

Having regard to these developments it may be advisable to consider the replacement of the existing scheme by a simpler one providing a flat rate of pension leaving it to the subscribers to make their own arrangements to supplement the income by investment or by taking complementary pension insurance policies from the LIC or the UTI who have introduced their own pension schemes.

Employees' State Insurance Act

This Act provides for a scheme for health insurance. The Act was passed in 1948 and it was introduced in 1952. The scheme is being implemented area-wise and employment-wise. Initially the scheme was made applicable in all areas where there was a concentration of 5000 or more insurable population. Later it was decided to implement the scheme in all areas where there was concentration of 500 or more workers. The Act was to apply in the first instance to all factories. It has since been extended to seven more classes of employments. It does not apply to mines and plantations. In terms of numbers the scheme covers hardly 15 million workers. There are several problems and issues affecting the expansion of the Scheme. One of the main difficulties in the expansion of the scheme is the inability of the ESIC to make satisfactory arrangements to provide medical benefit to the insured persons. The ESI Scheme is a composite scheme. It provides for medical benefit as well as for certain cash benefits. Because of the constraint in the expansion of the facilities for providing medical benefit it has not also been able to expand the scheme for purposes of cash benefits. It is therefore necessary to bring about a structural change in the scheme. In this connection the ILO has observed as follows:

> "The ESI is both a provider and a carrier of insurance in respect of medical care while it is mainly an insurer in respect of sickness, maternity disability and employment injury benefits. The combination of provision and insurance has impeded the

> coverage of ESI and its capacity to provide non-medical care benefits............
>
> Against this background the reform agenda cannot be confined to piecemeal improvements....It will have to include a radical restructuring of the entire framework along with legal and administrative framework."

One of the structural changes suggested is that the provision of medical care should be separated from the insurance function which is a purely financial function and that the ESIC should concentrate on the insurance function, the provision of medical care being entrusted either to the State governments or to other specialist organizations in the public and private sector or to another National Authority. The ESIC may enter into agreement with these organizations for providing the service for which payment maybe made by the Corporation.

If such a structural change is carried out it should be possible for the ESI to expand its insurance business throughout the country without any limitation and thereby relieve the employers of their liability under the Workmen's Compensation, Maternity Benefit and Payment of Gratuity Acts.

In this connection the ILO has recommended as follows:

> "The direct provision of medical care through its captive hospitals can be de-linked from the ESI with its hospitals being handed over to the State governments (or to other organizations created to take them over). The ESI can then be transformed into a National Social Insurance Agency with the mandate for insuring sickness, maternity, disability and employment injury. Termination benefits on retrenchment now eligible under the Industrial Dispute Act can also be insured with the National Social Insurance Agency. As any other insurer, the National Social Insurance Agency will liaise with a network of employers and providers for verification of claims and disbursal of benefits. Insurance with National Social Insurance Agency for all benefits involved should be made mandatory based on appropriate tripartite premia contributions, for employees in all enterprises, establishments, institutions etc. outside the public sector subject to a reasonable and feasible floor on the number of employees in regular employment (10 or 20). It is of essence that the administration of the National Social Insurance Agency should be efficient and economic. It should be based on modern lines,

> decentralized, responsible and accountable to employers, employees, and the government. Medical care can be separately insured through a National Health Insurance Agency (NHIA). The provision of medical care can be through hospitals and clinics in the public, private and voluntary sectors as well as private medical practitioners, identified and regulated by the National Health Insurance Agency subject to appropriate terms and conditions it might prescribe. Medical insurance can be mandatory for enterprises and establishments with regular employees in the non-government sector the National Health Insurance Agency can also provide voluntary health insurance with other health insurers (public, private or joint ventures). As a nationwide agency it can also form joint ventures with private insurers and provide reinsurance."

While the ESI Scheme is compulsory there is provision for grant of exemption under certain circumstances. Taking advantage of this provision many employers especially in the public sector have sought and obtained exemption from the application of the Scheme. The consequence of the grant of exemption is that the employers have themselves to provide to their employees medical and other benefits, which would otherwise be provided by the ESIC. The employees are happy with this arrangement as they can get privileged treatment at the hands of their employers to them. The employers will do well to consider whether such arrangements are in the best interests of their industry or business. The current thinking among experts is that the management should concentrate on its core functions, hiving off the ancillary functions to other specialist organizations, which will be more economical and more efficient. Such a policy would demand that the responsibility for providing medical care to the employees of an establishment should be transferred to an institution, which has specialized in providing that service through a health insurance scheme instead of seeking exemption from the scheme.

An employer organization has drawn attention to a problem employers are facing in the administration of the ESI Scheme. In essence what it says is as follows:

> Section 2(9) defined the term employer in wide terms to include contract workers.......There is no minimum qualifying period and the contributions under the Act are payable from day one of employment. Though an employee is entitled to the medical and employment injury benefits from the very first day of his

> employment he/she becomes entitled to sickness and maternity benefits only if he completes the contribution period of six months. The persons engaged in construction repair and maintenance of buildings do not stay for long period in one unit.......Therefore the construction workers are not able to derive the benefit on account of sickness and maternity from the limited membership of the ESI Scheme, as they, more often than not cease to be in employment during the corresponding benefit period....... Therefore these workers are not in favor of any deductions being made from their wages for contribution to the Scheme......For this reason it is suggested that construction workers employed through contractors should be excluded from the scope of the ESI Act, and Section 14 of the Workmen's Compensation Act should be amended to make it obligatory on the part of the employer to insure his liability under that Act in respect of construction workers engaged through a contractor. This would save the employees 1.5 per cent of their wages, which they have to contribute to the Scheme.

The ESIC is opposed to this suggestion for the valid reason that the contract workers need health insurance more than others. But it seems that in their enthusiasm to cover the contract workers they have not paused to verify whether the workers are able to take advantage of the scheme. It appears from what the employer organization has said that the Scheme operates more as a tax on the poor worker than as a social security measure. The ESIC may therefore be asked to conduct a survey as to whether and if so to what extent the contract workers are able to avail of the benefits of the scheme and whether they would like to be covered. If the survey confirms the views expressed by the chamber they should take steps to exclude the contract workers from coverage.

Industrial Disputes Act, 1947

This Act was enacted to replace the then existing Trade Disputes Act under which the Government could intervene in an industrial dispute and Rule 81 A of the Defence of India Rules under which the government could refer a dispute for compulsory adjudication. The object of the Act was limited to provide for settlement of industrial disputes through conciliation and adjudication. The procedures and machinery provided under the Act have been modified from time to time in the light of the actual working of the relevant provisions, the decisions of the judiciary and the influence of bipartite and tripartite agreements. Even so, with the passage of time further amendments have been found necessary. The working of the Act was reviewed by the National Commission on Labour, and subsequently in a series of Indian Labour Conferences recommendations were made for comprehensive amendments to the Act.

At one stage in 1978 the then government brought forward a bill to replace the Act by a more comprehensive Act but it fell through. Subsequently, after ten years, in 1988, another bill was introduced to amend the various provisions of the Industrial Dispute Act and the Trade Unions Act. That was not passed. In the wake of the announcement of the new Industrial Policy the organizations of employers have been pleading for carrying out changes in certain provisions of the Act, which in their opinion are impeding the healthy growth of industries in the country. Certain official committees such as the Bajaj Committee and the Omkar Goswami Committee set up by the government have also recommended major changes in the law. The National Labour Law Association a voluntary organization carried out a review of the labour laws including the Industrial Dispute Act and the Trade Unions Act with a view to suggest simplification, rationalization and consolidation of the laws. It has also proposed certain basic changes which are as follows

> "As the purpose of the entire project was to codify the laws applicable to all working people and as the intention was to cover persons employed in diverse capacities in all kinds of establishments irrespective of their size, nature of activities, ownership patterns etc., this part of the Code is called Labour Relations rather than Industrial Relations. Consistent with this decision the term labour has been used in other cognate expressions instead of the term industry as in the case of 'labour dispute' 'labour relations commission', etc.
>
> The basic approach of the Code with respect to labour relations is to devise a system, which would considerably reduce, if not altogether do away with, the intervention in labour relations by the State. It seeks to ensure that ultimately State intervention in labour relations should aim at promoting autonomous bilateral negotiations between employers and trade unions. It provides for third party intervention for resolution of disputes between the parties not by government agencies but by statutory authorities created for the purpose independently of Government. The Code makes bipartite negotiated settlements freely entered into by he employers and the workers paramount by providing

that the terms and conditions of employment at levels above the minimum standards laid down in the Code should be determined by mutual agreement between the employers and the employees concerned through collective bargaining. The Code also lays down the procedure for collective bargaining.

The Code defines Employers Associations and Trade Unions separately and also makes separate provision for their recognition. The Code prescribes the minimum number of employees required for registration of a trade union. This is on accepted lines. However as far as Employers Associations are concerned a similar limit is not considered possible as it may happen that a very large number of employers may account for only a small number of employees; likewise a single employer may account for the bulk of the employees in an activity in a local area. A different criterion has been prescribed for the purpose.

Taking account of the poor financial position of trade unions it is provided that the minimum rate of subscription for membership of a trade union should be 0.5 per cent of the wages subject to a minimum of one rupee.

The extent of unionization varies so considerably from state to state, from industry to industry, from urban to rural areas that no uniform minimum percentage can be thought of for purpose of recognition. It is therefore left to the Labour Relations Commission concerned to decide the matter on case-by-case basis.

Likewise the procedure for determining the bargaining agent, whether it should be by check off or by verification or by secret ballot is left to be decided by the Labour Relations Commission concerned which is expected to take into account all the relevant factors before deciding the issue.

The Code provides for conciliation, mediation, arbitration as well as adjudication for resolution of disputes.

It envisages the establishment of Labour Relations Commissions at the National, Central and State levels with the wide-ranging functions and powers. The Code has vested considerable amount of authority on the Labour Relations Commission. This is deliberate as only high-powered Labour Relations Commissions would be a safeguard against undue intervention in the labour relation's matters by appropriate Governments. It is envisaged that the National Labour Relations Commission may be invested with the powers of even the Supreme Court under Clause 3 of the Article 32 of the Constitution. Consistent with the status and authority of the members of the Commissions it is provided that their appointment will be made on the recommendations of a National Judicial Commission.

In regard to strikes and lockouts the Code does away with the existing distinction between public utility services and the rest. The Code requires a strike ballot to be taken with the support of a minimum of 51per cent of the members of the bargaining agent or the bargaining council before going on strike. The corresponding provision in the case of a lock out is for a decision on a lockout to be taken at the highest level of management. There is a separate provision for settlement of individual grievances."

The author of this paper was associated with the project under which these recommendations were made and therefore I commend them.

Trade Unions Act

One organization of employers has pointed out that under the existing law registration of unions is optional and even unregistered union can raise disputes. It has expressed the opinion that unregistered union should be regarded as non-existant. and accordingly recommended that registration of unions should be made compulsory as suggested by the National Commission on Labour. The Ramanujam Committee has also recommended that in the organized sector registration of trade union should be made compulsory. As there is consensus on the subject it may be suitably incorporated in the law.

The Ramanujam Committee had recommended that no trade union should be registered if its membership is restricted to a particular craft, occupation, caste, creed, community, race, religion or persons originating from a particular region. The CII has reiterated this recommendation. The Indian Labour Code has banned the registration of such unions. This prohibition may be inscribed in the law.

The Ramanujam Committee had recommended that the minimum strength of registration of trade unions should be 10 per cent of the employees in the establishment or 100 whichever is less subject to a minimum of 7 persons. The Government had also made a similar provision in the Amendment Bill of 1988. There seems to be a consensus on this proposal and it may be implemented.

The Ramanujam Committee had recommended that election of office bearers and committee members should be held once in three years if not earlier. This is a salutary provision. It may be incorporated in the law.

The Committee had also recommended that outsiders should not exceed 1/3 of the number of office bearers and committee members. The government had also proposed in the Amendment bill of 1988 that all except two of the total number of office bearers should be persons engaged or employed in an establishment or class of establishments with which the trade union is connected. The PHD Chamber had recommended that no outsider should be a member or office bearer of a trade union. As the recommendation of the Ramanujam Committee is based on consensus it may be incorporated in the law.

One organization of employers has pointed out that most of the trade unions revolve round a couple of outsiders who do not hold regular meetings with the result that the workmen are not very much involved in the functioning of trade unions and fail to evince any genuine interest in their activities. The Chamber has therefore recommended that the Act should be amended to provide for periodic general meetings besides the meetings for election of the office bearers at least once in two yeas and also for recording of the minutes of these meetings.

The organization of employers has further pointed out that most of the trade unions do not keep proper records and accounts and has suggested a provision for the appointment of inspectors to check the register of members, record of the meetings and the statement of accounts.

It is felt that the arrangements for exercising checks on the working of trade unions should be similar to those of cooperative societies and societies registered under the Cooperative Societies Act and Societies Registration Act.

There is no provision in the existing law to resolve intra trade union disputes, for instance, to determine who is the lawful office bearer of a union or to declare the election of office bearers as unconstitutional. As such disputes affect industrial relations in the establishment provision should be made for their resolution. The India Labour Code (draft) has provided that such disputes may be referred to labour courts. The PHD Chamber has suggested that the Registrar may be empowered to resolve them. The Registrars of Cooperative Societies have powers to intervene in intra society disputes. Similar powers may be conferred on the Registrars of Trade Unions.

There is no provision in the existing law for recognition of union for purposes of collective bargaining. Proposals for recognition of a bargaining agent or a bargaining council have been made by several bodies. The Ramanujam Committee has recommended as follows:

"There shall be a negotiating council in all establishments employing 50 or more persons. The negotiating Council shall have equal number of employees and employers.

In the case of employees where there is no union a team of five persons may be elected to represent the workmen and they will form members of the negotiating council. Where there is only one union that union will be entitled to nominate all the employees' representatives on the negotiating council irrespective of its membership. In case where there are multiple unions while employers' representatives the INTUC and the NLO opted for verification of membership and the check off system the other trade unions opted for secret ballot."

The Indian Labour code has made provision as follows:

Section 121:

1. There shall be a sole bargaining agent in each establishment to represent the employees of that establishment in collective bargaining, mediation and arbitration on matters relating to a collective demand;
2. There shall be a bargaining council for each activity or area to represent the employees in the activity or area in collective bargaining conciliation, arbitration or adjudication on matters of collective demand;
3. Subject to the provisions of this code the Labour Relations Commission shall, after such enquiry as it deems fit, specify the percentage of minimum membership a trade union should have to be eligible for recognition as a bargaining agent or as member of the bargaining council;
4. Subject to the provisions of this code the Commission shall determine the membership of a union by means of check off, secret ballot, general verifications or any other procedure, as the case may be, in consultation with the unions concerned and the decision of the Commission regarding the procedure for determining the strength of a union shall be final;
5. The union having the largest membership in an establishment

shall be recognized as the most representative union of that establishment provided it has the minimum number of members as specified and the Commission shall issue a certificate in token of that recognition; the union possessing such a certificate shall be the sole bargaining agent on behalf of the employees of the establishment;

6. The unions having the minimum membership in the activity of area specified by the Commission shall be recognized as members of the bargaining council for the activity or area as the case may be and the trade union having the largest membership in the activity or area shall be recognized as the principal bargaining agent for that activity/area.
7. No union which is not registered shall be entitled to recognition as a bargaining agent or as the member of the bargaining council;
8. No union with a membership of less than 15 per cent of the number of employees shall be eligible for recognition as a bargaining agent unless the registered union is the only union in the establishment, activity or area;
9. No craft union shall be eligible for recognition as a bargaining agent;
10. Recognition of a union or the sole bargaining agent shall be in force for a period of three years which may be extended from time to time unless challenged;
11. An employee who is a member of a union at the time of verification of the strength of that union shall not change his membership and join another union within less than one year; he may however withdraw his membership of the union".

The Indian Labour Code has also made provision for recognition employers' association.

The provisions of the Indian Labour code may be adopted.

Industrial Employment (Standing Orders), Act, 1946

This Act requires every industrial establishment to which it applies to frame standing orders and to submit them in draft for certification to the certifying officer.

The application of the Act is highly restrictive. It is applicable to every industrial establishment wherein one hundred or more workmen are/were employed on any day of the preceding twelve months. As standing orders are the basic instrument which regulates the conditions of service of the workmen it is necessary that the Act should be made applicable to all classes of establishments without limitation as to the number of persons employed.

Framing of the standing orders is a matter between the employer and his workmen. The Government has hardly any role to play in it. The requirement that the standing orders should be submitted for certification by the Certifying Officer may be omitted.

In this connection the Indian Labour Code has provided as follows:

"Section 27:

(1) The Central Government shall prescribe one or more sets of model standing orders on matters specified in Schedule II.

(2) Every employer shall make standing orders setting out the terms of employment of his employees which shall be as close to the model standing orders as possible but in no case less favorable to the employees;

(3) (a) In making the standing orders the employer shall consult the recognized trade union/s;

(b) Differences if any between the recognized trade union and the management in respect of the standing orders shall be referred to the Labour Court for decision;

(4) Where the employer has not made his own standing orders the model standing orders will apply;

(5) The terms of employment set out in the standing orders shall be subject to the provisions of this code;

(6) If any question arises as to the application or interpretation of a standing order it may be referred to the Labour Court and that court shall decide the question after giving the parties an opportunity of being heard.

(7) The decision of the Labour Court under this Section shall be final and binding of the parties."

It is suggested that the Act may be amended as above.

Contract Labour

The system of contract labour has been in vogue in this country for a long time. The term is associated with the concepts of migrant labour and bonded labour. In the past large numbers of Indian workers were sent to Ceylon, South Africa, West Indies and the East Indies under various forms of indentures, meaning contract. Within the country itself workers migrate from State to State in search of employment. The labour employed in the tea plantations of Assam are traditionally migrant labour from Bihar or Orissa. The system of employment of interstate migrant labour known in Orissa as Dadan labour are recruited from various parts of the State through contractors or agents called sardars/khatadars for work outside the State in large construction projects. This system had lent itself to various abuses and came under adverse notice on the part of several committees. The Whitley Commission recommended the abolition of the system.

As a result of the findings and recommendations of the various committees several measures were introduced to regulate the employment and conditions of service of contract labour. The definition of 'worker' in the Factories Act, the Mines Act and the Plantations Act was enlarged to include contract labour by amendment of the definition of the term immediate employer in the ESI Act. The Dock Workers' (Regulation of Employment) Act, 1948 protected the employment, wages and welfare conditions of specified categories of contract labour employed at major docks. As a result of the recommendations of the Industrial Committee on Coal Mines contract labour was abolished in railway collieries. The CPWD Rules for contractors required that job contracts should be given to contractors on the approved list who had agreed to pay fair wages and to provide welfare services and housing of the specified standard. A similar system was introduced by the railways. The Minimum Wages Act was made applicable to contract labour. The Bombay Industrial Relations Act and similar Acts in MP and UP were made applicable to contract labour.

The Second Five Year Plan stressed the need for improvement in the working conditions of contract labour and to ensure continuity of employment. The matter came up for discussion in the Indian Labour Conference and the Industrial Committee on Construction, the upshot of which was a general agreement on the need to abolish the system of contract labour wherever possible and to regulate it in other cases. Eventually the Contract Labour (Regulation and Abolition) Act was passed in 1971.

Since then the movement to abolish contract labour has gained increasing stridency. The recent judgments of the Supreme Court have made the employment of contract labour unprofitable and unattractive. At the same time there is also a rethinking at the highest levels on the necessity to permit the system of contract labour.

The Chief Minister of Karnataka while making a statement at the

Chief Ministers' Conference held in May 1997 is reported to have "Suggested a review of labour laws particularly those which could enable contracting out of services".

The Fifth Central Pay Commission has made several positive recommendations in this regard. The more important of these recommendations are reproduced below:

> "Contracting out of services
>
> There is a widening area of services which are currently being performed in-house in the Government but which can be conveniently outsourced to the private sector.
>
> These may include designing, construction and maintenance of Government buildings, factories, workshops, residential colonies, railway stations, equipment and transport, cleanliness, sanitation and housekeeping, maintenance of monuments, lawns and gardens, catering (including catering in airlines, trains, canteens), provision of transportation services (to replace the fleet of staff cars), postal deliveries, carriage of mail, security of all non-sensitive buildings and installations, reservations in railways and airlines, printing, reprography, photography, audio visual publicity, translation, interpretation, computer related services, maintenance of accounts etc."

Although this recommendation has been made in the context of regulating employment in the Government of India the logic of the recommendation is equally, if not more, applicable to the corporate sector. If the government can be permitted to contract out some of its services there is no reason why non-governmental organizations cannot contract out similar services for the same reason/s.

The Pay Commission has also recommended that employment on contract basis should be recognized as one of the legitimate forms of employment and should be resorted to more frequently inter alia for the purpose of maintaining a certain flexibility in staffing and moderating the numbers deployed depending on the exigencies of work.

They have specifically stated, "It may be necessary to amend the labour laws in the country to send out a clear signal to the courts that short term employment should be recognized as a legitimate mode of engagement of labour and job security should not be accorded the preponderant attention that it has received in the past"...

Let us now consider what changes in the law/s are required to bring them in line with the current thinking. There are primarily two laws regulating contract labour: the Contract Labour (Regulation and Abolition) Act 1971 and the Inter State Migrant Workmen (Regulation of Employment and Conditions of Service) Act 1980. We shall first review the Contract Labour Act.

Contract Labour (Regulation and Abolition) Act 1970

Clause (a) of Sub Section 5 of Section 1 of this Act provides that the Act shall not apply to establishments in which work only of an intermittent or casual nature is performed. According to the explanation below the Section a work performed in an establishment shall not be deemed to be of an intermittent nature if it was performed for more than 120 days in the preceding twelve months or if it is of seasonal character and is performed for more than sixty days in a year. Section 10 of the Act requires that the State government may prohibit employment of contract labour in any process etc. having regard to the conditions of work and benefits provided for the contract labour and other relevant factors including whether it is of a perennial character. Use of the term perennial in labour law is somewhat unusual; a more appropriate term would be "permanent". In other words, permanency of a job is one of the primary reasons for prohibiting contract labour in an establishment. It follows that contract labour may be permitted in casual, intermittent and temporary jobs. This is also what the Pay Commission has recommended. There is however no definition of the terms 'temporary' or 'casual'. The Model Rules framed under Industrial Employment (Standing Order) Act define the term temporary workman as one who has been engaged for work which is of an essentially temporary nature likely to be finished within a limited time. The period within which it is likely to be finished should however be specified. Similarly the term casual workman is defined as one who has been engaged for work, which is of an essentially casual nature. In Government a person who has been in temporary employment for more than three years is required to be declared as quasi permanent. Having regard to these facts it is proposed that Section 1 of the Contract Labour Act may be amended; to read as follows:

> **"Section 1(5)(a) :**
>
> "It shall not apply to establishments in which work only of a temporary or casual nature is performed."
>
> Consequential amendment may be carried out in clause (b) thereof

The explanation below the Section shall be amended as follows:

"For purpose of this Act, work performed in an establishment shall be deemed to be

- of casual nature if it lasts for less than 120 days
- of temporary nature if it lasts for less than 36 months continuously or intermittently as the case may be.
- of permanent nature if it lasts for more than 36 months".

Clause (b) of Section 2 defines the term contract labour to mean a person who is employed in or in connection with the work of an establishment when he is hired in or in connection with such work by or through a contractor with or without the knowledge of the principal employer. The key elements of the definition are that if one is hired by or through a contractor he will be contract labour. But there could be a difference between a person hired by a contractor and a person hired by another employer through a contractor. In the former case, the contractor would himself be an employer and is sometimes described as an intermediate employer. In the latter case the contractor could only be a recruitment agency. Employment is provided by the principal employer.

The Emigration Act provides an analogy. This Act requires that no foreign employer may recruit an Indian citizen for employment outside the country except through a recruiting agent registered under the Act. It is conceivable that within India also a person may be recruited through a recruitment agency. Indeed there are several agencies providing this service. They bring the employer and the aspirant for a job together and facilitate recruitment. Once a person is recruited he becomes the employee of the employer.

A distinction would therefore have to be made between hiring by a contractor and through a contractor. A person may be hired by a contractor for casual or temporary job in an establishment. The object of the Act is to regulate the employment of such persons. Clause (b) of Section 2 may therefore be amended to read as follows:

> "A workman shall be deemed to be employed as 'contract labour' if he is employed in an establishment for work of casual or temporary nature on contract entered into either directly or through a contractor".

Clause (e) of Section 2 defines a contractor as one "who undertakes to produce a given result for the establishment other than a mere supply of goods or articles of manufacture to such establishment through contract labour or who supplies contract labour for any work of the establishment and includes a sub-contractor."

According to this definition the provisions of the Act are attracted if a contractor is engaged for any job other than supply of goods and articles of manufacture. In modern day industry and business contracts are entered into not only for supply of goods and articles of manufacture but also for performance of construction and other works as well as for supply of services. Indeed the service sector is getting more and more sophisticated and specialized. Industrial and business establishments find it necessary and advantageous to let out many of the ancillary services which they had been performing in-house in the past not only for reasons of economy but also for reasons of technological advancement. This is one of the reasons why the 5th Pay commission has recommended contracting out services in government. If contracting out of services is permissible in government there is no reason why it should not be permitted in the industrial and business sector. It is therefore proposed that the definition of the term contractor may be amended to read as follows:

> "Contractor in relation to an establishment means a person who supplies labour or functions as an agency for recruitment of labour for any work of the establishment and includes a subcontractor".

The object of this amendment is to permit an establishment to enter into contract not only for supply of goods or articles of manufacture but also for work and for supply of goods or articles of manufacture but also for work and for supply of services and to permit a firm to function as an employment agency or as a recruitment agency to help secure the services of labour they require.

Section 10(1) provides for the abolition of contract labour and specifies the factors that should be taken into consideration before issuing the notification in that regard and these are –

(a) Whether the process, operation or other work is incidental to or necessary for the industry, trade, business, manufacture or occupation that is carried on in the establishment.
(b) Whether it is of perennial nature, that is to say it is of sufficient duration having regard to the nature of the industry etc.
(c) Whether it is done ordinarily through regular workers in that establishment or an establishment similar thereto;

(d) Whether it is sufficient to employ considerable numbers of whole time workers.

It appears that these facts were specified on the basis of the observations of the Supreme Court in the Standard Vacuum Refining Co. case. These observations were made at a time when it was customary for an industrial organization to do everything required for production of an article within its own premises. Ancillarization whereby the practice of using bought out items produced by ancillary industries was not very much in vogue; now even some of the service functions are being farmed out. The first and the third criteria do not seem therefore to be quite relevant in the current context. The only criterion that is still relevant for abolition of contract labour is whether the work belongs to the core function of the organization and whether it is of perennial or permanent nature. Having regard to these facts Section 10 may be amended to read as follows:

> Employment of contract labour for any process or operation or other work of permanent nature in any establishment relating to its core function is prohibited.

If a doubt arises whether a work is of permanent or temporary nature and whether a function is a core function or not the decision of the Labour Relations Commission shall be final.

Chapter IV and V of the Act relate to regulation of contract labour where it is not abolished. These chapters require registration of contractors and specify what facilities they should provide for contract labour. The basic need of contract labour is security of service. The Contract Labour Act does not provide for it. On the other hand the Act requires the establishment where contract labour is employed should provide canteens, restrooms and other facilities. These facilities would normally exist in any organization and they could be available to contract labour also. It is therefore a moot question whether it is necessary to make special provisions in the law in that regard exclusively for contract labour.

There are, however, a few other Acts such as the Dock Workers (Regulation of employment) Act and the Kerala Head Load Workers Act which provide for de-casualisation of casual and contact labour without imposing any unreasonable burden on the employers. Similar provision may be made for regulating the employment and conditions of service of contract labour in other employments also.

Practically every establishment employs labour on casual or

temporary basis either directly or through a contractor at one time or the other. It is doubtful if any useful purpose is served by requiring them to register. There would be no harm if the relevant sections 6 to 9 were deleted.

If the foregoing proposals are accepted consequential changes may be carried out in the other sections of the Act.

Inter-state Migrant Workmen (RECS) Act 1979

This Act seeks to regulate employment of interstate migrant labour through contractors. A contractor who supplies labour performs the role of a recruitment agency. Considering the state of the market for migrant labour it may not be possible to do without them unless a substitute mechanism is created for the purpose. The Sixth Five Year Plan had envisaged the establishment of a statutory Migrant Labour Board with advisory as well as executive powers to look after the interests of the migrant labour. A tripartite Committee set up to evolve a legislative framework for brick kiln workers consisting mainly of migrant labour had recommended the establishment of one or more Boards to regulate their employment and conditions of service. The Indian Labour code also envisages the constitution of Boards for regulation of employment and conditions of service of certain categories of rural and unorganized labour including migrant labour. It is suggested that the Act may be recast on the lines indicated in the Indian Labour code.

The Act requires that migrant workers should be paid the same wages as are applicable to local labour. In addition they are to be paid displacement allowance and journey allowance. They are also to be provided residential accommodation and other facilities. If they are all taken together the cost of employing migrant labour would be higher than that of local labour and the employers may not find it economical to employ them. If these provisions are enforced rigorously it is likely to be counter productive and deprive the migrant labour of the opportunities for employment instead of promoting their employment. The conditions of service prescribed in the Act therefore calls for a review. What the law needs to ensure is that there is no discrimination against migrant labour in the matter of wages or other conditions of service and that they are not deprived of their dues by the extortionist middlemen.

Welfare Funds for Mine Workers

Welfare funds have come to be realized as a suitable instrument for providing social security to large numbers of workers in the organized, more so, in the unorganized sector. This instrument has to be fine tuned so as improve its effectiveness. The ILO says:

> "Welfare funds are appropriate in industries and activities in which workers are geographically concentrated and welfare benefits for them can be financed through a cess or surcharge relatable to the manufacture or sale of their output. There is scope for extension of this modality.".

One important change to be made in the laws relating to the welfare funds set up by the Government of India is to broaden the end use of the funds so as to convert the funds into social security funds and to provide for all the benefits under the various branches of conventional form of social security.

Another change that needs to be carried out is to make the Funds to function as insurance agencies financing the services instead of undertaking to provide the services themselves, which call for expertise and specialization.

Maternity Benefit Act 1961

The most important reform required in this Act is to convert it from an employers' liability to a social insurance scheme. There are widespread allegations of the liabilities under the Act being evaded on one ground or another. The National Commission on Labour had therefore recommended the establishment of a fund for payment of maternity benefit. The ESI Scheme was intended to take over the liability under a social insurance scheme. Indeed the maternity benefit is one of the benefits provided under the ESI Scheme. As however its coverage is limited due to its inability to make adequate arrangements for providing medical benefit which is regarded as the kingpin of the scheme its coverage for purposes of maternity benefit has not been extended to the extent it was necessary. If the ESIC is restructured as proposed above this lacuna will be filled. If that does not happen the government would have to consider creating a separate social insurance organization for the purpose.

Minimum Wages Act 1948

This Act provides for fixation/revision of minimum wages separately for each employment enumerated in the Schedule to the Act. The process involves first inclusion of an employment in the schedule; appointment of tripartite a committee to advise on the rate/s of minimum wages to be fixed, to give notice of the proposals calling for objections and then to issue the notification fixing the wages which will come into force after a while. Under this system minimum wages have not been fixed in respect of many employments for which it should have been fixed for the reason that they are not included in the schedule. There is considerable delay in fixing and revising the wages even in the case of scheduled employments and there are wide variations in the rates of wages fixed for various employments for which there is no reasonable justification. Several suggestions have therefore been made to fix a national/general minimum wage, which would be applicable to the workers at the lowest level in all employments.

The Indian Labour Code provides as follows:

(i) The Central government shall fix a National Minimum wage (Section 59).
(ii) Every State government shall fix a General Minimum Wage payable to the employees employed in employments in the State or in each zone or region thereof, as the case may be (Section 60).
(iii) The appropriate government shall review the minimum wage and if necessary revise it at intervals not exceeding three years (Section 61).
(iv) The general minimum wage fixed and revised by a State government shall in no case be less than the National Minimum Wage fixed by the Central Government as revised from time to time (Section 62).
(v) In fixing or revising the minimum wage the appropriate government shall take into account the basic needs of the employees as specified in Schedule IV and the cost of living (Section 67).

The Minimum Wages Act may be amended on the lines of the provisions made in the India Labour Code.

Payment of Bonus Act

The object of the Act is to provide for payment of bonus on the basis of profits or on the basis of production or productivity. In course of time however the Act has been amended to provide for payment of minimum bonus without regard to profits, production or productivity. As the practice of payment of minimum bonus has come into vogue it would be difficult to go back on it. It is therefore suggested that the object clause be changed and provision may be made for payment of the minimum bonus at the rate of 12.5 per cent of the wages as a deferred wage. The payment of bonus, on the basis of profits and production or productivity, is being kept out of the Act to be settled by collective bargaining or otherwise.

Payment of Gratuity Act 1972

This is also an employers' liability Act. Many employers are known to have defaulted in discharging their liability under the Act due to financial constraints. It is therefore necessary to convert it into a social insurance scheme. A better course would be to amalgamate the scheme for payment of gratuity with the EPF Scheme by suitable adjustment of the rates of contribution whereby the employers may be able to discharge their liability by payment of the contribution, which will be comparatively low. In that case the scope of the Act may also be widened.

Payment of Wages Act 1936

This is one of the basic laws. It seeks to protect the wages of workers. This protection is required by all classes of employees. But unfortunately the application of this Act is very limited. It needs to be broadened so as to make it applicable to all classes of establishments and workers. The wage ceiling prescribed for its application should be raised if not removed.

Workmen's Compensation Act 1923

This Act provides for payment of compensation in the case of disability or death in the course of employment. It is one of the earliest and primary forms of social security. But again application of the Act is subject to severe limitations and restrictions for which there is no obvious justification. So long as the Act requires compensation to be paid for injuries caused in course of employment and arising out of employment there is no reason why the Act should not be made applicable to all workmen.

There is however no doubt that broadening the scope of the Act will add to the liabilities of the employer. Some of the small employers may not be able to bear the liability especially after the minimum quanta of compensation payable under the Act was enhanced. It is therefore necessary that provision should be made for compulsory insurance of the liability under the Act. Where an establishment is covered by the ESI Scheme this problem does not arise. The solution would therefore lie in extending the coverage of the ESIC or to set up a separate corporation for the purpose.

Records and Returns

A Chamber (PHD Chamber) has pointed out that the existing laws involve lot of paper work, which imposes a heavy burden on the employers. It says:

> "Almost every Act requires the employer to maintain a set of registers, submit periodic returns and display certain notices. The load of the paper work involved is felt rather badly by the employers especially those in the small scale sector. Moreover the effort spent to complete these formalities is not commensurate with the utility of such registers returns and notices.
>
> It is suggested that the requirement of display of notices should be dispensed with and maintenance of records and submission of returns should be simplified.
>
> There should be one inspection book wherein all the inspecting officers may record the observations of this visit.
>
> A common format may be developed for accident reports under the Factories Act and the ESI Act.
>
> It is suggested that there should not be more than one register under each Act.
>
> It is further suggested that there should one comprehensive annual return instead of different returns with varying periodicity under various labour laws as at present.
>
> The Payment of Wages Act requires the preservation of registers and records for a period of three years after the date of the last entry made therein. This should be the position for registers and records under all the labour laws so that three years old records may be weeded out.
>
> Inspecting officers may be directed to accept computerization as a modern phenomenon and not require the maintenance of manual records. Whatever information or statement is required can be immediately supplied in the form of neat and clear print out without any misprint or overwriting or cutting."

All these suggestions are unexceptionable. Indeed an exercise to simplify the records and returns was done some years ago when the Labour Laws (Exemption from furnishing Returns and Maintaining Registers by certain Establishments) Act was passed. The problems cited by the Chamber have been minimized by the passage of that Act. Further simplification of the procedures can be done only if the laws themselves are simplified and codified. One should aim at that objective.

IV
Labour Law Enforcement

It is needless to state that training is essential in any field of administration. It is particularly so in the Labour Department where the officers need training, firstly, in the subjects that are handled in the Departments and secondly, in the manner of dealing with those subjects. In other words, the participants would have to acquire expert knowledge in the laws which they will have to administer and also in the methods and techniques of administering those laws. It should be noted that Labour laws are concerned primarily with human relations. The administration of the labour laws therefore calls for a human approach. It requires an understanding of the psychology and the culture of the people one deals with and a degree of sensitivity to the human situation in which the laws have to be administered.

The Central Industrial Relations Machinery (CIRM) as well as the Inspectorates of the State Labour Departments are the cutting edges where the Departments come into contact with the public and they are the agencies through which implementation of the labour policy is secured. They, therefore, represent the key element in the system of labour administration. If they have to function effectively they have to have adequate knowledge of the labour policy of the government and the system of labour administration set up for its implementation.

Labour policy of the government has not been declared in the same manner as the Industrial Policy or Health Policy has been spelt out through a resolution of the Government. But the basic elements of the policy are outlined in the Constitution itself and the various laws which have been enacted by the Parliament and the State Legislatures. The Five Year Plans also refer to them as they provide the basis on which the plans are prepared.

The Constitution declares that India is a Socialist Democratic Republic. It aims at securing to all its citizens justice – social, economic and political. The Supreme Court has declared that social justice is the signature of tune of the constitution. The Directive Principles of State Policy contained in Part IV of the Constitution specify inter alia the principles of social policy, administrative policy, and the socio-economic rights of the people. It is said to give a broad picture of the progressive philosophy on which the Indian Republic is founded. It makes the constitution an instrument of social resolution.

Article 41 of the Constitution requires that the state should make effective provision for securing the right to work, to education, to public assistance in case of unemployment, old age, sickness and disablement and other cases of underserved want. Article 42 requires the State to make provision for securing just and humane conditions of work and maternity relief. Article 43 imposes the obligation on the State to secure to all workers a living wage, conditions of work ensuring a decent standard of life. While the Directive Principles of State Policy generally represent the agenda for the whole nation the principles contained in these Articles represent the charter of the Departments of Labour of the various Governments. This should be kept in view in any discussions as the functions of Labour Department.

India is a member of the International Labour Organization. The main aims of this Organization are to remove injustice, hardships and privation of large masses of toiling people all over the world and to improve their living and working conditions and this establish universal and lasting peace based upon social justice. In pursuance of these aims the organization has adopted a numbcr of International Labour Standards in the form of Conventions, Recommendations and Resolutions. India has ratified a few of the Conventions but subscribes and committed to the principles contained in the others though it has not been possible to ratify them. A few of these are particularly relevant in the context of this courses. They are Convention No.150 and Recommendation No.158 concerning Labour Administration and Convention No.81 and Recommendation No. 81 concerning Labour Inspection.

The Convention concerning Labour Administration requires that each Member which ratifies the Convention shall in a manner appropriate to national conditions ensure the organization and effective operations of a system of labour administration the functions and responsibilities of which are properly coordinated. It also requires that each Member should make arrangements to secure consultations, co-operation and negotiations between the public authorities and the most representative organizations of employers and workers or their representatives. The bodies responsible for labour administration are specifically required inter alia to study and keep under review the situation of employed, unemployed and under-employed persons, taking into account national laws and regulations and national practice concerning conditions of work and working life and terms of employment, draw attention of defects and abuses in such conditions and terms and submit proposals on means to overcome them. The corresponding recommendation envisages that these bodies should take an active part in the preparation, development adoption application, and review of labour standards, including relevant laws and regulations, that there should be programmes aimed at the promotion, establishment and pursuit of labour relations which encourage progressively better conditions of work and working life. Convention No.81 concerning Labour Inspections requires that each Member should maintain a system of labour inspection in industrial work plans. The functions of the system of labour inspections have been specified. They are (1) to secure the enforcement of legal provisions relating to conditions of work and the protection of workers which engaged in their work, such as provisions relating to hours, wages, safety, health and welfare, the employment of children and young persons, and other connected matters, to bring to notice of the competent authority defects or abuses not specifically covered by existing legal provisions. There are similar Conventions concerning labour Inspection in Agriculture and Mining and Transport undertakings. I have dealt at length with these conventions because most if not all of you hold position in systems of labour administration or labour inspection in the Central Government or the State Governments and these conventions/recommendations provide guidelines for your effective functioning.

Labour is a concurrent subject on which both the Centre as well as the State Governments can legislate and they have in fact enacted several laws. There are about 40 laws enacted by the Parliament itself. There are many more laws enacted by the State legislatures. These laws are at once the cause as well as the effect of social change. Laws are framed when need is felt to bring about some change in society and changes are necessitated in the laws when social conditions change. Presently we have nearly 20 proposals for fresh legislation or amendments tc existing legislation.

These laws cover subjects broadly—Employment, training, wages, working conditions, labour welfare and social security and industrial relations. Besides the Departments of Labour have undertaken certain activities related to labour through administrative decisions; for example, Worker's Education, Workers' participation in management, etc.

It should be evident from the foregoing analysis that the Labour Departments have clearly two types of activities, namely, enforcement of the laws and administration of the Programmes. The nature of duties and functions of the personnel employed in the Departments vary accordingly. There is however one type of activity which cuts across this classification, namely conciliation or mediation for settlement of disputes and promotion of harmonious industrial relations. This is a special type of activity which is sui generis. The image of the Department depends to a large extent on the effectiveness with which this function is performed. The subject is so important that the labour law enforcement machinery in the Centre is called the Central Industrial Relations Machinery though it has many functions other than those relating to industrial relations. Healthy labour management relations are vital to national development. Strikes and lock-outs entail a heavy cost in terms of lost production damage to equipment and raw materials, added start-up costs in addition to the damage caused by dislocation of workers' families, and in the case of certain industries the permanent injury to public welfare. The conciliation officers render a national service by preventing work stoppages.

There is a general criticism about the ineffectiveness of the enforcement of labour laws. The Supreme Court has recently given authoritative voice to this criticism publicly. There is a general feeling that while we have several laws they are merely on paper. This feeling has been generated by the extensive violations of the laws and inadequacy of the administrative machinery to enforce them. Violation of the laws could be deliberate or due to ignorance it could also be due to genuine difficulties. The enforcement machinery will therefore have to function with imagination and constructive spirit. No social law can be administered mechanically. There has to be a human touch. Unfortunately in the social milieu in which we are working, any softness on the part of the law enforcement machinery is apt to be viewed with suspicion. It therefore calls for the highest degree of integrity and rectitude on the part of the officials to be able to act with courage according to their convictions. Administration of the labour laws particularly the beneficent laws require that the administration and the administrators concerned should be infused with the social purpose. They should realize that before every complaint and every application for a benefit there is a human being in dire need of sympathy, understanding and assistance.

The National Commission on Labour laid much stress on the need for training of the staff and officers employed in Labour Administration. They observed inter alia as follows :

Several questions which are being dealt with in the offices created by the Labour Ministry/Department have not acquired their own technicalities which require to be understood by persons charged with the responsibility of dealing with them.

What we have said about induction of a worker to industrial establishment equally applies to persons to be initiated to labour administration. But apart from induction certain aspects of training and retraining in the course of employment are equally important. As a matter of training, persons recruited to the junior-most technical posts in the inspectorate under any legislation should be made to spend some time with an office of a trade union. They should also acquire familiarity with the working of industrial establishments. Visits to places where workers live should also be a part of the initial training.

The other aspect of training is initiation into office procedures.

At the senior level, apart from familiarity with the items mentioned above- (relating to office procedure) the officer should have arrangements to understand the breeder perspective within which he has to establish his utility to the public. For new incumbents in such positions, it may not be out of place, where the parties have no objection, to attend collective bargaining sessions, trade union meetings, and discussions organized by trade unions and professional organizations....

Situations which an officer has to meet during the course of his work require to be lived with for their better comprehension. I do not know if the programme drawn up for this course provide for these; if not, it would be worthwhile making suitable alterations to accommodate the suggestions of the commission.

In this connection it may not be out of place to mention how training is provided in some of the advanced countries. In Australia every person recruited to the position of Inspector is given an induction training. The initial phase of this programme provides an introduction to the organization of the Department, its functions and responsibilities under the legislation by which it is established and operates its role in industrial relations and the duties of inspectors within this framework. In later phases, new inspectors are given training in inspection and investigation procedure and methods including exercises on award problems. Training is also given in report and correspondence writing and in dealing with enquiries. In subsequent stages of the programme the trainees accompany experienced inspectors on familiarization visits to work-places and to court hearings and in the last week carry out inspections under supervision. Progress in training is evaluated by the Senior Inspector through observations, discussion and assessment of abilities in dealing with practical problems.

At a Regional workshop on 'Making Labour Inspections More Effective' held under the auspices of ARPLA in 1978 a number of suggestions were made some of which are noteworthy :

- Improving the identification of the range of employers/ establishments to be inspected;
- Ways and means of co-ordination between the work of various kinds of inspectors;
- Action to be taken to overcome reluctance of many workers to make complaints;
- Focusing attention on employers with non-unionized labour or with inherently dangerous or unhealthy working process of materials;
- Creation of psychological impact through emphasis on quality of inspections, publicity to prosecutions and Convictions and area saturations campaigns;
- Involving employers and workers in remote areas to central locations for inspection and review.

Need for Systematic Evaluation of Implementation of Labour Laws

Government receives several complaints about non implementation of labour laws generally or in particular areas, industries or establishments. These call for investigation cutting across the jurisdiction of the various inspection agencies appointed under the various labour laws. Complaints of general nature also underline the need for evaluation of the implementation of the laws. While every Government has a machinery for enforcement of labour laws, there is at present no arrangement for an evaluation of the working of the inspection machinery The existing system of monitoring the implementation of the laws through the Labour Bureau cannot be said to be satisfactory.

A National Seminar on Administration of Minimum Wages in Agriculture was held in collaboration with Asian Regional project for Labour Administration of the ILO. One of the conclusions reached at the Seminar was:

> "There seems to be need for a periodical evaluation concurrent with the adjustments or revision of wages to ascertain why minimum wages are not being paid and, where they are being paid, what effect it has had on the rural economy, what

> countervailing forces are working in the economy and how they could be counteracted."

There is a similar need for evaluation of the implementation of other laws to enable Government to consider whether there is need for any change in the laws or for any other measures to improve the administration of the laws. It is felt that such an evaluation should be built into the system of labour administration.

The responsibility for administration of labour laws rests mostly with the State governments. As however, labour is a concurrent subject, and the national policy is evolved by the Government of India the responsibility for conducting evaluatory studies which may be directed towards modification or of better implementation of the policy will have to be assumed by the Central Government itself.

These studies may be organised through the Labour Bureau, the NLI and/ or other institutions engaged in research in the field of labour.

NOTES

1. Address delivered at the National Labour Institute on 23.1.1984.

V
Major Issues Concerning Labour

There are certain fundamental issues concerning labour generally which need to be addressed in formulating policy for the future. These issues are mentioned below.

1. The World is witnessing climatic changes in the political, economic as well as social spheres. In the context of these changes the basic question that has arisen is whether the State has any role to play in the field of labour and, if so, what is the nature and scope of that role.

   As the State normally operates through law this question can be formulated in a different way, that is, whether, in the changing situation, labour relations can be regulated by law, if not, what is the alternative to protect labour from exploitation.

   The facts relevant to these questions briefly are as follows:

   There is a fundamental cleavage of opinion regarding the role of the State, and therefore of law, in the economic sphere, between market economy and socialist countries. The market economic countries lay greater faith in the operation of the market forces for achieving economic as well as social objectives. The socialist countries, on the other hand, consider it to be the function of the State to ensure Social justice for its people. Consequent on the failure of the Socialist experiment in the East European countries, the erstwhile Socialist countries are transforming themselves into market economies. The hallmark of a market economy is the freedom of the individual and organizations to act as they deem fit without impinging on the rights of others to do so. The hallmark of a socialist economy is State ownership of the means of production, State control over the activities of the individuals and organizations and State regulation of the relationship between management and labour. Conversion of a socialist economy into a market economy would mean abandonment of State regulation leaving the relationship between labour and management to be regulated by the Operation of the market forces.

Indeed, the World Bank experts have been advocating a policy of deregulation, simplification of labour laws permitting closure of sick units and retrenchment of labour. Following the lead given by the World Bank, Indian economists are pleading for a new approach to industrial relations and exit policies. It is said that our present emphasis on overprotecting organized labour is not conducive to development. It has been announced that under the new policy for small-scale industries they may be exempted from some of the labour laws.

On the other hand, there is a move to insert a Social Clause on Worker's Rights in the General Agreement on Tariffs and Trade. Such a clause would allow cases to be brought under GATT procedure for alleged breaches of internationally accepted workers rights leading to imposition of sanctions against the abuse or repression of worker's rights.

Thus the Third World countries like India are subjected to contradictory pressures.

2. If State regulation of labour relations is to be eliminated or reduced the only alternative to safeguard the interests of the workers is organization of the workers and collective bargaining. But the current trend indicates a decline in the strength and importance of the trade unions. In the circumstances the question is whether collective bargaining can be an effective alternative to State regulation.

   There are two reasons for weakening of the trade unions. Firstly, due to the technological revolution that is sweeping all over the world the number of blue collar workers is dwindling and the number of the so-called knowledge-workers is growing. It appears that there is little in common between the blue-collar workers and knowledge-workers. The lack of homogeneity among the working class has affected the solidarity of the labour movement.

Secondly, and more importantly, is the growth of flexibility in the organization of work. Flexibility is being introduced in every aspect of employer-employee relationship, employment, remuneration as well as condition of work. It is leading to a variety of atypical employment relationships characterized by increasing labour casualization, decentralization of production, sub-contracting, homework, use of temporary workers and networking. This tendency has contributed significantly to the breakdown of the solidarity of the working class.

For both these reasons questions have arisen about the future role of collective bargaining in regulating the relations between labour and management.

3. The foregoing developments raise a further question about the role of the ILO itself and its future.

The basic function of the I.L.O. is to set international standards in the field of labour.

The international labour standards become effective only when they are ratified by the Member Governments. They can be ratified only when the laws and practices obtaining in the countries conform to the standards. It is therefore a pre-requisite for ratification of the I.L.O. conventions that the national laws should be brought in line with them. If the laws cannot be upgraded for the reason that they provide undue protection to the workers the purpose of the standards set by the I.L.O. and hence the purpose of the I.L.O. itself would be defeated. The current trend is to dismantle state control and state regulation in the field of labour strikes at the very root of the international organization.

The ILO is one of the few post World War I institutions which have survived. It was created to operate as a countervailing force to the communist movement. With the retreat of communism the ILO seems to have lost its raison d'etre.

The International Labour Standards emphasize the right of the workers to organize them serves and to bargain collectively. They also emphasize consultation with the organizations of employers and workers before taking any decision affecting labour.

The decline in unionization and consequent weakening of the trade union movement have resuscitated a change in the outlook In the circumstances the question is whether the ILO can continue in its present form or whether any change in its organization and function is warranted.

4. Although there has been a phenomenal growth in the world economy during the recent years there has been no comparable development of the human resources. On the other hand, the **World Labour Report Vol. III (1987)** has pointed out that the world labour situation has deteriorated since the first two volumes of the Report were published. The question is as to how the trend can be reversed, what policy changes if any are required and what programs are necessary to alleviate the conditions of labour especially in the rural and unorganized sectors of the developing countries, and what new forms of social and economic organization need to be created.

   In this connection the following facts brought out in the World Labour Report are relevant:

   Real incomes from work have fallen in many parts of the world. A significant proportion of workers in some Asian and industrialized market economy countries have also experienced declining real incomes. Trends in employment show the same depressing picture. In the rural areas of the developing countries inappropriate systems of land revenue, introduction of modern agricultural techniques and mechanization have pushed millions of people out of farming. They have gone to swell the ranks of the unemployed, been forced to find casual wage employment where and when they can or to take precarious and insecure jobs in small urban enterprises. In many market economy countries unemployment has remained at unacceptably high levels while in both Developing countries as well as market economies increasing number of workers have become more vulnerable to insecurity of income and employment. The move towards more flexible forms of employment and remuneration may aid greater efficiency and economic growth but in many cases it means that increasingly large groups of workers are driven to the margins of the labour market. Reduced government social expenditure has often led to reduced opportunities for the vulnerable groups in society who are not generally protected by collective bargaining. New forms of social and economic organization are therefore needed to defend their rights and collective interests.

5. This brings us to the appropriate development strategy for developing countries.

The development objectives have undergone a metamorphosis during the last four decades. Initially maximization of economic growth was the primary objective. It has given place to what is called human development and improvement in the quality of life. Prof. Amartya Sen has pointed out that some countries like Sri Lanka with relatively low level of GNP have achieved comparatively higher standard of living. The project on "objectives processes and indicators of development" sponsored by the U.N. University has highlighted the shortcomings of the conventional theories of development introducing the concept of mis-development. It has concluded that optimum development should be measured in terms of quality of life.

In spite of these changes in the theory of development some of the industrialized countries of the West, the World Bank and the IMF have advocated that the third world countries should take a cue from the happenings in East Europe and opt for a laissez faire policy. In this connection a writer has observed that in all the socialist countries which have started opting for a market economy ownership of resources has been leveled down and an equity base has been built on which the edifice of the market economy is to be built. In the case of most of the developing countries such a leveling down has not taken place and it is a moot point whether a market economy would work out satisfactorily in these countries. Hegel has argued that the organization of life through the market produces great poverty alongside great wealth. This is corroborated by the experience of development in many developing countries where there is concentration of wealth in a few hands while the majority of the people suffer privation.

It is therefore obvious that a more equitable development strategy needs to be evolved.

A remarkable feature of the economic situation in many developing countries is the surplus of labour in rural areas. The surplus labour is moving towards urban areas in search of employment but as there are not adequate opportunities of employment even in those areas they are living in sub-human conditions. Any scheme of development has to address itself to this situation. In this connection two alternative models of development, are suggested. One is to develop self-sufficient village economies so as to arrest the growth of urban centers.

The second is to develop growth centers, a set of intermediate points between towns and villages, which supply the necessities of the villages on the one hand and serve as a market for the village products on the other. Whatever model is adopted it is necessary to build a proper nexus between rural and urban areas so that they may be complementary to each other. No conscious effort has been made in this regard so far and it needs to be made. The question is whether such a strategy has any bearing on the labour policy.

VI
Globalisation and its Impact on Labour[1]

Globalisation means many things to many people. The Human Development Report 2001 has defined globalisation as "the free movement of goods, services, people, and information across national boundaries". In other words it means movement of goods and services across nations without any restriction by way of tariffs and quotas. Just as goods and services move freely without any restriction within a country globalisation requires movement of goods and services equally freely across different countries.

Traditionally, nation states have tended to insulate themselves by imposing tariff barriers so as to protect their industries against competition from abroad. The current thinking is that such protectionist policies tend to make local industries inefficient, non competitive and uneconomical. The countries of the world have therefore entered into an agreement and created a new international organization called World Trade Organisation which requires that the member countries should pull down all the trade barriers and allow goods and services to move across countries freely without any restriction. This is described as integration of national economies with the global economy.

In theory the concept of free trade is based on the principle of comparative advantage. Every country produces those goods and services for which it has the necessary advantage and purchases the other goods and services from countries which have the comparative advantage for producing them. "International trade depends fundamentally on international specialization and localization of production on sites of minimum costs, and that, in turn, requires unrestricted movement of capital, labour raw materials, and finished goods. In world conditions of free trade the world's relative scarce factors of production will be distributed by natural forces in such a way that they will be used to maximum advantage. The volume of world trade will be the largest possible., and every country will benefit either as a producer or as a consumer and in many cases from both points of view."[2]

Globalisation is based on the principle that competition promotes growth and consequently betterment of the living conditions of the people generally. It is the means and the end of marketisation of national economies in contradistinction to State control and regulation of the economy. Its object is economic development shorn of all equity considerations. The advocates of globalisation assume that economic growth brings in its wake social development and that no special effort need be made for the protection of the poor and the excluded.

Free trade and globalisation work well if there is perfect competition among the countries. But the world economy is characterized by imperfect competition. For competition to succeed all countries should have a level playing field. As the world is divided between the developed and the developing countries, countries endowed with natural and human resources and those who do not have such resources competition among the countries cannot be equal. In the circumstances the countries who are economically better off are apt to take advantage of those who are worse off.

The New Economic Policy initiated by the Government of India in 1991 aims at integrating Indian economy with the global economy. In other words it seeks to globalise the Indian economy. In pursuance of this policy the Government of India has signed the World Trade Agreement which requires removal of all restriction on international trade by way of tariffs and quotas and the policy is being implemented vigorously. The Study Group on Globalisation of the Second National Commission on Labour examined the working of the economy since the introduction of the New Economic Policy and came to the following conclusions

(1) During the 20th century, wide spread poverty and unemployment resulted in significant interventions by the State in all major countries, regardless of their ideological differences and models of economic policies. These interventions while resulting in widening and deepening of protection for labour were increasingly seen as leading to economic stagnation.

(2) During the past two decades, there is significant tendency worldwide for withdrawal of state from many areas of economic life coinciding with lowering of national barriers to international capital and financial flows. At the beginning of the 21st century the world is once again at cross roads and there is a search for

balancing the concerns of competitiveness of enterprises with maintaining the rights of labour for decent working and living standards.

(3) These concerns emanate from some of the most important trends of globalisation processes directly affecting labour in our country. In so far as major trends in employment and employment relations are concerned the following are the major conclusions:

- Employment growth has slackened in the last decade coinciding with high rates of growth of the national economy
- Employment in primary sector, the largest employer of labour force in the country is declining, while the manufacturing sector employment has recorded only marginal growth. The major growth area of employment is in the service sector.
- Casualisation of the labour force has increased *vis a vis* self employment and regular and salaried wage employment.
- Proportion of organized sector in total employment has declined steadily.
- Declining employment elasticities imply declining employment absorption capacities.

All the above labour market trends indicate increasingly insecure and unstable nature of employment growth, which has major implications for income inequality and regional disparities. Globalization in the present form holds little promise for ensuring decent working and living conditions for the majority. These pessimistic conclusions however need to be tempered by the fact that there is a trend towards rise in real wages and productivity along with significant decline in poverty levels. In the area of employment relations, some important trends noticeable are as follows:

- There is decline of union density across the board in all sectors.
- The decline of organized employment coupled with increasing voluntary separation is significantly reducing the space for trade union activities in the organized sector.
- Increased emphasis on technology and productivity based bargaining has emerged along with tendency towards decentralized collective bargaining.
- Declining incidence of industrial conflicts over the last two decades is accompanied by increased lockout to strike ratio.

In the emerging global economic environment the following are the main conclusions concerning the performance of Indian economy:

- Although the process of economic liberalization has provided increased opportunity for trade and investment inadequate competitiveness in Indian economy has deterred the capacity of Indian industries to harness the opportunities presented by globalisation.
- Constant increase of productivity has become the cornerstone for increasing overall competitiveness. Here again productivity levels in the economy are much less than the desired levels.
- Liberalization and globalisation has accelerated technology flows across national borders. However the key issue here is the ability to adapt new technology and engage in continuous product and process innovation. The present industrial structure is still not conducive to adoption of new technology at a fast rate.
- There are lots of resources locked in sick and unviable industrial enterprises. While having a deleterious impact on those who are employed in these enterprises it also deters in the overall employment generation. The current legal and bureaucratic institutional processes obstruct rather than aid in the unlocking of these national resources.

It is important to recognize that the above problems are not exclusively due to the processes of globalisation. These processes may have accentuated or exacerbated several of the socio-economic and labour problems, which persisted for a long time. There is a need for restructuring the economy and enterprises for more efficient utilization of national resources. Processes of globalisation have only made this an urgent and imperative need. The emerging trends in labour market and employment relations on the one hand and the urgent need for restructuring necessitated by the changing global business environment on the other hand warrants that appropriate strategies be adopted to make globalisation work for the people of India. What is clear however is that this cannot be achieved by blindly pursuing the present agenda of globalisation. Simultaneously it is also evident that greater preparedness is required by all the social partners both to confront the ills of globalisation and to harness the process for national benefit. The recommendations made by the study group reflect this need for balance.

Thus globalisation has had both beneficial as well as adverse consequences. While it has contributed to the growth of the economy to a certain extent benefiting the middle and the upper classes of people it has had a deleterious effect on employment and the conditions of life of the people in the lower segments of the society. The Study Group has pointed out that on the basis of principal status, the rate of growth of employment in the economy has slowed down from 2.27 per cent during the years 1993-94 to 1997-98 to 1.55 per cent p.a. during 1993-94 and 1999-2000. On the basis of usual status and subsidiary status taken together, the rate of growth in employment comes to 0.82 per cent. The rate of growth of labour force during the same period, taking into consideration the backlog of the unemployed is 3.63 per cent. This is more than double the rate of growth in employment during the period. Whatever growth has taken place is in the unorganized sector. There is an increase in casual and contract labour. The proportion of casual wage labour which was 29.9 per cent in 1987-88 went up to 32.6 per cent in 1999-2000 with a corresponding reduction in the percentage of the self employed which went down from 56.3 per cent in 1987-88 to 52.51 per cent in 1999-2000. The absolute magnitude of the unemployed in 1999-2000 was 9.7 per cent. The size of the organized sector shrunk and that of the unorganised sector increased. The size of the unorganized sector in 1999-2000 was 92.9 per cent of the total labour force.

The growth in the numbers of the unemployed and casual wage employed suggests deterioration in the conditions of life of the people. The reduction in the number of self employed suggests that a large number of self employed people took to wage employment not being able to sustain themselves by their traditional employment. This explains to some extent the large scale death by suicide in several parts of the country.

This situation is not peculiar to India. It is a global phenomenon. It is particularly acute in some of the Latin American countries and it has generated a movement to oppose globalization.

This movement has been spearheaded by trade unions and NGOs all over the world who have formed an organization called World Social Forum to agitate against the policies and programmes of globalisation with the slogan "another world is possible".

The World Social Forum was first constituted about four years ago at a place called St Allegro in Brazil. It is stated that in the four years since it came into existence, the World Social Forum (WSF) has developed a large and growing family of converts. "Characterised variously as a platform, a movement and a space – the precise choice would involve a quite needless diversion into terminology - the WSF has played the role of uniting diverse concerns into a singularly forceful assertion of the need for alternatives to today's dominant political and economic paradigms."[3]

The process of globalisation has several aspects. Unfettered free trade is one. It is associated with liberalisation and privatisation.

Privatisation is a process under which many of the public utilities and other undertakings in the public sector are being transferred to the private sector and in this process some of the public enterprises are being taken over by multinational companies. It is looked upon as a measure "dictated by the economic super powers whose priority is to gain control over the resources and ensure that neo liberal capitalism becomes irreversible."[4]

Globalisation has thus come to be treated as synonymous with the growing instability, inequity and uncertainty in many parts of the world.

What is the remedy?

The key to the problem of globalisation lies in promotion of employment. The Study Group on Globalisation of the NCL has therefore made the following recommendations for promoting employment:

> " An important aspect of globalisation has been its adverse impact in the field of employment. Provision of gainful and decent employment to the mass of Indian people remains the strongest bulwark against the insecurities and instabilities generated by the present form of globalisation. In creating such employment growth, all the social partners have a role to play. What is crucial is that there should be synergy between the competencies and roles played by each of the partners."

The role of the state in directly creating employment is no longer a viable option. State role is now to be reoriented from being a generator to facilitator of employment growth. State can effectively promote employment growth while following a high economic growth strategy in the following manner.

- By clearly enunciating a national employment policy as a strategic response to the globalisation process.
- By formulating appropriate employment planning at the sector/ decentralized level on the basis of an effective labour market information system.
- By prioritising physical and social infrastructure development

both to jump start employment growth and to enhance employability of the population.

- By giving priority in hearing and considering positively the trade union views.
- By identifying employment potential of different sectors where the country has comparative advantage. Available evidence shows that the areas where such growth potential are present are:
  - Service sector including information technology enabled services
  - Forestry and logging
  - Energy from biomass
  - Renewable sources of energy
  - Watershed management
  - Animal husbandry and Horticulture
  - Value added products and services i.e. Gems and Jewellery, Special Chemicals, Fragrance.

Apart from identifying the growth sectors, it is also crucial to ensure that there is prospect for continuous up-gradation of the sector and the employment thus created to move up the value chain as follows:

- By facilitating up-gradation of skills and restructuring the educational system to enhance employability.
- By providing positive incentive structures and appropriate infrastructural support to ensure that informal sector generates quality employment.
- By protecting through provisions in international agreements (WTO) agricultural sector and small industries for international competition in order to protect livelihoods of persons in occupations potentially affected.
- By indentifying successful non-state employment generation models based on community participation, cooperatives, self help groups etc., and facilitating their replication.

NOTES

1. The MP Cement Manufacturers' Association held a Seminar on "Impact of Globalisation on Industry and Labour" on February 1 and 2, 2003 at Hotel Satya Ashok Jabalpur. I was invited to prepare a background paper for the Seminar and to present it. I presided over the inaugural session and made

two presentation in the subsequent sessions; one on the "Challenges of Globalisation and their Impacts" and the other on the Report of the National Commission on Labour. This the paper I presented on Globalisation and its impact.

2. P. 529 Text book of Economics, Briggs and Jordan University Tutorial Press Ltd., London.
3. Globalised Struggle by Sukumar Muralidharan Frontline February 13, 2004.
4. P.K. Tripathy.

VII
Problems of Unorganised Labour

Bonded Labour

Individual Freedom is a basic condition of a democratic society. The constitution of India guarantees the right to freedom, which includes freedom of speech, freedom of association, freedom of movement, freedom of residence, freedom of trade and occupation etc. The Constitution also confers a right against exploitation and prohibits traffic in human beings and forced labour. Parliament by a separate Act, the Bonded Labour (Abolition) Act, 1976 has abolished bonded labour. It is however believed that the system of bonded labour still exists in various forms. There are varying estimates of the number of bonded labour in the country. According to one estimate there are over two million bonded labourers in the country. According to another there are about 1.5 million bonded labourers. These are however statistical projections. The actual number of bonded labourers identified by the various State Governments for purposes of release and rehabilitation is less than 2 lakhs. There is thus a vast difference. The Government of India has therefore exhorted all the States to take vigorous steps to identify bonded labour where they exist and to have them released and rehabilitated. The response from the State Governments has not been very encouraging. At a national seminar on bonded labour held in February 1983 it was observed that in certain States much larger number of bonded labourers had been identified than elsewhere and this was attributed to lack of administrative will and to the fact that sometimes administration was touchy and avoided admitting existence of bonded labour. On the other hand several academics have concluded that bonded labour in the strictly legal sense has disappeared. There is thus a wide divergence of opinion and it is necessary to determine the fact whether there is bonded labour in India and if so in what form and in what numbers. It is needless to say that this has several policy implications.

Firstly, having passed an Act abolishing bonded labour no Government worth the name can allow bonded labour to continue to exist.

Secondly having ratified the ILO Convention No. 29 on forced labour, the Government of India is now open to the supervisory jurisdiction of the ILO and is answerable to that organization for the existence of forced labour in the form of bonded labour in violation of the Convention.

Thirdly, Rehabilitation of Bonded labour is one of the items of 20-point programme and if a large number of bonded labours still exist unidentified unreleased and un-rehabilitated it represents a failure of the 20-point programme.

On the other hand, if bonded labour exists on such a mass scale as estimated by the Gandhi Peace Foundation or the NSS their sudden withdrawal from their present position is likely to cause a social upheaval and their rehabilitation will impose a heavy burden on the Government.

Some international agencies are giving wide publicity to the existence of bonded labour in India, which has been affecting the image of the nation. It needs to be, but it has not been possible effectively to counter the above publicity.

There is also good deal of confusion among persons working for social change. They need to know whether the existence of bonded labour is real or imaginary:

- Is the concept clear? When some say that bonded labour exists and other deny it. Do they refer to the same phenomenon?
- What is the hallmark of bonded labour? Is it non-payment or short payment of wages? If so what is the difference between Rehabilitation of Bonded labour and enforcement of minimum wages, which are distinctive items of the 20-point program.

These are questions for which we have find to an answer. I cannot say that I have an answer but I have a hypothesis, which I wish to place before you.

The term-bonded labour has two connotations. According to one it signifies forced labour – labour one is required to provide involuntarily against one's will without any wages or at low wages. According to the other it signifies lack of freedom of movement.

There is no mention of bonded labour in our Constitution, which talks only of forced labour. The ILO Conventions also refer to forced labour and not to bonded labour. We should determine whether the two expressions are synonymous. In my view they are not.

During discussions in the tripartite committee on brick kiln industry I got the impression that in referring to bonded labour stress was laid on the lack of freedom of movement as though the workers were illegally confined and not so much on compulsion to work.

These are two distinct rights – the right to freedom of movement and the right against exploitation. Denial of the freedom of movement may exist where there is forced labour but one should be able to conceive of forced labour without denial of freedom of movement.

V.D. Mahajan in his commentary on the Constitution of India says:

> "Article 23 prohibits forced labour, i.e,. labour or service, which a person is forced to provide. Forced labour may arise in several ways. It may be physical force which may compel a person to provide labour or service to another or it may be force exerted through a legal provision such as provision for imprisonment or fine in case the employee fails to provide labour or service or it may even be compulsion arising from hunger and poverty, want and destitution. Any factor which deprives a person of a choice of alternatives and compels him to adopt one particular course of action may properly be regarded as force and if labour or service is compelled as a result of such force, it would be forced labour".

Again he says –

> "Begar" means involuntary work without payment. It commonly connotes forced labour for which wages are not paid. Even if some payment is made, it is grossly inadequate. However, a voluntary agreement to do extra work for payment is not begar or forced labour".

The Supreme Court has ruled that where a person is required to work for wages, which are lower than minimum wages, there is forced labour.

There is perhaps no disagreement on the prevalence of forced labour in this sense. Politicians, public administrators as well as academics accept the existence of forced labour in the sense of a person being forced to work at low wages for economic reasons. But there is disagreement on the existence of bonded labour. The differences in my view, lies in the inclusion of the element of denial of the freedom of movement in the concept of bonded labour.

If this is correct it would be obvious that the objective of the legislation would need to be reconsidered and restated. It should be made clear what the Parliament sought to achieve in legislating for abolition of bonded labour – whether payment of minimum wages, freedom of movement or freedom of occupation or protection against forced labour.

In his commentary Mahajan identifies three types of circumstances under which forced labour may exist:

- Physical force may compel a person to provide labour to another.
- There may be legal compulsion.
- There may be compulsion arising from hunger and poverty.

It may be possible to prevent forced labour caused by physical force or by a legal provision. It may not be possible to do away with forced labour arising out of poverty and distribution by issue of a fiat. It calls for an economic regeneration. This is a longtime process. The National commission on Labour has observed that mere legislation is no remedy for difficulties arising out of economic compulsions. With slow improvement in economic conditions, enforcement of tenancy laws, security of tenure and opportunity for employment, the system has shown signs of disintegration. We should therefore aim at further and rapid improvement in these directions to eliminate the evil of forced labour.

In the meantime it will be necessary to remove the ambiguity underlying the term bonded labour as distinguished from the concept of forced labour so that the administrators have a clear focus for action.

Child Labour

Child labour has been in vogue, all over the world, for a long time but it was not considered as evil till recently. On the other hand it was considered as part of the process of socialization and therefore beneficial. It has however now become a social problem due to the development of the tendency for employers to exploit children employed as wage labour calling for measures to protect the children against abuse. This is the product of the growth of capitalist mode of production and consequent changes in social relations.

The Indian economy is in an evolutionary stage; it cannot be said to be entirely capitalist. There are pre-capitalist, feudal as well as capitalist elements in it. The form of child labour prevalent in the economy is therefore not uniform.

In discussing child labour, we should therefore distinguish between different forms of labour and isolate those which are harmful so that appropriate measures may be evolved for protection of children who are working under exploitative conditions.

Traditionally in a rural economy based on agriculture, children are used to work in family circles, learning the family crafts on the job through observation, association and imitation. There may be an element of exploitation even in such work but there are hardly any harmful effects. It is regarded "as one form of participation in community life an intrinsic part of adaptation to and internalization of adult roles". It is likened to "those present day tasks, which by nature are light, sporadic, interesting, educational and socially useful and which serve to integrate the child in the social life of the group to which he belongs". Children may enjoy working for or with their parents, brothers and sisters. This tradition continues in large areas of the Indian economy in spite of its growing modernization. This tradition is not to be caviled at although one might like those children to learn in schools rather than in the fields.

It does not mean that all is well with the children in this sector and that there is nothing that needs to be done for them. Indeed there is much that needs and should be done for these children because many if not most of them are underfed, undernourished, uneducated and fall in to bad ways. But the problems of these children are the general problem of poverty and child development. It is not the problem of child labour as such. In my opinion this distinction is important.

The problem of child labour exists where children are made to do hard work, excessively long hours, on low wages, under unsafe and unhealthy conditions against their will stifling their physical as well as mental development. It is said that these things are necessary to bring the work of a child within the concept of child labour. Firstly, the child should be employed in a gainful occupation. Secondly, the work must be hazardous and thirdly it must deny to him the opportunity for development. When these or similar conditions exist there is exploitation of child labour that will have two aspects. Firstly, a part of the production of the workers is expropriated by others and secondly the working children are discriminated against relation to their abilities and development needs.

Child labour in this sense is prevalent in village and small industries, hotel and restaurants, plantations and other services. In match factories children are put to work at frame fitting, box filling, and bundle rolling. In beedi industry they help in cutting and cleaning the leaves and binding and closing the ends of the beedies. Some children also do the rolling. In cashew factories children are employed in peeling of nuts after they are roasted and shelled. In carpet weaving the children help in the middle of the looms while the weavers work on the corners. In the glass industry they help in joining of ends, cutting, patching, sorting and ornamental work. In stoneware industry they are engaged in brushing, polishing, labeling and packing. In construction industry they carry loads. In plantations, children are employed in weeding, manuring, care of nurseries, harvesting etc.

Urbanization is a concomitant of modernization. Urban centers offer opportunities for services and self-employment of children. A large number of children are employed as domestic servants and as workers in hotels, restaurants and wayside dhabas. Many of them are employed as shoeshine boys, coolies, newspaper vendors, hawkers etc. In some places beggary has become a profession and children are employed for begging.

The fact that children are put to work is not by itself a matter of concern. It is the nature of the work, the age at which they are made to work and the conditions under which they work, it is these that make child labour, it is these that make child labour reprehensible. Children are employed in domestic service at the age of 9 or 10. There are cases where even younger children in the age group from 6 to 9 have been put to work. A study carried out in Bombay a few years ago revealed that nearly 25 per cent of the child workers were in the age groups of 6 to 9, nearly 50 per cent in the age of 10 to 12 and the remaining in the age group of 13 to 15. Thus bulk of the children at work are below 12 years of age. Children below the age of 12 are employed in manufacturing or construction activities of hazardous nature and those working under conditions of bondage call for priority attention of the State and Social Action groups.

For the purpose of policy child labour can therefore be classified into the following categories:

1. Those employed in agriculture and related activities within family circles and those apprenticed for family crafts.
2. Those employed in manufacturing or construction activities. These can be subdivided into those employed in hazardous occupation and others.
3. Those employed in services. These again can be sub-divided into those who are working under condition of bondage and others.
4. Those self-employed.

These can be reclassified age-wise as follows:

Those who are below the age of ten.
Those who are between 10 and 12, and
Those who are between 13 and 15.

A demographic profile of child labour has been circulated. It may be seen there from that nearly 87 per cent of the children at work are in agriculture, livestock, forestry, poultry and related occupations. This corresponds to the first category. Manufacturing and construction activities account for approximately 7 per cent. Services including trade and commerce account for 6 per cent.

Statistics relating to the number of children employed in hazardous occupations or those employed in conditions of bondage are not available. Statistics showing the analysis of the number of workers age-wise is also not available. It would be worthwhile collecting it.

It has been reported that large industrial firms and other sizeable capitalist enterprises do not make much use of child labour perhaps because of the labour legislation. The practice of employing child labour is therefore common in smaller establishments, which are outside the scope or beyond the reach of the law. I therefore propose that this Seminar will do well to concentrate on the problem of child labour in such units.

Minimum wages have been fixed by the appropriate governments for large number employments. In Gujarat the Government of Gujarat have prescribed minimum wages for 38 employments. These rates are applicable to adults. It is provided that children would be entitled to a certain percentage of these rates; the percentage varies from 50 per cent to 80 per cent, according to the nature of employment. In the employment in any pulp and paper or board manufacturing the minimum rates of wages payable to a child is 50 per cent of the rates fixed for adults; in the bone crushing industry it is 75 per cent; in some cases the notifications are silent about this; in all other cases it is about 80 per cent. The rationale for these variations are however not clear and would have to be looked into.

Under the Minimum Wages Act the appropriate Government is also required to prescribe the hours of work which will constitute a normal working day for which minimum wages at the prescribed rates are payable. Government of Gujarat have prescribed that 9 hours would constitute a normal working day for adults and 4½ hours for children. It is however not clear whether the percentages of minimum wages as applicable to children are for 9 hours of work or for 4½ hours. Where children are entitled to 80 per cent of the rates applicable to adults and they are to be paid at that rate for 4½ hours of work only there would be a premium on child labour. On the other hand if the children are to be paid 50 or 80 per cent of the wages reduced proportionately for the reduced hours of work they will be at a discount. This calls for a review.

The actual number of hours worked by children each day varies considerably depending upon many factors, mainly the nature of the work they perform, whether they go to school or not, the attitude of their parents and their employers. It is said that as the child workers are usually at the mercy of the employers, working days of 10, 12 or 14 hours seven days in a week are not uncommon. Self-employed workers have to adjust their working hours to the needs of their customers. It has been observed that 8 or 9 year olds remain at work till late at night trying to sell their morning newspapers outside the big hotels. A study carried out in Bombay has revealed that children employed in hotels and restaurants were working for more than 11 hours a day on the average.

Very often children are employed as unpaid household servants where they have to work for indefinite hours in return for the board and lodging of minimal standards provided by the householder. In the past there was a practice of pledging the children as workers in repayment of debt taken by the parents. This practice was legally prohibited as early as in 1933 but the practice cannot be said to have disappeared altogether. Certain types of apprenticeships have the marks of bondage.

Workers generally are exposed to occupational risks of accidents and diseases. These risks are greater for child workers because of their lack of experience, concentration and strength to bear the strain of work. Besides the incidence of these risks is also greater in the types of work in which children are employed. For example, there have been many accidents resulting in loss of life in match factories. In glass works children sustain cuts and burns. In carpet manufacturing they are liable to bisinosis type of diseases for they constantly breath in wool dust. In construction projects the children are exposed to danger of falls and injuries.

If the working conditions of the children are bad then living conditions are worse. They are deprived of the care and affection of their parents when they need it most. They find the world cruel and harsh and it affects their mental make-ups in their formative stage. Generally speaking they live in unhealthy conditions on the pavement or in the workshop or kitchen where they work lacking nourishment, badly clothed with no protection against the climate. Vitamin and protein deficiency is common. Incidence of T.B. and other dreaded diseases is also high. It is therefore said that the conditions in which children usually work are harmful to the child, the results of which are carried to the adult life. The ill treatment and the sense of neglect injustice and frustration they suffer will have bad effect on the young minds and they fall prey to social evils. These destroy the elements, which constitute the cementing force of the society and pose a grave danger to the future a well-ordered civilized life.

International Programme on the Elimination of Child Labour

The International Labour Organisation has launched a programme for elimination of child labour on global basis; India has joined the programme by signing a MOU with the ILO. The highlights of the programme include :

- Rehabilitation of tribal child labour
- Pilot work on a 3 tier strategy for rehabilitation of child labour on Railway Platforms
- Attempt to combat child labour in municipal waste dumping yards
- Combating child labour in plantations
- Creation of awareness etc.

It is well known that a large number of children in India are employed for wages under exploitative conditions. According to the 1981 Census, the estimated number of working children was 13.6 million. This figure rose to 17.02 million according to the estimates of the 43rd round of the National Sample Survey conducted in 1987-88. According to the Census of 1991 the number of working children was 11.28 million. More than 90per cent of child labour is engaged in rural areas, in agriculture and allied occupations like cultivation, agricultural labour, livestocks, forestry and fisheries. The estimate of child labour thus varies widely but is admittedly very large.

It is generally agreed that that child labour is a pernicious practice which needs to be eradicated. The International Labour Organisation has launched a programme for elimination of child labour on global basis, India has joined the programme by signing a MOU with the ILO.

The Government of India has made a declaration of the National Policy for Elimination of Child Labour and has also adopted an action plan towards that end. The policy of the Government with respect to Child Labour is to ban employment of children below the age of 14 years in factories mines and hazardous employment and to regulate the working conditions of children in other employment. In pursuance of this objective the Government has adopted an action plan consisting of the following elements:

- a legislative action plan
- focusing of general development programmes for benefiting children wherever possible and
- project-based action plans in areas of high concentration of child labour engaged in wage, quasi-wage employment.

This plan is being implemented.

As per the legislative action plan the Child Labour (Prohibition and Regulation) Act, 1986 has been enacted. Through a notification dated 26.5.1993 the working conditions of children have been regulated in all employments which are not prohibited under the Act. As per a Notification dated 29.3.1994 Government have also prohibited employment of children in five more occupations/processes adding to the six occupational and fourteen processes already scheduled under the Act for such prohibition.

A high powered body called the National Authority for Elimination of Child Labour was constituted in Sept. 1994. The Authority adopted a programme for securing convergence of services of the Ministries of the Government of India and the Department of State Governments which implement child related programmes at the national state and field levels so as to provide education, health and other inputs.

Under the project based action plan 12 national child labour projects were started in various States. Initially the projects were sanctioned as part of a central scheme in the following areas:

- Match Industry in Sivakasi, Tamilnadu
- Precious Stones Polishing Industry in Jaipur, Rajasthan
- Glassware Industry in Ferozabad, Uttar Pradesh
- Brassware Industry in Moradabad, Uttar Pradesh
- Hand made Carpet Industry in Mirzapur-Bhadohi, Uttar Pradesh
- Lock making industry in Aligarh, Uttar Pradesh
- Tile Industry in Jaggampet, Andhra Pradesh
- State Industry in Markapur, Andhra Pradesh
- State Industry in Mandsaur, Madhya Pradesh

The following activities are taken up in theses project areas:

- Stepping up of Enforcement of Child Labour Laws;

- Non-formal Education;
- Adult Education;
- Income and Employment Generation;
- Special Schools;
- Raising Public Awareness; and
- Survey and Evaluation.

A major activity under the plan is the establishment of special schools to provide non-formal education, vocational training, supplementary nutrition, stipend, health care, etc., to children withdrawn from employment. In addition stipends are paid to children withdrawn from employment.

A project level society is required to be constituted for each project to supervise the programme with the District Magistrate/Collector of the district concerned as its chairman and representatives of the other departments concerned and voluntary organisations. Execution of the project is entrusted to a Project Director who is assisted by field officers or social workers. The society is a registered body with a distinct legal status.

During 2000-2001 there were 96 National Child Labour Projects in child labour endemic States for rehabilitation of about 2.0 lakh children. For the 8th Five Year Plan ₹15 crores were provided for the scheme. During the ninth plan a sum of ₹250 crores was allocated for the scheme.

Financial assistance is also given to voluntary organisations for implementation of on going as well as new projects for the welfare of the working children. Under the grant in aid scheme voluntary agencies are being financially assisted to the extent of 75 per cent of the project cost for taking up welfare projects for working children where they are provided with non-formal education, supplementary nutrition, health care and vocational/skill training. The current emphasis of the programme is to create capacity among NGOs to undertake rehabilitation of child labour instead of undertaking the work directly. Several institutions have been involved in the programme such as the National Labour Institute, National Institute for Rural Development, PHD Chamber of Commerce and Industry etc.

The projects are stated to have been evaluated by certain independent agencies. It is claimed that the projects have achieved their objective to a large extent.

It is doubtful if these measures have made any significant dent on the problem of child labour and whether the incidence of child labour has been reduced. Considering that the total number of children at work at the minimum is nearly 12 million the number of persons covered under the child labour projects which is about 0.02 million is insignificant. There seems to be no possibility of covering the entire child labour force under the child labour projects in the near future.

The main objective of the National Child Labour Projects has been to withdraw children working in hazardous employments and mainstreaming them to the formal school system. The total number of children who were employed in such employments, the number of children who needed to be withdrawn from such employment and the actual number withdrawn are not known. The ultimate goal of the child labour projects cannot be just withdrawal of children from employment in hazardous employments but their rehabilitation which lies in their education vocational training and reemployment in appropriate jobs Otherwise the possibility of the children weaned away from work going into the streets which would pose a greater problem cannot be ruled out. It seems therefore necessary to ascertain the condition of the children who have been withdrawn from work. Without this information it cannot be said that the projects have been successful in their objective.

Employment of children in hazardous employments was already prohibited since the adoption of the Constitution and the number of children employed in such employments in violation of the provisions of law could not have been large. The incidence of child labour is much larger in non hazardous employments. But there are no projects to withdraw them from such employments. It is necessary to extend the scope of the projects to such employments also.

While the law prescribes the minimum age for employment in hazardous employments and processes there is no such law prescribing a minimum age for employment in non hazardous employments. It appears that the first step towards elimination of child labour is to enact a general law prescribing the minimum age for employment in any occupation in conformity with the ILO Conventions and Recommendations except in hazardous industries and processes.

It has been recognized that the basic cause for the sad state of children in India is poverty. Unless this problem is tackled it cannot be improved. There is therefore a social security dimension to the problem of child labour. In most cases children are sent to work because of the inability of the parents to educate them and their need to supplement their income with the income of the children. If the families below the poverty line can be given some financial assistance for the maintenance of their children in the form of a family benefit it may go a long way to enable them and to encourage them to withdraw their children from labour. Such schemes already exist in some States where financial assistance is given to SC/ST families as an incentive to send their children to school. The scope of such schemes needs to be widened. The National Commission on Labour has therefore recommended introduction of a national scheme for the payment of a children's allowance on a universal basis, subject to a means test, to persons below the poverty line. "This would be one way of integrating social security schemes with poverty alleviation programmes", the Commission has said.

The Study group on social Security of the national commission on Labour has pointed out that the Government of South Africa has introduced a Scheme of State Support of Children of Poor Families and indicated that a similar scheme should be introduced in India. The Study Group has also pointed out:

> "According to the 1991 Census the total population of children was about 320 million. Assuming that this number has gone up to 350 million by the year 2001 and that 25 per cent of them are below the poverty line, the number of children for whom such assistance would have to be given would be about 90 million per month. Assuming again that the rate of children's allowance to be paid would be ₹ 50 per child per month the total cost of the scheme would be about ₹ 5400 crores per annum."

In absolute terms the estimated cost of the scheme may appear to be large but in terms of the GDP of the country it is very small and it is a small price to pay for the wellbeing of the future citizens of the country.

Disabled Child Labour

The problem of child labour, especially disabled children is matter of deep concern to all of us. In terms of the numbers the problem is gigantic. The number of children all over the world is estimated to be over 50 million. The estimated number of disabled persons is over 450 million. Unfortunately we do not have separate figures of disabled working children.

Disability may be congenital or it may be caused by malnutrition or accidents. According to one estimate 60 to 70 per cent of poor children show signs of growth retardation which in turn leads to physical and mental disabilities and also impair their functioning. It is said that while physical disabilities lead to impairment of functions the drab social environment in which such children grow up cripple their intellectual growth.

The problem of child labour is a product of the socio economic conditions obtaining in the developing countries and it may be difficult to totally eliminate child labour unless those conditions improve. It is however necessary for public authorities to ensure that in cases where children have of necessity to work they do not suffer disabilities on that account. A two fold strategy will have to be adopted to deal with the problem. One is to improve the economic conditions of the people whereby the need for the children to go to work can be avoided or minimized and the other is to provide for the welfare of the children who have necessarily to work for their living.

The welfare of the working children has many facets. Primarily they should be provided with adequate nutrition; secondly, it should be ensured that they are not subjected to occupational hazards; thirdly, they should be given suitable education whereby their physical and mental development is assured. There should be arrangements for development of the skills of the children particularly the disabled ones by testing their aptitudes and to guide them to a proper vocation after necessary training without letting them develop any complexes. In other words, the design of the welfare programme should be such as will enable the children, though employed, to grow into normal adulthood and to enter the mainstream of life.

A programme of this kind is by no means simple; it calls for enormous resources and above all it requires dedicated workers. It is obvious that it cannot be implemented through normal government channels. Private voluntary organisations are better suited to undertake them.

Migrant Labour

Historically, migration of labour represents a phase of development characterized by lack of stability in employment. In the early years of industrialization, workers came from villages; they retained contact with the villages and returned to them from time to time. They were mostly agricultural workers who came to towns and cities when they had no work in the villages but returned during the sowing or the harvest seasons. They could also be village artisans who went to the towns to improve their conditions whey they could no longer live on the meager earnings from their crafts, which had suffered under competition from factory production in the modern industry but cherished the freedom of their crafts and return to the joys of simple life in the villages.

Migrant labour is thus essentially temporary or seasonal in character; it comes and goes. Migrant workers never become residents of the place where they work. The term migrant labour is also associated with the concepts of contract labour and bonded labour. In the past, large numbers of Indian workers migrated to Ceylon, South Africa, West Indies or East India under various types indenture – meaning contract. Their wages were low, their working conditions difficult, unhealthy or dangerous, and their living conditions far worst. Even now large numbers of Indian workers have been migrating to the Gulf countries under similar conditions.

Within the country itself workers migrate from state to state, district to district or from place to place in search of employment. The labour employed in the tea plantations of Assam are traditionally migrant labour from Bihar or Orissa. The conditions under which plantation labour were working in the past, have been portrayed vividly by the famous novelist Mulk Raj Anand in his book *Two Leaves and a Bud.* Similar conditions are known to exist in the construction industry, brick kilns and other seasonal industries like the sugar industry. The statement of objects and reasons of the Inter-sate Migrant Workers (RECS) Act has described the situation as follows:

> "The system of the employment of interstate migrant labour (known in Orissa as Dadan labour) is an exploitative system prevalent in Orissa and in some other states. In Orissa, Dadan labour is recruited from various parts of the state through contractors or agents called *sardars/khatedars* for work outside the state in large construction projects. This system lends itself to various abuses. Though the *sardars* promise at the time of recruitment that wages calculated on piece-rate basis would be settled every month, the promise is not usually kept. Once the worker comes under the clutches of the contractor, he takes him to a far-off place on payment of railway fare only. No working hours are fixed for these workers and they have to work on all the days in a week under extremely bad working conditions. The provisions of the various labour laws are not being observed in their case and they are subjected to various malpractices."

Migrant workmen represent a section of unorganized labour who have not been able to protect their own interests by organizing themselves due (in the words of the National Commission of Labour) to the various constraints such as the casual nature of employment, ignorance and illiteracy, the scattered nature of establishments and superior strength of the employers operating singly or in combination. The early legislative measures were protective of the employers rather than of their workers. Owing to the scarcity lf labour in Assam, workers for the tea plantations had to be imported from the other provinces. The Workmen's Breach of Contract Act 1859 and the Employers and Workmen's Disputes Act 1860 which regulated the conditions of employment of plantation labour made it a penal offence for a worker to breach the contract of service. The first legislation, which gave some measure of protection to the workers, was passed in 1901. It was called he Assam Labour and Emigration Act, 1901. The Act prohibited the recruitment of labour except through licensed contractors. It was amended in 1908 abolishing the system of penal contract and prohibiting recruitment by unlicensed contractors; it was again amended in 1915 abolishing the system of indentured labour in Assam and recruitment by all sorts of contracts. The Act provided for the establishment of the Assam Labour Board for supervision by the tea garden *sardars.* It was replaced by the Tea Districts Emigrant Labour Act, 1932. The object of this Act was to regulate the recruitment of migrant labour. It did not contain any provision regarding their wages, conditions of work or their welfare. It was therefore found to be totally deficient and it was in due course replaced by the Plantation Labour Act. There was no such legislation in respect of migrant labour in other sectors of the economy.

The Minimum Wages Act 1948 was the first attempt at statutory regulation of wages and to some extent working conditions of workers in labour-intensive industries. The Third Five Year Plan drew attention to the great deal of leeway yet to be made up in respect of such workers and observed that their conditions should become a matter of special concern to Governments as well as labour organizations. Since then two major central Acts have been enacted to regulate the employment and conditions of service of contract labour and the Interstate Migrant Workmen.

The Contract Labour (Regulation and Abolition) Act requires every employer employing 20 or more persons to be registered under the Act and every contractor employing 20 or more persons to take a license. It prohibits employment of contract labour for work of a permanent nature. In cases where contract labour is allowed it requires the contractor to provide canteens, restrooms, latrines and urinals for the convenience of the workers and to supply wholesome drinking water. They are also required to provide first-aid facilities. Wages of contract labour are to be paid in the presence of a representative of the principal employer. If there is failure on the part of the contractor to pay the wages, the principal employer is made responsible for the payment. The principal employer is also held responsible for providing the required facilities if there is default on the part of the contractor to provide them.

The Inter-state Migrant Workmen (Regulation of Employment and Conditions of Service) Act, 1979 also requires registration of employers employing interstate migrant workmen. Likewise every contractor who proposes to recruit or employ interstate migrant workmen is required to obtain a license from the specified authority both of the state to which the workmen belongs and the state in which he is proposed to be employed. The contractor is required to furnish particulars regarding the migrant workmen so employed. He is also required to issue to every workman employed by him a passbook containing the details of the employment. The Act provides that the migrant workman would be entitled to the same wages as applicable to another workman in the establishment for work of the same or similar kind. It also provides for payment of displacement allowance to the migrant workman and journey allowance in addition. The employer or his contractor is required to provide to the workmen suitable residential accommodation, adequate medical facilities, protective clothing to suit varying climatic conditions and suitable conditions of work taking into account that they have migrated from another state. Both the Acts provide for inspection and punishment of the contractor by the law.

The appropriate Governments are required to frame rules for carrying out the purposes of the Acts. These enactments have not solved the problem of migrant labour. There are a number of issues on which public opinion does not seem to have crystallized, with the result, the policy of the Government with respect to migrant labour is open to question on several counts, and the implementation of the policy leaves much to be desired. An attempt is made in this paper to enumerate a few such issues, which call for consideration.

On a study of the relevant laws and their implementation the following facts and questions emerge:

> What is the objective of the law? Is it to prevent or stop migration of labour, or to protect and to promote the interests of the migrant labour? Mobility of labour and capital is one of the characteristics of modern society. Freedom of movement and free choice of employment are regarded as some of the fundamental rights of man. It is therefore obvious that whatever is done to protect migrant labour should not affect the mobility of the labour. This is where the dilemma of a policy maker lies. While mobility of labour in search of better opportunities should be respected and

promoted, migration of labour out of economic necessity under exploitative conditions should be prevented. But the line between the two types of movement is somewhat thin.

Both the Acts, namely the Contract Labour Regulation and Abolition Act and the Interstate migrant Workmen (Regulation of Employment and Conditions of Service) Act, 1979 are designed to protect the labour against the evils of the contracting system. The objective of these laws is to eradicate these evils. It is however, not clear whether it is also the intention to eliminate the contracting system. It is well known that the labour market for migrant workers is so notoriously disorderly and disorganized that the employers do not know where the labour is available and the workers do not know where the jobs are available. Employment Exchanges do not generally register the migrant workers and there is no other systematic means of disseminating labour market information to them. It is because of these difficulties in the labour market that the contract labour system has come into being and is thriving. If, therefore, the evils of the contract system are to be eradicated, the system under which the contracting arrangements are in vogue would have to be replaced. It would call for a system approach. The question therefore is, if the contract labour system is to be abolished what is the alternative system that needs to be developed to provide the kind of service that the contractors provide to the employers and the labour?

Both the Acts seek to regulate the terms of employment and conditions of service of migrant labour through a licensing procedure. They are reminiscent of the early legislation in respect of the plantation industry, which sought to regulate the recruitment of migrant labour through a similar procedure. It is obvious that this procedure has really not helped the workers. Is there any alternative way by which the employment of migrant labour and their conditions of service can be better regulated?

Both the Acts require registration of the employers and licensing of the contractors. The registration under these Acts is in addition to the registration under other Acts, namely, the Factories Act, Industries (Development and Regulation) Act, the ESI Act, the EPF Act and other Acts. It is a moot point whether, and if so to what extent, the multiplicity of registration and licensing procedures help the workers and whether they cannot be reduced, simplified or rationalized?

Similarly, both the Acts provide for inspections and penalties for violation of the law. Every labour law has similar provisions and inspections are being carried out under each law at different times by different inspection agencies. The consequence of such inspection by multiple agencies can be imagined. The question again is whether the inspection system can be rationalized?

The Interstate Migrant Workmen (RECS) Act defines an interstate migrant workman as one who is recruited by or through a contractor in one state under an agreement, or, by other arrangement for employment in an establishment in another state. The Act is applicable to interstate migrant workmen as defined above. In other words, it does not cover:

(i) interstate migrant workmen who come by means other than through a contractor; and
(ii) workmen who migrate from one place to another within the same state either directly or through a contractor.

Also an interstate migrant workman who having been recruited by or through a contractor under an agreement with one employer, switches his job to another employer will not be entitled to the protection admissible under the Act. This leads to malpractices whereby employers entice the workers to join them by offering higher wages or other perks which would still be lower than what they would have to pay under the Act placing the original employer or his contractor who would have paid the displacement allowance, journey allowance and advances at a great disadvantage. A point therefore arises whether there is any significance in the distinctions the law makes between the workmen who migrate from one state to another, and those who migrate from one place to another within the same state; again between the migrant workmen who are recruited by or through a contractor and others. The pertinent question is whether interstate migrant workmen recruited through contractors are at a greater disadvantage than other migrant workmen deserving of special protection, or, whether all migrant workmen need the same kind of protection?

Neither of the Acts can be implemented unless rules are framed by the appropriate Sate Governments and authorities are specified for the various purposes. It is noteworthy that rules have not yet been framed under the Interstate Migrant Workmen Act by many states. In the absence of the rules it should be assumed that the Act is not being implemented n these states. The Act has therefore remained only on paper at least in so far as those states are concerned which have not framed the rules.

The Supreme Court has commented on the delay in implementing the law. Yet the progress has been slow. What is the reason for the procrastination on the part of the states in giving effect to the law?

The primary purpose of the Contract Labour Abolition and Regulation Act is to abolish contract labour. Barring a few cases of employment in which contract labour has been abolished by the Central Government and a few State Governments, the system of contract labour remains intact. Contract labour has not been abolished in any establishment or employment in many states.

The most important feature of migrant labour is lack of continuity or stability in employment. There is no provision in either of these Acts to provide job security. In the absence of job security labour migration is likely to persist with all its attendant consequences. Can anything be done to stop it? It may be noted that the tripartite committee on the brick kiln industry has recommended the establishment of a direct employer-employee relationship in the industry by introducing a system of payment of a retaining allowance to the workers for the off season periods, so that the workers remain on the rolls of the employer and come back to them whenever necessary. Can such a system be introduced in other employments where migrant labour is employed?

The second major problem of migrant labour concerns their wages. The Interstate Migrant Workmen Act requires that they should be paid the same wages as are applicable to other workmen for the same or similar work. The Act also requires the employers to pay to the migrant workmen, displacement allowance and journey allowance in addition to the wages. They are also required to provide residential accommodation and other facilities to the workers. If the Act is implemented effectively with all such provisions it would appear that the migrant labour would be at an advantage over local labour. As migrant labour is normally imported because of its cheapness, the law which places a premium on migrant labour *vis-à-vis* local labour in the long run is likely to be counter-productive and operate against the interests of the migrant labour by reducing their employment opportunities.

It is well known that the rates of wages for the same employment vary from state to state; indeed, even within the same state from region to region. Take the case of agriculture. The rates of minimum wages prescribed for agriculture as on 15th April 1985 range from ₹ 6 in Maharashtra to ₹ 16.44 in the Punjab; a worker of Orissa where the minimum wages are ₹ 7.50 per day would stand to gain if he could get even ₹ 10 by migrating to another state when his travel expenses and cost of housing etc., are met by the employer. In the circumstances, is it necessary to insist that he should be paid the same wages as are applicable to other workmen?

For example, in the Asiad Case (Writ Petition No. 8143 of 1981) the Supreme Court ruled the minimum wage for the time being in force, or if the wage payable is higher than the minimum, such higher wage shall be paid by the contractors to the workmen directly, without the intervention of the *jamadars*, and that the *jamadars* shall not be entitled to deduct or recover any amount from the minimum wage payable to the workmen as and by way of commission or otherwise. Subsequently, in the Sallal project case (Writ petition (Crl) No. 1179 of 1982) the Court added that if there are any advances repayable by the workmen to the *khatedars* they may be paid by the workmen to *khatedars* after they receive the full amount of wages due to them. But on no account can any deduction be made from such wages and they must be paid to the workmen directly without the intervention of any middleman. They further added: "The Central Government must ensure, that every payment of wages whether it be normal wages or overtime wages, shall be made directly to the workmen without deductions...".

Although the law provides that migrant workmen should be paid at the same rates as are applicable to other workmen for the same or similar kind of work, the fact however is that they do not always get the same wages. The actual wages paid are much lower than the prevalent wages.

Further, whatever be the rates of wages agreed upon they are also not paid regularly. It is alleged that the workmen are often cheated of the low wages they earn by unauthorized deduction. The practice in many cases is to make on account payments periodically just enough for the current expenses, the final payment being made when the workers leave for their homes after adjusting the advances. The commission payable to the recruiting agents is also deducted from the wages.

The law requires that wages should be disbursed in the presence of a representative of the principal employer. This provision is neither observed nor is it effective. The Supreme Court has made it the responsibility of the Central and State Governments to ensure that wages are paid properly. It has also ruled that recovery of advances paid by the recruiting agents and the commissions payable to them are not legal. But the enforcement machinery of Government is not strong enough to prevent such malpractices altogether.

When the inspector notices an irregularity he can prosecute the employer and/or the contractor. But the cases linger in the Courts far too long and when they are decided the offenders are let off with small fines. The punishments are never sufficiently deterrent.

It would be obvious from the above that the conditions under which migrant labour is employed are determined by certain socio-economic forces. It is a moot question whether these forces can be controlled entirely through the instrumentation of law or whether it would call for any major structural or other changes in the society or in the economy of the country.

Section 19 of the Interstate Migrant Workmen (RECS) Act provides that it shall be the duty of every contractor and every employer to ensure that any loan given by them does not remain outstanding after completion of the period of employment and if any such amount remains outstanding it will be deemed to have been extinguished. It is customary for the contractors to pay advances to the workmen when they are recruited and to recover the same from the wages. As recovery of advance from wages is governed by the provisions of the Minimum Wages Act and the Payment of Wages Act, there is a tendency on the part of employers to protect themselves from the loss by the extinguishments of outstanding advances to the extent of resorting to certain unwholesome practices. It would be unrealistic to expect that the employers will give up such practice merely for the asking. A way has to be found to protect the rights of workers without undue loss to the employers. This provision therefore leads to certain practices, which the employers use to prevent the workers from leaving their employment prematurely. They are then accused of illegal confinement. The question therefore arises as to how the rights be exercised to protect workers without loss to the employers?

The problem of advances paid by the employers to the migrant workmen is an age-old problem. The early legislation relating to plantation labour sought to deal with it in one way. The Inter-state Migrant Workmen Act has sought to deal with it in another way. But the problem remains. These are some of the administrative problems to which there seems to be no ready answer.

The next problem concerns the working conditions of labour. In most cases the migrant workers are employed on piece rate basis but they are not always given full credit for the volume of work they do. Some employers resort to various subterfuges to avoid payment of wages at the full rates such as overloading trucks, which are taken as measure of work, or rejecting the things produced on ground of bad workmanship or quality. The workers have therefore to work very long hours to maximize their earnings. The legal limitation of the hours of work as regards either the total number of hours of work or their spread over the day or the night is rarely observed, if ever. The workers themselves may not be in favor of imposing any limitation on their hours of work, as it would affect their earnings. The law becomes therefore unenforceable.

The law requires that the contractor or the employer should provide various types of amenities at the workplace such as canteens, restrooms, latrines and urinals and first aid facilities. Migrant labour is employed mostly at construction sites. The employers have pointed out constraint of space to provide such facilities especially in towns and cities. There was a common complaint that such facilities were not provided in Delhi when the various stadia and other buildings were under construction for the Asiad/Commonwealth Games.

In many cases the workers migrate with their families and the whole family works. Since wages are usually paid on piece rate basis the work done by the wife and children is not reckoned separately. They are not always enrolled as workers so that the laws applicable to the employment of women and children are not attracted. Thus the women workers are denied maternity benefits and the restrictions regarding the minimum age of entry to employment and the limitation of the hours of work for children are freely violated. The children are the worst sufferers, as they have no place for education or recreation.

The Interstate Migrant Workmen Act requires that every contractor should provide and maintain suitable residential accommodation to such workmen during the employment. The rules framed under the Act specify the type of accommodation to be provided. But these rules are rarely observed. The workers usually live in slums, which come up at the work sites in the most unsanitary and unhygienic conditions.

The Interstate Migrant Workmen Act also requires that the contractor should provide the prescribed medical facilities to the workmen free of charge. The rules framed by the Central Government in this regard require that the contractor should provide at his cost the facilities for outdoor treatment and also for hospitalization wherever necessary. Every contractor is also required to provide and maintain first-aid boxes in sufficient numbers at accessible positions. There facilities are rarely provided.

Migrant workmen by definition have no organizations. If they fall foul of their employer and are removed from employment without payment of wages they have no power to sustain themselves till their claim or dispute is settled through the labyrinth of the judicial process. It is therefore natural that they prefer to forfeit their claims and go back to their own homes in dire distress. We have yet to discover a way for rendering quick justice to such hapless people. The rules framed by the Central Government under the Interstate Migrant Workmen Act provide for legal aid for such workmen. How effective this provision is, has yet to be verified.

The Sixth Five Year Plan had envisaged the establishment of a statutory Migrant Labour Board with advisory as well as executive powers to look after the interests of the migrant labour. It does not seem that any such Board has been set up. It needs to be considered whether such a Board/s would be useful so that the Government may take appropriate steps to constitute the Board/s.

The Inter-state Migrant Workmen (RECS) Act appears to be a self-contained Act. The provisions of the various other existing laws namely the Payment of Bonus Act, the EPF Act, the ESI Act and the M.B. Act etc., have been made applicable to the workmen. But considering the nature of their employment it is doubtful if the migrant workmen are able to take advantage of the benefits admissible under the various laws. For example, bonus under the Payment of Bonus Act is payable after the close of the accounting year and if the worker is no longer in the employment when the amount of bonus payable is computed he will not get he bonus unless he employer takes the trouble to remit the amount wherever he is by money order, or otherwise, which rarely happens. When a worker meets with an accident in the course of employment and he either dies or becomes an invalid, he or his family goes back to their native place. In the event of his death the claimant has to submit an application for payment of compensation to the commissioner who determines the admissibility of the claim and arrears for disbursement. The claims are often contested. If the claimant is not there to pursue his/her claim it will go by default. Similarly in the case of ESI Scheme there is a time lag between the contribution period and the benefit period his claim for the various benefits under he law may go by default. In the circumstances suggestions have been made for evolving a separate scheme of social security for such workers. These suggestions are yet to be considered and given shape.

Migrant workmen are employed largely in the construction industry. It has been reported that the incidence of accidents is very high in this industry. A sample survey carried out in August 1982 has brought out that the incidence of accidents in the industry is 1814 per 1000 as against 110.8 in textile industry and 50.1 in manufacturing industry. In some types of construction fatal accidents are reported to be as high as 1.0 per 1000 as compared to 0.14 per 1000 in factories. Yet no safety regulations have been framed in this industry. The industry is also not covered by the ESI Scheme. If a person meets with an accident in the course of his employment he can only go for treatment to the public hospitals. Otherwise, the liability of the employer is only to pay compensation under the Workmen's Compensation Act and as indicated above, there are difficulties in realizing the compensation also.

The foregoing is a list of problems that face the policy makers as well as the administrators. None of them is new. The Government has been grappling with them for long with not much success.

Rural Labour[1]

The problem of rural unorganized labour is indeed the problem of rural development. It has many facets. We are, however, primarily concerned with the problems of employment, payment of wages, working conditions, social security, industrial relations, etc. of rural unorganised labour

The major problem concerning unorganized labour is the lack of continuity of employment. The question of payment of minimum wages is linked with inadequacy of employment opportunities. Neither agriculture nor industry is well organized in the rural areas. The employers are, therefore, not able to provide good working conditions or security of income to these workers.

The primary need of the workers in this sector is organization, not necessarily as trade unions but as industrial or agricultural organizations. This need has been recognized and efforts have been made to help the workers to organize themselves by education and appointment of honorary organizers. But much more needs to be done. In industrial organizations the workers require capital and managerial assistance. I am not certain that the honorary organizers that we have appointed will be able to provide such assistance.

In the past much emphasis has been laid on organization of workers in the form of trade unions. The main function of trade union is collective bargaining. This pre-supposes organization of employers as well as workers. If the workers organize themselves into trade unions and the peasants organize themselves into farmer associations, both have to grow pari passu. It seems, therefore, that in the present circumstances the formation of trade unions may not be so urgent. What is urgent, however, is to provide the workers a modicum of welfare and social security. The question whether social security can be extended to the rural sector has been considered in the past.

Social security can be provided in two forms: By way of social insurance and social assistance. Social insurance requires collection of contributions from the employers as well as the employees. Under the conditions available in the rural sector it will be difficult to collect contributions from the workers or even the employers. In the circumstances if social security has to be provided to the workers, the State will have to intervene and provide the necessary assistance.

Social security is primarily needed for protection of income during sickness, accidents, maternity, unemployment, old age and death. Whether it will be within the means of the various Government to provide this kind of assistance to all the persons in the rural sector who represent the majority of the work force is the moot point.

The whole question relating to unorganized labour, therefore, hinges on the economic development of the country. Whatever measures that are taken for the amelioration of the economic conditions of the weaker sections of the people will benefit these categories of sections also.

Laws can be framed but implementation would be difficult. We have recently had the phenomenon where the attempts made by the State Governments to enforce the labour laws strictly in the brick kiln industry resulted in the complete closure of brick kilns in many States. It shouldn't happen that in our anxiety to enact labour laws and to enforce them we kill the goose which lays golden eggs.

Progressive reduction in the incidence of poverty and unemployment, improving the quality of life of the people in general with special reference to economically and socially handicapped population and strengthening the re-distributive bias of public policies and services in favour of the poor, contributing to a reduction in the inequality of income and wealth are the central objectives of the Five Year Plans. It is well-known that a large section of the population in our country live below the poverty line and majority of them live in the rural areas. A number of studies and researches conducted in the past have shown that the fruits of development are still not equitably shared by all sections of the community, causing, in the process, many gaps in the social ladder and bringing in their trail many undesirable consequences. In other words, inequality and poverty are the direct outcome of inequitable distribution of resources on the one hand and denial of access to the opportunities available for their physical and economic development on the other. This imbalance must be corrected if the Central Objective of our planning as aforesaid is to be achieved. Organization of the rural poor is one of the instruments for removing this imbalance.

Secondly, and this follows from the first, organization of the rural poor would make them feel that they, as free citizens of a free country, are as much entitled to the inalienable social, political and economic rights as the rest and it is not by way of charity but as matter of right that they must be provided with the right climate and environment for a free and full evolution of their personality and realization of their cherished human rights.

Thirdly, organization leads to participation of one in the affairs of many in an atmosphere of freedom and spontaneity and helps to build up a participative culture which is so essential for the functioning of democratic institutions. It instills a sense of new awakening through which the individual wakes up from a culture of silence, alienation and inertia, to one of collective action for realization of collective goals and gets a fresh lease of life.

Fourthly and most importantly organization leads to realization of the ultimate goal of collective self-reliance. It helps the rural poor to reach a stage where they will no longer be wedded to a highly fatalistic way of life, nor will they be prone to look up to government and other external agencies with a culture of helpless dependence. Instead, they will learn and be motivated through organization to fend for themselves. In other words, through organization, development, physical, emotional and spiritual, becomes self-generating and self-propelling.

We are in the most crucial phase of implementation of the new 20 point programme. This is a National Programme which today has almost become a charter of hopes for the common man. Whether it is provision of employment or guaranteeing minimum wages, rehabilitation of freed bonded labourers, allotment of land to the landless or asset to the asset-less, construction of dwelling units or provision of a clean and slum-less living surrounding, the relevance of the programme for the life of the common man was never before felt more acutely than it is today. But in order that the benefits of the programme reach the common man in time and in adequate measure, it is necessary that there are organizations of the rural poor who carry the message behind the programme to them, create a mass awareness through intensive orientation and training, and build up a link between the programme and the common man.

A major percentage of the rural workforce is in he category of agricultural labourers, followed by bidi workers, workers in brick kilns, building and construction workers, fishermen, handloom weavers, leather workers and workers employed in forest operations. The agricultural workers in rural areas have certain common characteristics. Many of them have little or no security in relation to the land on which they work. In majority of the cases, particularly in case of the small and marginal farmers, there is no distinct employer-employee relationship and the peasant and the tiller work shoulder to shoulder. In such cases, even those who are employed and who may be covered by the provisions of labour laws relating to wages, overtime, weekly off etc. enforcement of law becomes difficult. The agricultural labourers are subjected to excessive seasonality of employment and cycles of unemployment. There is also a large scale incidence of disguised unemployment. Despite perceptible lack of avenues of employment in agriculture on an assured basis, there has been a significant increase in the number of agricultural labourers. This increase, coupled with inadequate change in the agrarian structure and decline in avenues of employment in rural areas, has given rise to large scale migration to alternative and apparently more attractive avenues of employment in both urban and semi-urban rural areas, like brick kilns, building and construction etc. The last and the most important characteristic is that there is a direct co-relation between unemployment, low wages, poverty, landlessness and assetlessness and malnutrition in rural areas, and any attack on the one will necessarily have to be combined with the removal of the other.

In such a situation, rural workers' organizations need to be conceived, promoted and sustained with multiplicity of objectives, both at the micro and macro level. At the micro level, it could be for creating better avenues of employment, for enforcement of minimum wages, for making the workers aware of the development programme of government, to help in identification of beneficiaries under these programme with a view to securing the physical, social and economic advancement of the workers. At the macro level it could be aimed at democratizing the process of economic development, and to ensure the free, spontaneous and willing participation of the people in the process of social and economic transformation in the rural areas.

I am acutely conscious of the fact that in carrying out their onerous duties and responsibilities, the rural organizer will be confronted with many challenges and constraints. These constraints arise out of the legal, sociological and administrative framework through which the present system functions. The fight against landlessness and assetlessness, and for land, assets and minimum wages may eventually become a fight against the vested interests in the rural community. The magnitude of the problem becomes more real than apparent when we think of the two sections of the rural society whose interests are in sharp conflict with each other.

Notwithstanding the above challenges and constraints, Government is promoting the cause of rural workers organizations. This flows partly out of the constitutional obligations reflected in the Directive Principles of State Policy, and partly out of the obligation arising out of the ratification of ILO Convention No. 141 concerning Rural Workers Organizations in 1977. The sincerity and earnestness of Government in translating this laudable objective into reality would be evident from the series of Rural Labour Training Camps which are being conducted by the National Labour Institute, right from 1975. The Central Board of Workers Education is also organizing 2 day and 5 day awareness camps and adult literacy camps in rural areas intended to help rural workers to develop and strengthen their organizations, to build up the required cadre, and to promote among workers a greater understanding of the problems of their economic environment, their privileges and obligations as union members, union officials and citizens.

Despite the importance of governmental intervention, I would like to clarify that Government can mostly act only as a catalyst for change through such organizations. In other words, government can create conditions conducive to organizations but it cannot directly take up the work of organization of rural poor by itself. This role has to be appropriately left to voluntary agencies, social action groups and individual animators. That many of you are already committed to and engaged in this extremely sensitive task is well-known. We in Government do not have any pretensions about the ordeals and challenges associated with that process. The road leading to the ultimate goal of an effective and successful organization is also long and difficult. I am, however, confident that nothing can prevent or inhibit the process which is in the direction of good of humanity. On this happy occasion, let us consecrate our time, energy and resources to the cause of total advancement and upliftment of the rural poor through strong, united and viable organizations so that the vision of the apostles of our Constitution could ultimately be translated to reality.

Journalists

A union of journalists has to exercise dual functions. While as a professional organization, it has to maintain the highest standard of journalism in the country, as a trade union, it is expected to promote and safeguard the interests of its members. These dual functions have necessarily to be performed, within the parameters of national interest which must be considered supreme.

Journalists as a class have a significant role to play in educating the public and moulding the public opinion. While it is accepted that they should enjoy the freedom of expression and independence in their writings it should be remembered that this freedom carries with it a great responsibility as well. They can make a tremendous impact on educated population in various ways and can serve varied interests, whether these be in the political, economic, social, cultural or literary areas. Since they wield immense power to arouse the conscience of the people it must be channelized properly so as to be beneficent. Journalists have, therefore, to use the power of their pen with discretion; they have also to discriminate between matters of substance and triviality. A healthy approach on their part can greatly help in building up the image of the country. As members of a journalist union you are all eminent in your profession. You will no doubt provide enlightened leadership in this regard.

In our country we have always stressed on the promotion and maintenance of the highest standards of journalism. The performance of our journalists has been as good as their counterparts in any other country. By the very nature of their profession, journalists are required to play a delicate and difficult role in a complex society. Their task is also onerous as their quest for information may take them to remote areas of a district or State or even the country so as to be able to gather correct information which can stand to scrutiny. Their analysis of the information so gathered has to be made interesting and yet should be based on facts and figures. Such investigative journalism needs encouragement. It has its own sweet and invaluable reward.

All the Plans arouse great hopes and aspirations among the vast mass of our countrymen who are below the poverty line and whose standards of living have to be raised. The fight for eradication of the twin evils of poverty and unemployment requires a massive effort on the part of all of us. It has to be fought relentlessly, and with a sense of determination and discipline.

One of the objectives of the five Year Plans is to promote the active involvement of all sections of society in the process of development through appropriate education, communication and institutional strategies. I am sure the journalists can contribute immensely towards the successful implementation of the programme laid down under the plan. They can enlist popular participation and disseminate information about the human endeavour and the persistent efforts being made in various parts of the country to secure completion of projects undertaken for the benefit of the people. Such propagation of information will greatly enthuse people, keep up their morale and motivate them to continue their efforts to achieve the objectives we have set for ourselves.

In all the processes of development, the welfare of the human-being must receive the first priority as man should be the center of all our policies. For effective implementation of the objectives outlined in the Plan, people's willing cooperation and their active involvement are essential pre-requisites. Working journalists can play a significant role by creating awareness among the people regarding the objectives of the Plan and the efforts needed on their part to achieve them to speed up economic progress for attaining better standard of living, as well as the dangers that lie ahead if these are not done soon enough. People must be made fully conscious of the problems confronting the country and their own contributions for satisfactory solutions.

Journalists can extend their valuable cooperation in launching a countrywide movement for motivating the people to contribute their best for raising production and productivity, whether they are working in factories, fields or plantations or offices. Unless we are able to attain the highest levels of efficiency, increase the availability of goods and services and also establish an effective system for their distribution we cannot hope to secure rapid economic progress. Without such progress it would be difficult to raise the living standards of our countrymen and fulfil their aspirations.

Productivity is an essential part of our urge for self-improvement and the achievement of excellence which must form part of any dynamic society. A nation which does not move forward will be forced to lag behind. The aspirations of our people are rising. The world is also changing fast. To be content with status quo in any area of human endeavour and technology is to relegate oneself to the limb. It is, therefore, essential that any change which leads to productive efficiency and also safeguards the interests of people involved in the production apparatus is accelerated and channeled into desired directions. In fact, productivity must be built into our basic attitudes towards all branches of national endeavour.[2]

So far as the emoluments and conditions of service of the Working Journalists are concerned they are already well protected under the Working Journalists Act. Wages of the Working Journalists as well as non-Journalists employees are being revised periodically on the recommendations of the Tribunals set up under the Working Journalists Act.

The Working Journalists Act was passed at a time when the industry was nascent and neither the employers nor the workers were organized.

Now that the newspaper industry is flourishing and the workers are well organized, it should be possible for them to look after their interests without the intervention of the Government. State intervention in matters concerning employer-employee relationship is justified only where the industry is new or the workers are weak and unorganized and need to be protected from exploitation. It has therefore been one of the primary objectives of Government's Labour Policy to educate the workers and to help them to organize themselves and to be self-reliant. I feel that the newspaper industry has attained the stage in which Government can quietly withdraw and leave the employers and the employees of the industry to settle their problems through collective bargaining bilaterally.

This is the age of information. Information is one of the basic inputs to modern business in any field of activity and it is one of the basic elements of modern organization. The social economic and cultural development of the country depends to a large extent upon dissemination of information of what is happening in various parts of the world. There is therefore a great need for small and medium newspapers catering to the needs of the people in the moffusil. As I foresee, the future of the newspaper industry lies not so much with the large newspapers based in metropolitan cities but with those at State headquarters and District towns. There is a bright future for enterprising journalists in this field. As Gandhiji said India lives in villages. It is therefore important that all of us, whatever be our avocation, should develop the means of serving the vast humanity living in the country side.

NOTES

1. Speech delivered at the valedictory function of the National Seminar on Rural labour held on Jan. 8, 1984.
2. Speech addressed to Journalists on Feb 2, 1982.

VIII
Legislation for Unorganised Workers

India has about 40 per cent workers of the total population. About seven to 8 per cent of workers are in the organized sector and the rest in the unorganized sector.

The unorganized sector consists of workers employed in a wide variety of employments classified as follows:

- Persons who being self employed have no employers
- Persons who have employers but being employed on wages on casual temporary or intermittent basis their relationship with any single employer would be discontinuous and no one can be identified with any particular employer over a length of time
- Persons who have employers but being employed in small or tiny establishments are largely excluded from the purview of the existing labour laws.
- Persons who have no employment

A characteristic feature of the workers in the unorganized sector is that they lack legislative protection. The Directive Principles of State Policy contained in the Constitution of India require that the State should make effective provision for securing

(a) the right to work, to education and to public assistance in cases of unemployment oldage, sickness and disablement (Art.41)
(b) just and humane conditions of work and for maternity relief (Art. 42)
(c) a living wage, conditions of work ensuring a decent standard of life and full enjoyment of leisure and social and cultural opportunities (Art. 43); etc.

These directions have not generally been fulfilled in the case of workers in the unorganized sector. There is therefore a demand for a legislation to convert these assurances into statutory rights which may be enforced through courts of law.

The organizations of workers have been demanding a legislation for protection of unorga nised labour. They have pointed out that that the welfare and well being of the workers in the unorganized sector cannot be ensured without an appropriate legislation. They have further pointed out that governments in the past have introduced a large number of non statutory schemes which have either failed or have been discontinued for various reasons not publicized. The experiences with the Khetihar Mazdoor Bima Yojana and the Unorganised Sector workers Social Security Scheme illustrate point. They are of the view that the welfare of the 93 per cent of the workers should not be left to the fleeting policies of changing governments. They therefore strongly urge the UPA Government to translate its commitment to ensure the welfare and well being of the workers into a statutory obligation.

In this background, the outline of a model law for workers in the unorganized sector would be as follows:

There are broadly three categories of workers in the unorganized sector, viz., wage employed, the self employed and the unemployed.

The Wage Employed workers who work under the control of employers require a comprehensive legislation covering the following aspects

(a) Regulation and Protection of Employment
(b) Regulation and Protection of Wages
(c) Regulation of Conditions of Service
(d) Regulation of Conditions of Work
(e) Provision of Social security
(f) A mechanism for settlement of disputes
(g) A mechanism for enforcement of the law.

The self-employed workers may not require regulation of their employment, wages, conditions of work or service but they do require legislative provision of social security.

In the case of the Unemployed persons also the question of regulation of employment, etc., does not arise but they need to be provided with work failing which a measure of social security in the form of unemployment allowance or other such benefit to enable them to subsist

Regulation of Employment

A labour law makes provision normally for the following matters for regulating employment

- Employment on casual, temporary and permanent basis
- Minimum age for employment
- Age of superannuation
- Disciplinary Action
- Termination of service at the instance of the employer., etc.

There are at present several laws at the Centre as well as in the States to regulate employment and the conditions of service or conditions of employment of workers in the organized as well as the unorganized sectors

At the Central Level there are the following Acts to regulate employment

- The Beedi and Cigar Workers (Conditions of Employment) Act 1966
- Building and Construction Workers (Regulation of Employment and Conditions of Service) Act
- Cine Workers And cinema Theatre Workers (Regulation of Employment) Act, 1981
- Dock workers (Regulation of Employment) Act, 1948
- Factories Act, 1948
- Industrial Employment (Standing orders) Act, 1946
- Inter State Migrant Workers (Regulation of Employment and conditions of Service Act, 1979
- Mines Act, 1952
- Motor Transport workers Act, 1961
- Plantation Labour Act

At the State Level there are the following Acts:

- Kerala Headload Workers Act 1978
- Maharashtra Mathadi, Hamal and Other Manual Workers (Regulation of Employment and Welfare) Act, 1969
- Tamilnadu Manual Workers (Regulation of Employment and Conditions of Work) Act, 1982

Each of these laws has prescribed a different procedure for regulating employment.

As mentioned earlier, workers in the unorganized sector are generally employed on casual, temporary or intermittent basis either directly or through contractors. They lack security of employment. Their primary need, therefore, is continuity or regularity of employment. This need can be met only by appropriate decasualisation measures. The Dock Labour Act, the Mathadi Workers Act of Maharashtra and the Kerala Head Load Workers Act serve as the models for such measures.

The India Labour Code drafted by a Committee of Experts under the auspices of the National Labour Law Association had recommended that employment of workers in certain employments where there is no continuity of employer and employee relationship should be regulated in the manner in which employment of dock workers and *mathadi* workers is regulated. It had said: "The appropriate government may make provision by one or more schemes for the registration of workers and employers in the activities specified in clause (b) with a view to ensuring greater regularity of employment and for regulating the employment of the employees therein whether registered or not in a specified place or area." The Code has specified the activities for which such schemes maybe prepared and also what the schemes should provide for.

The National Campaign Committee for Central Legislation for Construction Workers has also been making the same demand.

The Study Group on Social Security of the National Commission on Labour has recommended the adoption of the Mathadi Workers Welfare Board model for the following classes of workers :

- Headload workers
- Security guards
- Beedi workers
- Building workers
- Fish Processing workers and
- Rag pickers

The Commission has suggested that it may be tried on an experimental basis in some States in the building industry.

Minimum Age for Employment

The law should lay down the minimum Age for Employment

There is a constitutional bar to employment of children below the age of 14 in factories mines and hazardous industries. There is no such bar on employment of children in other non hazardous employments with the result that the incidence of child labour has been very high.

ILO convention No. 138 concerning Minimum Age for admission to employment requires that each member who ratifies the convention should make a declaration speçifying the minimum age for admission to employment or work which should not be less than the age of compulsory schooling or 15 years and that no one under that age should be admitted to employment or work in any occupation. This Convention has not been ratified by India

It is therefore proposed that the law should prescribe a minimum age for employment which should not be less than 15 years in any employment hazardous or non hazardous and to ratify the relevant ILO Convention. The Government of India have since decided to ban employment of children below the age of 14 in any industry.

After prescribing a minimum age for employment the government should also take necessary steps to ensure that all children especially the girl children are placed in full time mainstream schools receiving quality education under the responsibility of the State.

Regulation and Protection of Wages

The Minimum Wages Act provides for fixation and revision of minimum wages. The Act also provides that where a minimum wage has been fixed the employer should pay to every employee engaged under him wages at a rate not less than the minimum rates of wages so fixed

But the Act is applicable only to those employments which are included in the Schedule to the Act. Although the Act provides for making additions to the Schedule the process of making such additions has been so cumbersome there are many employments which are not covered.

The rates of wages prescribed also vary employment wise and State wise.

There are several recommendations for fixation of minimum rates wages on a uniform basis and to make them applicable to all employments as general minimum wage at the State level or as a national minimum wage at the national level. This is an appropriate opportunity to implement the recommendations in this regard and to make legal provision for fixation and periodical revision of general minimum rates of wages at the State level and a national minimum wage on that basis

Appropriate provision should also be made for protection of the wages payable to the workers on the lines of the provisions of the Payment of Wages Act or the Minimum Wages Act.

Age for Superannuation

Article 38 (e) of the Constitution requires that the health and strength of workers, men and women, and the tender age of children are not abused and that citizens are not forced by economic necessity to enter avocations unsuited to their age or strength. In the absence of social security in old-age many workers have had to work up to a very advanced age without regard to their health or strength. No civilized society or State should permit it. It is therefore proposed that the maximum age for employment may be fixed in the form of the age of superannuation beyond which a worker may not be allowed or required to work unless his health and strength permit. It is also proposed that having regard to life expectancy and other relevant factors the age of superannuation for the workers in the unorganized sector may for the present be fixed at 65.

Disciplinary Action

"Hire and fire" is the current practice in the unorganized sector. Although the Courts have ruled that even a casual or a temporary worker should not be removed from service as a punitive measure without following the procedure for conducting disciplinary proceedings many employers are known to terminate the services of such workers by way of discharge before they have completed their work or their tenure without bothering to conduct an enquiry to establish the culpability of the workers. This is one of the greatest handicaps the workers in the unorganized sector are facing.The law should therefore lay down the procedure for terminating the services of the workers before they attaining the age of superannuation or before completion of their tenure

Regulation of Conditions of Work

The Preamble to the Constitution of the ILO, stating the reasons for the establishment of the organization says:

> "Whereas universal and lasting peace can be established only if it is based upon social justice;
>
> And whereas conditions of labour exist involving such injustice hardship and privation to large numbers of people as to produce unrest so great that the peace and harmony of the world are imperilled; and an improvement of those conditions is urgently required; as, for example, by the regulation of the hours of work including the establishment of a maximum working day and week, the regulation of the labour supply, the prevention of

> unemployment, the provision of an adequate living wage, the protection of the worker against sickness, disease and injury arising out of his employment, the protection of children, young persons and women, provision for old age and injury, protection of the interests of workers when employed in countries other than their own, recognition of the principle of equal remuneration for work of equal value, recognition of the principle of freedom of association, the organization of vocational and technical education and other measures;
>
> Whereas also the failure of any nation to adopt humane conditions of labour is an obstacle in the way of other nations which desire to improve the conditions in their own countries."

The same reasons are applicable in the context of the unorganized sector of workers in India.

It is a characteristic feature of the unorganized sector that the hours of work are not regulated. There is no provision for rest, weakly holidays or leave. The work environment does not give adequate regard for safety or health of the workers. Welfare provisions are virtually non existent.

The law has therefore to prescribe the hours of work. It is suggested that no worker should be required to work for not more than 8 hours a day with, half an hour for rest, or 48 hours a week. Work for additional hours limited to two hours per day should be compensated at double the normal rate of wages. The spread over should be limited to 10 hours per day.

Every worker should have a weekly paid holiday.

In addition every worker should be entitled to two days of earned leave and one day of medical leave.

As the safety and health conditions vary with the employments the umbrella legislation may only make an omnibus provision to the effect that every employer would be responsible for the safety and health of the workers at the workplace. The specific measures to be taken by them may be prescribed separately under rules or schemes as the case may be employment wise.

As regards welfare measures provisions corresponding to Sections 16-19 of the Contract Labour Abolition and Regulation Act and Sections 16 of the Inter State Migrant Workmen (RECS) Act (or Rules 36 to 46 of the Inter State Migrant workmen (RECS) Rules,) may be made

Settlement of Disputes

The Law Commission in its 114th Report has suggested an alternative deprofessionalised participatory system of settlement of disputes generally. Such a system seems to be ideally suited for settlement of disputes in the unorganized sector. Appropriate provisions may therefore be made accordingly in the law for the Unorganised Sector.

Enforcement of Laws

Inspector Raj is under attack. It has also not been effective in enforcing the existing laws. It is therefore proposed that a de bureaucratized participatory system of enforcement of the law may be prescribed. Bipartite or tripartite bodies may be set up in each area or organization to keep a watch over the implementation or observance of the law and to bring to notice of the head of the organization and/ or the Government as the case may be infractions of law.

Social Security

Employment Guarantee

Workers in the unorganized sector live, hand to mouth they work on a day to day basis being without a long term employment Continuity of employment or employment security is the most important security that the workers in the unroganised sector require, where work is available but the terms of employment are unfavourable. The suggestion made above to regulate employment on the model of Mathadi Boards will be functional. But where work opportunities are not adequate it would be necessary to create such opportunities by means of appropriate public works programme. It is therefore proposed that a national employment guarantee scheme on the lines of the Maharashtra Employment Guarantee Scheme may be introduced in the form of an enforceable legislation. The Common Minimum Programme of the UPA Government also requires the introduction of such a law. The Scheme when introduced should be integrated with the social security system. The Government have since introduced such a scheme, called Mahatma Gandhi National Rural Employment Guarantee Scheme on a statutory basis.

Other Social Security Needs

Next to employment the workers require health security income security during invalidity and old-age, maternity benefit for women and survivors benefit in the event of the death of the breadwinner.

Every worker should be entitled to basic medical care for himself and his family.

If a worker is incapacitated and is unable to work and earn his living because of an accident occupational disease or other reasons he should be provided with the means of livelihood by means of a pension.

When a person attains the age of superannuation and stops working or is stopped from working he should be provided with the means of livelihood by means of a pension.

When a woman becomes pregnant and is unable to work she should be compensated for the loss of income by means of a lump sum or periodical payment.

When the breadwinner dies his dependants should be paid an amount which will be adequate for their subsistence until they are able to find an alternative source of income.

Financing of Social Security

There are various techniques of providing social security, namely, social assistance, social insurance, subsidized insurance, welfare funds, etc. In the case of persons who have little or no income and are unable to make any contribution towards their security the State will have to provide the same at its own cost meeting the expenditure from its general revenues fed by tax resources and that is social assistance. Except in the case of persons in respect of whom contributions are paid for a pension scheme by their employers the old-age pension will have to be paid by the State. The Central Government has already introduced a National Old-age Pension Scheme which is supplemented by some state governments. The eligibility criteria for admission to the scheme are very narrow and the quantum of benefit is also very low. If the Scheme is liberalized many of the workers in the unorganized sector can be covered under it.

In this connection it may be mentioned that many countries have a universal public pension scheme under which a pension is paid to the elderly from the general revenues of the state without regard to the status of the pensioners. There is a case for introducing such a scheme in India

The Government of India has already introduced a National Maternity Benefit Scheme which is applicable to all women below the poverty line. If it is suitably enlarged all the women workers in the unorganised sector can be covered under it. It may however be necessary to enhance the quantum of benefit payable under the Scheme.

There is another national scheme called the National Family Benefit Scheme under which some assistance is given to the members of the family in the event of death of the breadwinner. This scheme is applicable to all persons below the poverty line. In the case of persons above the poverty line the LIC has introduced an insurance Scheme called Jana

Shree Bima Yojana which is subsidized to the extent of 50 per cent of the premium. These schemes need to be further liberalised.

So far as medical care is concerned the workers can avail of the Primary Health Care System that exists in the rural areas and is being improved from time to time. For secondary and tertiary care the Government have since introduced a health insurance scheme called Rastriya Swastya Bima Yojana which again needs to be liberalised.

Workers employed in tiny and small industries which are at present outside the scope of the existing social security laws may be covered under appropriate social insurance schemes either by reducing the threshold limit for application of the existing laws or by introducing new schemes applicable to small units on the model of the Unorganised Sector Workers Social Security Scheme which was introduced by the NDA Government but is currently kept in abeyance pending a review.

A Social Security Fund may be established at the Central and each state level.

A social security tax or cess may be levied to meet the expenditure on social assistance schemes and the subsidies to be paid under subsidized insurance schemes. The proceeds of the tax /or cess may be credited to the Fund. The contributions collected from the workers and employers may also be credited to the Fund. Any short fall in the Fund may be made good by the Government by way of special purpose grants or loans as the case may be.

Administration of Social Security

A tripartite Board may be set up in each State which will be responsible for administration of the law including the social security scheme. The Board may set up area committees at district taluk and lower levels as may be found necessary for collection of contributions and delivery of services.

Exceptions

The foregoing proposals are for an umbrella type of legislation covering all or most of the employments in the unorganized Sector. In the case of major employments however like Agriculture, Beedi, Building and Construction industry etc., the existing laws may continue with suitable modifications or similar special laws may be enacted.

IX

Labour Management Issues in the Third World[1]

Developing societies confronted by poverty, unemployment, exploitation and inequality are striving hard to establish a new socio-economic order, based on dignity and equality of men to ensure social justice and improvement in the quality of working life. These challenges call for greater commitment and dedication from all sections of society including employers and workers. Such dedication cannot come unless there is a reorientation of the traditional methods of management. We have to recognize the basic fact that yesterday's management policies and practices cannot cope with today's needs and problems. What applies to managements, applies equally well to trade unions also. There is, therefore, an urgent need for a new pattern of management – whether of an enterprise or of a trade union – which affords a developmental and constructive role for both of them. This is the challenge which confronts the Industrial relations scene. Many of the basic assumptions call for a rethinking and much of the strategy needs recasting. Like other living institutions of society the trade unions and managements must outgrow the past and adapt themselves to the needs of the present and future. Together, they are in a position to accelerate or slow down the process of social change.

Besides, labour and social policy is an area where priorities have to be laid down, choices made and values weighed one against another. It is an area where the opposing interests of more or less influential groups in the industrial system will have to be reconciled. This is an area of power struggle and hence the only practical and possible mode of resolving matters of dispute is negotiation between trade unions, employers and government. This is the institutional approach to development. In this process of social negotiation, labour laws have a decisive role to play as they create the framework, the rules and the procedures under which such negotiation must take place.

The most notable characteristic in every field of activity is the constant attempt to reconcile conflicting views or actions to discover a workable compromise. In an industrial system, as in any other walk of life, there is no such thing as fight to the finish. It is always a reconciliation exercise over opposing views and differences. Even if we fail to get fully satisfactory results from such reconciliation, efforts must be continued in future to ensure that the inadequacies are made up in a spirit of mutual cooperation and understanding. In other words, the relationship between the employers and the employees should not be considered as a fleeting episode but of a continuing nature.

An industrial relations policy should be such as promotes industrial harmony which emphasizes the absence of strife and struggle and is, therefore, positive and comprehensive. It postulates the existence of understanding, cooperation and a recognition of the inter-dependence of the interests between employers and workers. A search for industrial harmony is indispensable where a country has chosen the path of planning to secure economic progress. Economic progress is itself bound up with industrial harmony, for the reason that such harmony inevitably leads to more cooperation between employers and workers. This would naturally result in higher productivity which would contribute to all round prosperity of the country.

Healthy industrial relations on which industrial harmony is founded cannot be regarded as a matter of concern only to employers and workers. It is of vital significance to the community as a whole. That is why the concept of industrial harmony involves cooperation not only of employers and workers but also of the community at large. Such cooperation stipulates that employers and workers recognize that although they are justified in safeguarding their respective rights and interests, they must also bear in mind the interests of the community and the fact that the national interest must be considered supreme. This is the true scope of the concept of industrial harmony. It follows that industrial harmony ought to emphasize the importance of not only uninterrupted production of goods and rendering of services but also of raising productivity so that that the resulting accelerated rate of growth will benefit the community as a whole.

Government's role in maintaining industrial harmony arises from its desire to bring industrial relations practices in line with the requirements of economic development and achievement of the objectives set pout in the Five Year Plans. It is on this account that in India emphasis has been laid on negotiation, conciliation and arbitration of disputes and differences between employers and workers. Government action in this area can, however, be of a promotional nature and of providing the infrastructure for settlement of disputes. The initiative for effective purposeful action would lie primarily with the managements and workers.

Industrial relations in our country are generally conditioned by beliefs and practices borrowed from western countries. The theory of inherent conflicts of interests between workers and employers has been influencing the behaviour pattern in the industrial society for sufficiently long. This has led to an antagonistic approach which has generally vitiated to climate of industrial relations and generated mistrust and suspicion between the two parties. The approach is alien to the Asian Psyche which looks for harmony in all kinds of inter-personal and inter-group relationships. It does not also serve the objectives of a developing economy. There has been an increasing scepticism about the relevance and validity of this philosophy, particularly in developing societies which are struggling to attain stability and self-reliance. Any seismic disturbance is, therefore, likely to upset the equilibrium. It is not fully appreciated that workers and employers are not the only parties to the society who can be left to themselves to settle their problems at the work place, that there is a third party – the community at large - whose interests transcend those of the different sections and that the seemingly opposing interests need not be considered as warranting an adversarial approach. These interests have to be harmonized as there is complexity of interests in the socio-economic development process. There is, therefore, an urgent need for a reassessment of their respective roles in our own context and devise a pattern of industrial relations which is indigenous and more authentic to our own needs and aspirations, though one can surely take lessons from other countries which have succeeded in establishing a sound basis of relationship.

In a developing economy like India, the industrial relations policy has to meet two conflicting requirements. It has to protect the rights of the working class to organize and to strive for its economic and social betterment. At the same time, the policy undertaken must ensure the speedy growth of investment, productivity and production at a satisfactory rate. Without such growth, employment opportunities will not increase rapidly enough to absorb the large mass of unemployed and semi-employed. This inevitably underscores the need for industrial harmony.

Industrial harmony serves another purpose. Attainment of development objectives and efforts for raising productivity can be facilitated by creating a climate of industrial harmony. Development itself has to strike a fair balance between stability, production and distribution. Following from a developmental approach to industrial relations, participative style of management assumes vital significance, as it encompasses industrial relations policies which aim at cooperation between employers and workers. It seeks to promote a relationship based on mutuality of interests. In the land of Mahatma Gandhi, who enunciated the principle of trusteeship in industry, industrial harmony through a cooperative and consultative model is not incompatible with the relationship between employers and workers. In fact, it provides an alternative model of employer-employee relationship in the industrial system which is truly Asian and can contribute greatly to a reduction of conflicts. But both managements and workers have to introduce such a system with conviction in its efficacy and the realization that in the absence of such a system one has only the conflict and strife.

There are various issues confronting our industrial relations scene. One of these relates to the laws on industrial relations. One has to make a continuous assessment of the efficacy of these laws to find out if they are able to cope with the emergent problems in the fast changing industrial scenario. For instance, are the workers able to secure speedy redress of their grievances and do the managements realize the significance of prompt resolution of such grievances so as to keep up the morale of the workers and building among them an image of fair play and justice. These are some of the issues which, though they may appear simple, have a great impact on the employer-employee relationship. An employer can ignore them only to his own peril. In India, we have recently brought some changes in the industrial relations laws to improve their working while further improvements are under debate at the tripartite level.

Another problem which often affects industrial relations, particularly, in India, is the multiplicity of trade unions in the same enterprise, each vying with the other to increase their membership and not hesitating make exorbitant demands or adopting unconstitutional methods to have them fulfilled. This phenomenon of multiplicity of trade unions has weakened their bargaining position and resulted in their fragmentation at various levels. Added to this is the politicalisation of trade unions which has not always guided them in pursuing their policies only for the furtherance of the workers' interests. This is not a very healthy development in the trade union movement. Very often, multiplicity of trade unions has introduced extraneous mattes in the area of employer-employee relationship and upset this relationship, though a solution of such mattes lies elsewhere.

There is yet another aspect which assumes great significance in a developing country like ours. Majority of the trade unions cater to the needs of organized working class but the interests of the unorganized and rural workers, who constitute most of the work force, are not looked after adequately. Government effort in this area has been to provide minimum wage protection to them, as their conditions are far worse in comparison to the organized workers though their contribution to the national income has been substantial. Unless the conditions of the vast mass of unorganized and rural workers are improved there can be no real change in the quality of life of the people. The trade unions will have to give serious thought to this aspect while advocating the cause of the organized workers.

One of the major problems of the modern industrial society has been the alienation of workers from the work process. By doing a rapid and monotonous job day or night the workers become an appendage to the machine. From this alienation flow various evil consequences which affect not only the process of production but also the workers' way of life. To combat these evils, it is necessary to promote the involvement of workers in the process of production. It is here that the management will have to take the initiative to bring about the appropriate motivation. The field of industrial relations is basically one of human relations and is not, therefore, fully amenable to rules and regulations. Further, the human relations approach does not envisage only the relationship of one person and another at the same level of hierarchy but to the entire workplace upward and downward. It is now well recognized that a work place or an industrial enterprise is a special system composed of various sub-systems. There is also an awareness that very often management policies and practices aimed at increasing efficiency and productivity may have negative effects on the people at the work place, if their aspirations and attitudes are not understood and utilized. It is essential that the managements fully recognize the utility and the inevitability of the human relations approach and make an earnest attempt to understand the human behaviour at the workplace and utilize or modify that behaviour to achieve the objective of the organization while fulfilling also the aspirations of the workers. Such an approach based on consultative and cooperative model can help in speeding up the process of integration of workers with the organization and creating an awareness of the mutuality of interest for harmonious working. And yet, how many managers can sincerely say that they follow such approaches for tackling the problems of industrial relations and accept the workers as indispensable partners in the production process. One glaring instance of neglect is generally the absence of an effective machinery for the redress of individual grievances of workers which, if allowed to continue unresolved, can eventually lead to explosive situations. The value of a grievance redress machinery has not been fully appreciated by many managements. Nor have they taken effective steps with a sense of determination to create trust and goodwill among the workers by following a participative approach as an integral and an important ingredient of their industrial relations system.

In the field of industrial relations one cannot expect that there would be no disputes or differences. But it is for the managements to provide an effective system by which the disputes and differences can be sorted out speedily and that they are not allowed to accumulate. Discontent and frustration if ignored would only endanger the relationship and harm the industry. Their causes have to be patiently analyzed and remedial action taken with the utmost expedition to create a sense of satisfaction among the workers and built up their loyalty to the industry, personnel practices and their implementation should inculcate among the workers a feeling that the management is firm and also just. Such practices should also render support to the participative system, wherever introduced. Once the management has created trust among its workers it would have laid the firm foundations of a sound industrial relations system.

There is yet another important aspect to which I would like to draw your attention. Industrial organizations are part of the society. They do not exist for their own sake but fulfill a specific social purpose and satisfy a specific need of the society which includes individuals. They are not ends in themselves but only means to achieve certain objectives. Managements being essential ingredients of such organizations have not only to perform the specific purposes of these organizations, but also make the work meaningful and help the workers achieve results. They have also to manage social impacts and discharge their social responsibilities. Social responsibility has emerged as a key area in which an organization must set objectives and secure results. Business survival depends upon this in many cases. Failure to recognize this reality may lead to industrial chaos. All these tasks have to be achieved at the same time and within the same managerial dimension. Any mismanagement of the social impacts is likely to minimize or eliminate the society's support for an industrial organization. This calls for a radical reappraisal of business philosophy and policies being adopted by industrial organizations so as to keep pace with the challenges of a changing environment. Workers and trade unions will also have to prepare themselves for a positive role in the socio-economic life of our country to make it different and better than what it is today. In the making of this new socio-economic structure both the managements and workers have a major share. It is towards this shining horizon of a just social order to which we have to set our sights and march with unflagging determination.

NOTES

1. Address at the International Seminar on Labour Management Issues held on 6.1.1983

X
Industrial Relations

Conflict or Cooperation

The term "industrial relations" stands for the system under which transactions take place between employers or their organizations, on the one hand and workers and their organisations on the other with the government playing the part of mediator between them. The system governs the role and functions of the parties concerned, the methods by which the transactions are effected and the general climate meaning the policy and legislative framework, the industrial and social structure, the traditions and cultures, within which they take place. A sound system of industrial relations consists of a machinery and the procedure for collective bargaining, settlement of disputes and grievances, communication between the employers and the workers. Development of an integrated system of industrial relations is expected to ensure industrial peace which is vital to achieve production and productivity at a high level. This depends upon the spirit, quality and strength of the cohesion and consensus that exist among the social partners.

The system of industrial relations varies from country to country and from enterprises to enterprise. There are a variety of practices relating to each element of the system.

Recommendation No. 94 of the ILO adopted in 1952 requires that appropriate steps should be taken to promote consultation and cooperation between employers and workers at the level of the undertaking on matters of mutual concern not within the scope of collective bargaining machinery or not normally dealt with by other machinery concerned with the determination of terms and conditions of employment. It is needless to emphasize the advantage of cooperation between workers and employers. Stronger employee commitment to the goals of the organisation and improved climate of industrial relations are the best insurance of productivity in business

Employers are demanding removal of restraints on lay off and retrenchment as a remedy to prevent sickness of industries. In a welfare society, no activity can be an end in itself.; it has to serve a greater social purpose. The workers are as much an organic part of an industrial unit as the employers and managers themselves. The health of the unit depends upon the health of its members. You cannot say that a unit is healthy by cutting out a limb thereof. Besides, how are the workers to live if their livelihood is taken away from them. This problem has to be viewed from a more human and compassionate point of view than from a purely economic point of view.

An organization of employers is apt to highlight the point of view of the employers on any issue concerning them while the organisations of workers present their views. There are always two sides to a debate on any subject representing the thesis and the anti thesis out of which a synthesis emerges. Thus to every thesis that is propounded by the employers there would be an antithesis of labour and *vice versa*; it should be the endeavour of the Government to bring about a synthesis between them The tripartite system is based on this philosophy.

The world is always in a state of flux and it is now more than ever before. The book Future Shock describes how the fast rate of change in various walks of life has revolutionalised the ways of life and thought. It appears that there is a collapse of values which is only symptomatic of the changes occurring in human culture. We cannot prevent the changes by treating the outward manifestations of the changes. The employers suggest that firm action should be taken to put down the activities of trade unions but that will only have the effect of suppressing the movement which is gathering strength with all the potential of an earthquake and may burst forth any time shaking the very foundations of our society. It will not do. We should go to the root cause of the problem.

The most important trend noticeable unmistakably in the field of industrial relations is that the very nature of the relations between the employers and the employees is undergoing a change. Following the establishment of the International Labour organization, Universal Declaration of Human Rights, the Covenant on Economic, Social and Cultural rights and the Philadelphia Declaration of the Aims and Objects of the ILO and the various Conventions and Recommendations of the ILO it has come to be accepted that labour cannot be treated as a commodity nor can workers be regarded as inferior human beings. The master-servant relationship which was prevalent in the past has given or is giving place to functional relationship where all persons are equal though they may perform different functions. It has come to be recognized that the workers have a vital interest in the working of an organisation. Correspondingly therefore, they should have a say in it. In dealing with labour related problems the rights, dignity and interests of the workers should be kept in view. There is therefore a growing emphasis on the rights of the workers to influence the decision making process. This trend is taking different forms. At one end there is collective bargaining where all important decisions are subjected to negotiation. At the other end there are arrangements under which labour replaces the private capitalist in the control of the industry. In between there are work councils, joint councils of management, codetermination and self management. The essential feature of all these arrangements is the recognition of the need for cooperation/collabouration between employers and employees. Even in a country like the USA where labour and management play adversary roles it has been felt necessary to organize a labour management consultative group at the highest level to see how they can deal with national issues of common concern jointly by mutual discussion. The Supreme court has recently ruled that the affected workers have a right to be consulted even on a proposal to wind up a company. The challenge that this trend poses is to provide institutional framework for a similar arrangement but suited to the culture of this country.

Another important development that has affected the nature of employer employee relationship is the growth of the Public Sector. It should be obvious to anyone that the nature of relationship between the employer and the employees in the public sector is not the same as in the private sector because there is a fundamental difference in the very objectives of the two sectors. While maximization of profits is the primary objective of the private sector the objective of the public sector is welfare of the people including labour which eliminates altogether any need for or intention to exploit it. In the public sector the State is the owner as well as the employer. All those engaged in it, whether they be in the management cadre or among workers are all employees. There is hardly any difference between the management and labour. Thus there is a fundamental difference in the nature of the problem between the private sector and the public sector and they call for a different approach and different institutional arrangement for settlement of labour related disputes. The problem however is that they are being handled much in the same way as in the private sector and it is not yielding the desired results.

Incidental to the first point is the development of social legislation. Laws have been enacted and more of them are being enacted at national and international levels to safeguard the rights of the workers and to protect/promote their interests. The ultimate objective of these laws is to provide social security to the workers. When I say social security I donot mean only protection against certain occupational risks but I use it in a broader sense meaning the protection of the social as well as the economic and cultural rights of the workers as envisaged in the Universal Declaration of Human Rights. The problem here is to bring forward necessary legislation covering all aspects and more inportantly to implement the laws which have been enacted. The Indian scene is characterized by piecemeal legislation, often overlapping and leaving several gaps. Attempts to bring forward comprehensive legislation in the past have not been successful for various reasons. We have therefore necessarily had to go slow. It is therefore said that there is too much of legislation in this country. There are certainly too many laws but I cannot say that they are enough. We are yet to cover a much wider ground. There is also a general feeling that most of our laws suffer in implementation. Although we believe in Dharma many of us have little respect for law and evasion of law has been turned into a fine art and it has become a profession. We need therefore strong enforcement machinery which has never been adequate.Even the existing machinery is breaking down under pressure of work. Workers lack organisation. They need to be educated. We have a long way to go in this area.

This brings us to another phenomenon of the Indian labour scene, i.e., multiplicity of trade unions. Freedom of Association is enshrined in our constitution as a fundamental right and this right has been excercised with great zeal. We have large number of trade unions conforming to different ideologies which come into conflict at certain levels. These conflicts have tended to weaken the labour movement. Divided as they are the trade unions have not been able to put up a united front on issues of basic nature. Solidarity which is essential for effectiveness of labour is unfortunately lacking in this country. This weakness manifests itself sometimes in violence and tends to discredit it. Consolidation of labour movement is therefore the prime need of the day. The labour leaders should put their heads together to bring about this consummation.

At government level too there is need for a measure of coordination among different Governments belonging to different parties. Labour is a concurrent subject Many of the laws enacted by the Parliament are to be administered by the state governments there has therefore necessarily to be a proper understanding between the Central and State governments.

It seems to me that the basic cause of all the disturbances taking place in the industrial world is the high expectations engendered by a free democratic society and the impatience of the people -the young, the weak, and the downtrodden- to assert their rights and to demand their share of the national wealth and income. This upsurge of aspirations of the common people for the higher values of life cannot be arrested by deployment of the police force and by the stricter enforcement of the criminal law. It calls on the other hand for a complete change in the very economic order.

The vast majority of the people are living below or on the poverty line or just above it while the affluent few are showing an ugly display of ostentatious consumption. The enormity of social injustice which permits such stark contrasts can no longer be hidden. There is an awakening among the people. They are becoming increasingly conscious of the disparities in income and wealth. They demand a correction of the existing social and economic order to make it more just, fair and equitable. This demand cannot be dismissed or suppressed.

The change is bound to come. If we can help it, it will be peaceful and orderly; if not, it will be violent and it will take a heavy toll. The choice is ours. We shall therefore do well to recognize the potential of the revolution in the making and see how this force can be canalized into constructive channels. I would therefore exhort you to consider the problem of employer employees relationship in this light.

There is no way that you can come up with a formula that could solve all problems. In dealing with people you need many factors. You cannot just say that this is the method, this is the technique. The most crucial factor in building human relationship is compassion. One of the means of developing compassion is empathy – the ability to appreciate another's suffering. It is extremely helpful to put yourself in the position of the other person and see how you would react to a particular situation.

Being honest and open minded are useful qualities. I have always felt that candour is the best policy in dealing with other people especially trade unions and staff associations.

Need for Harmonization of Interests

There is an implied or explicit assumption in all plans and programmes at the national level as well as at the level of an undertaking that the industrial relations situation will be peaceful but in reality this assumption appears to be a wishful thinking for we rarely find a case where the industrial relations situation has been peaceful consistently for a reasonable length of time. I was at one time associated with the evaluation of the record of the various undertakings in the field of industrial relations for purpose of an award and I found that there were few establishments having a good record. At the same time I am quite convinced that no country or no undertaking can make real progress in a state of friction or conflict. Notwithstanding what some social scientists may say, I am of the firm conviction that conflict is essentially destructive and anti-thetical to progress. I am of the view that progress is an act of creation and creativity cannot flourish in a state of disturbance. It is axiomatic that peace is an essential condition for progress in any field.

Dr. Calderon, former ILO Regional Adviser on Labour Relations, says that to achieve our development goals there is need to harmonize the divergent, even conflicting interests of the three participants, and that a failure to harmonize such interests could lead to work stoppages, disruption of essential services, poor investment climate, low productivity, social disorders, even a loss of faith in democratic institutions. He goes on to say that Industrial Relations is of relevance to nation building not only for its role to higher productivity and to economic growth but to its contribution to the spiritual foundations of the nation. "The most important resource of a nation is its people, in their initiative and imagination, in their skills, in their spirit of enterprises, in their love for honest of toil, in their love of truth and justice, in their sense of national purpose and in their faith in the dignity and worth of man. These are the values, which propel a nation to greatness and these values are best nurtured not only in schools, or in temples but also in factories, in offices and plantations, in short, in the world of work and employment. It would be difficult to develop and nurture such values if the workers are treated merely as units of production, if there is exploitation or discrimination, if they have a sense of wrong in their hearts, if tomorrow will just be another day".

There is however a notion that conflict is inherent in the relationship between employers and workers and it cannot be wished away. It is therefore held that the industrial relationship is adversarial in nature. While I agree that conflicts do arise between management and labour, I am not certain that it is correct to say that the relationship is adversarial in nature. If two brothers quarrel over division of property, can we say that the nature of relationship between brothers is adversarial? One can make an adversary of the other by denying him his due or by making unreasonable demands but one need not always be an adversary of the other.

I do not also agree that there is an inherent conflict of interests between an employer and his employee. The interest of the organization which transcends the interests of both the employers and the workers is a common interest. The organization is one. The management and labour are its constituents. In so far as the interests of the constituents have to be subordinated to or derived from that of the whole there can be no inherent conflict between the parts.

There is also a deeper aspect, which denies this conflict.

The employer or the management represents capital. What is Capital? It is the product of past labour. How can there be conflict between labour and its product? In this connection it is pertinent to quote what Pope John Paul said in his Encyclical called *Labourem Excercans*.

> "All the resources contained in this visible world are placed at the disposal of man. These resources can serve man only through work. And to be able through his work to make these resources bear fruit man takes over ownership of small parts of the various riches of nature: those beneath the ground, those in the sea, on land or on space. He takes all these things over by making them his workbench. He takes them over through work and for work.
>
> The same principle applies in the successive phases of this process in which the first phase always remains the relationship of man with the resources and riches of nature. Everything that comes from man throughout the whole process of economic production, whether labour or the whole collection of means of production and the technology connected with these means presupposes these riches and resources of the visible world, riches and resources that man finds and does not create.
>
> Since the concept of capital includes not only the natural resources placed at man's disposal but also the whole collection of means by which man appropriates natural resources and transforms them in accordance with his needs it must be immediately noted that all these means are the result of the historical heritage of human labour. All the means of production from the most primitive to the ultra modern ones – it is man that has gradually developed them, man's experience and intellect. Thus everything that is at the service of work is the result of work.
>
> At the present stage of technological advance when man who is

> the subject of work, wishes to make use of the means of production he must first assimilate cognitively the result of work of the people who invented these instruments, who planned them, built them and perfected them and also continue to do so. Capacity for work demands greater and greater preparation and proper training before all use. Obviously it remains clear that every human sharing in the production process is the real efficient subject in this production process of which the whole collection of instruments, no matter how perfect they may be in themselves, are only a mere instrument subordinate to human labour.
>
> In the light of the above truth we see clearly, first of all, that capital cannot be separated from labour; in no way can labour be opposed to capital or capital to labour and still less people behind these concepts be opposed to each other. A labour system can be right in the sense of being in conformity with the very essence of the issue and in the sense of being intrinsically true and also morally legitimate, if in its very basis it overcomes the opposition between labour and capital through an effort at being shaped in accordance with the principles: the principle of substantial and real priority of labour, of the subjectivity of human labour and its effective participation in the whole production process independently of the nature of the services provided by the worker".

I have quoted at length from the Encyclical because I am fascinated by the argument and I want to share it with the others. This argument, in my opinion, proves beyond a shadow of doubt that the conflict is not inherent in the nature of relationship between management and labour.

But unfortunately the entire system of Industrial Relations in this country has been built up following the example of some other countries on the premise of inherent conflict in the relationship. In the very structure of industrial relations workers and their unions are pitted against the employers and their associations. The concept of tripartism envisages that the State holds the balance between the warring parties. Collective bargaining which is the essence of the whole system has become a battle of wits.

It seems to me that the whole approach to Industrial Relations needs to be changed and a new industrial culture based on co-operation instead of conflict needs to be developed. Let us see what this means in practical terms.

First, the "we-they" concept which characterizes the present day industrial relations will have to yield to the 'We' concept; the management as well as workers will have to come to realize that they are members of one group with different functions. Workers will have to be incorporated in the management process. There should be greater flow of information and greater sharing of responsibilities. In this connection it may be of interest to you to note that even in the U.S., the bastion of free private enterprises and the champion of the market economy, there is a growing trend towards participative management programme that emphasise closer collaborations between labour and management. It has been reported that representatives of both labour and business in their words as well as in their action are trying to overcome the adversary relationship. The traditional attitude of the executives is evolving towards a greater acceptance of employee inputs into decision-making. At the international level workers' participation is viewed as a fundamental improvement in labour relations and a way of promoting better mutual understanding in the common interest of employers and workers. At the national level it is one of the directive principles of State Policy contained in the Constitution to promote workers' participation in management. It is also a policy of the ruling party. Several schemes of workers' participation in management have been introduced. They need to be given a trial in proper spirit.

Second, a fresh look needs to be given to the suitability of collective bargaining to our economy. One author described collective bargaining as a dangerous economic weapon; it can inflict hardship on millions of fellow citizens; it is a field in which ingredients of equity are impossible of acceptable definition and that muscle is enshrined as the indispensable element in giving reality to the entire process. He questions why in this institution alone, among the facets of our society we should exalt the right to make war as the hallmark of industrial civilization when we seek to exorcise it everywhere else.

Collective bargaining implies perfect competition between capital and labour. It is designed primarily for an economic system based on competition and free private enterprise. Is it relevant in a socialist or planned economy?

In this connection it may be pertinent to trace the history of the relationship between management and labour. In a feudal society the employer is all-powerful; the worker has no say and the Government is neutral. In an industrial society based on private enterprise the workers become equal to the employer and the Government holds the balance between them as an umpire. As the nature of society changes and socialism comes the state itself becomes the employer and the nature of this relationship undergoes a metamorphosis. The State enterprises all the people; it includes managers as well as the workers. Managerial personnel are also employees as the workers are. The employer and the workers are not separate entities and their relationship is that of the body and its limbs. How can there be collective bargaining in this changed situation between the whole and its parts?

India has been declared to be a democratic socialist state. In this State although private sector exists the public sector has been growing and dominating the economic scene; it holds the commanding heights of the economy. In terms of investment as well as employment the public sector today is larger than the private sector if we leave agriculture out.

Even the private sector is not totally free. It is subject to various kinds of regulations by Government according to a plan. There are severe restrictions on the operations of the market forces of demand and supply. In such an economy how can there by collective bargaining in the real sense?

The Sixth Five Plan document said that a State committed to social justice cannot leave the wage rates to be determined entirely by the market forces of demand and supply. At the same time it also said that the commitments to the principle of freedom or association and collective bargaining would require that state regulation should be minimized and that the tasks of policy are to evolve a wage structure without impinging on the freedom of the parties to negotiate wage arrangements. It is evident that the Planners face a dilemma and have tried to ride two horses at the same time without realizing that there is a contradiction in their statements. The problem is that in a planned economy the scope for collective bargaining is limited and it should be faced squarely. If we do so, we shall realize that it would be necessary to evolve alternative mechanisms and procedures to deal with matters connected with the management-labour relationships.

The traditional subject matter or industrial relations in general and collective bargaining in particular have been that of wage and wage determination procedures. Recently because of the changing economic conditions and growing concern on the part of national governments regarding income distribution there is a growing trend towards centralization of wage negotiations industry-wise or nationwide instead of collective bargaining at unit level so as to avoid disorderly and inflationary leap frogging wage settlements and to achieve greater coherence in the pattern of inter industry settlements. Macro issues have come to have a bearing on the wage negotiations. Governments have also had to intervene effectively in these wage negotiations through income policy statements or otherwise so as to ensure that wage settlements through collective bargaining do not frustrate national objectives. Tripartite arrangements are also made to ensure prior negotiation at the apex level to evolve a common approach for the wage settlements and to avoid excesses. It is obvious that in its present state of the economy the country can least afford the kind of leap frogging wage settlements that have been taken place. It seems therefore necessary to set up one or more national tripartite machineries for wage determination in the country.

Suggestions have been made for setting up a wage commission for the Public Sector. In the past, Wage Boards had been set up for most of the industries. The experiment was successful initially but owing to growing intransigence of the parties who preferred collective bargaining to wage Boards the latter have not been able to function effectively. But the system of Wage Boards can be a viable alternative to collective bargaining if they are placed on a statutory footing.

Another important aspect of industrial relations, which calls for change, is the arrangement for settlement of grievances and disputes of workers. These are at present largely left to the employers themselves or the Government failing which to the judiciary. The workers or their organizations have no role except as plaintiffs. There is good deal of dissatisfaction about the working of this arrangement. Recommendations have been made by the National Labour Commission as well as the Sanat Mehta Committee which was set up by the National Tripartite Conference held in 1982 that State level and National Industrial Relations Commissions should be set up to replace the existing arrangement. No decision has been taken in this regard. It is obvious that the grievance machinery should be such as will enjoy the faith and confidence of the workers if it has to function effectively.

The Planning Commission says that if adequate consultative machinery and grievance procedures are evolved and made effective, strikes and lockouts can become redundant. Nothing tangible has been done so far for the establishment of appropriate consultative machinery. It should in my personal opinion be given urgent consideration.

Today one of the causes for the estrangement between management and labour is the wide disparity in their ways of life marked by ostentatious consumption on the one side and privation on the other. It breeds cynicism on the part of the workers towards those who demand greater devotion from them while indulging in unsavory practices themselves. The management should discipline them before disciplining others.

New Culture in Industrial Relations

Lately there is much talk about the need for a new culture in industrial relations. Let us first try to understand the nature of the existing culture of industrial relations and what is meant by new culture. We may then consider how the new culture can be brought about.

It is well known that the climate of industrial relations in the country at present is characterized by conflicts of various kinds such as strikes, lockouts, go-slow, pen-down strikes, etc. There are also many instances of physical assaults and people being held under duress for conceding ones demands. Every day we read in the newspapers about a strike or a lockout in one or the other establishment and action being taken under various laws for irregularity in attendance, etc. These incidents tend to stop or to slow down the wheels of the industry, interrupt production, lead to lay off, closure and retrenchment causing untoward hardship to the economy in general and to the workers in particular. This is the culture that obtains at present in the field of industrial relations. It is the culture of conflict. Well-meaning people are therefore pleading for a new culture in industrial relations based on cooperation between labour and management instead of conflict. G. Ramanujam, the well known trade union leader once said, "Let us bring about a new order of society that would ensure mutual trust in the place of mutual suspicion, mutual service in the place of mutual exploitation, community of interests in the place of conflict of interests, and cooperation in the place of confrontation".

The Economic Resolution adopted by the Indian National Congress at its session held in Calcutta said that the new industrial culture in the public sector should be based on participative management. Workers must feel that they are not mere wage earners but also have a place in management. Both the workers and management must realize that the public sector is a national asset and it has great responsibility in maximizing production.

The problem of industrial relations is the problem of industrialization. The climate of industrial relations is a key element in the process of industrialization. The performance of an undertaking depends in a large measure on the degree of mutual confidence and respect between management and labour, in the manner in which effective communications are developed within and outside the enterprise and on the ways in which conflicts of interest are dealt with and reconciled. The question is how the climate of industrial relations can be changed. There are several ways in which this objective can be achieved.

First is education. The basic cause for misunderstanding, mis-trust and suspicion is prejudice born of ignorance and psychological fixation. These obstacles can only be removed by education. Education gives the light and leads to the right path. It helps to change the attitudes and paves the way for understanding. It helps one to realize that the interests of management and labour are not in conflict but they are mutually complimentary.

The workers benefit by the prosperity of the business in which they are employed and the business prospers if the workers are happy and put in their best for the good of the business. The best condition for progress is the identity of interests between management and labour. When this realization comes conflict disappears and the culture of cooperation dawns.

The second way is to establish a mechanism and a procedure by which the differences between labour and management are reconciled speedily, the legitimate grievances of labour are redressed and disputes settled speedily so that they do not snowball into becoming sources of major conflicts. The conciliation machinery should be such as will inspire confidence in its impartiality; the personnel comprising the machinery should be well trained to handle delicate situations. The adjudicative machinery should also be independent, impartial and quick so that people do not lose faith in the judicial process and try to take law into their own hands. Loss of employment due to lay-off, retrenchment or other reasons is the main cause of conflict between management and labour. While the employers seek to achieve economy by reducing the number of workers the workers seek to protect the same. If there is some means by which the income of the person who is likely to lose employment can be protected such as unemployment insurance, the friction between labour and management on this account can be minimized, if not, eliminated. There should be a code of conduct for both employers as well as workers. The law regulates closure, lay-offs and retrenchment. There is no such regulation of strikes, go-slow and other such practices except in the case of public utility services. Strikes and lockouts should be the courses of last resort, which should not be resorted to until all other measures for settlement of the disputes have been explored and even then great care and circumspection should be exercised in resorting to them especially in public utilities. There should be no place for physical violence.

Symbolical protests have as much force as any other and the sensitivity of the employer should not be put under great strain by extreme measures.

The best means of securing cooperation between labour and management is through workers participation in management. There is a growing tendency towards industrial democracy all over the world and several types of schemes of workers participation are being introduced through legislation or otherwise. Whatever the forms may be the basic object of such schemes is to involve the workers in the management process. This is a new technique of management, which is still in an evolutionary stage. There are certain impediments in its way, which need to be overcome.

The basic impediment is the attitude of the employers and the workers towards one another born of mutual mistrust and fear of losing power. Trade union leaders are hesitant to share responsibility with management because of their distrust of management especially when the management has to take unpleasant decisions affecting labour itself.

The workers who cooperate with management are likely to be looked upon with suspicion of having been bought over by management. Besides, the union leaders also find it difficult to adopt a conciliatory stance. Managers are equally hesitant to share the power of taking decisions with the representatives of labour. Being concerned mainly with making quick profits they fail to see the benefits they may secure in the long run by cooperating with labour. If the cooperative approach to industrial relations were to succeed management has to change its philosophy. It should recognize that decision-making is no longer its exclusive privilege and be prepared to enlist the rank and file in that process and associate the workers in the formulation of policies and solving problems. In the same way, union leaders should change their philosophy realizing that by actively participating in the management of an enterprise they can exercise greater influence on the policies and programmes of the organization on a continuing basis. Both groups should realize that the adversarial approach couldn't be relied on for settlement of issues on a permanent basis.

Another major impediment in the way of cooperation between labour and management is the lack of information. The management is hesitant to make the information required by labour for intelligent participation in the decision making process available to it for fear that it may take advantage of this information and pass it on to competitors. Even where such information is made available it is doubtful if many of the representatives of labour especially those who have risen from among the rank and file who may not be educated enough would be technically equipped to make intelligent use of it.

These difficulties can only be overcome by education and training. Both the managerial personnel as well as workers need to be educated on the value of cooperation and the methods of cooperative endeavour by which they can derive maximum mutual advantage. The managerial personnel should be provided with skills in human resources management and the workers representatives should be enabled to acquire enough knowledge of the technical as well as the economic aspects of the enterprise and the industry so that they may be able to take part in their management effectively.

The success or failure of cooperation in the field of industrial relations is determined largely by the views and attitudes of the national organizations of workers in industry. The policies and lines of action dictated by national leaders are usually followed by the rank and file. These are very often conditioned by ideological or other considerations. Unless there is agreement among the leaders of business and trade unions at the national level on the need and value of cooperation there is change of cooperation succeeding in the field.

At a seminar held in March 1965 a declaration on the social responsibilities of business was adopted. At another seminar held on March 1966 a similar declaration on the social responsibilities of Trade Unions was adopted.

The following paragraphs contained in the second declaration are noteworthy:

> "It is equally necessary that the trade unions encourage better communication with other sections of the community. In particular, because of their special interest unions should not only ensure minimization of industrial strife but also promote trust and confidence between labour and management. It is recognized that this is a task the responsibility for which has to be mutual. In recent years, there has been a welcome emphasis on bipartite discussion at various levels. The spirit of constructive cooperation, which will develop through such discussions, can be a great asset in festering of a large measure of collective bargaining between the parties.

The community can also be helped by trade unions when they offer responsible cooperation to management in improving levels of production and productivity. In this task, however, the initiative may have to come from the management. Workers' gain can arise mainly from the strength and dynamism of the economy, the enduring basis for which is provided by a rising level of productivity. The vicious circle of poverty, unemployment and low productivity can be broken only by all participants in the process of production. Such cooperation will enable the community, in its turn, to understand the workers' claims for sharing the gains of productivity.

The task of socio-economic transformation in India is not limited to getting some higher benefits for labour or even to telescoping the process of economic development into a short span of time, but extends to a basic transportation of the relationships among the different groups in society and of their status. A fundamental alteration in the scheme of values in the society is called for. Trade unions, as one of the major instruments in the society for such transformation, will have to develop their own thinking and methods to contribute to this process, just as other groups are expected to."

The Role of State in Industrial Relations

In considering the role of State in Industrial Relations, we should first have an understanding of what the term Industrial Relations means as it connotes different things in different contexts.

In its broadest sense the term Industrial relations encompasses the entire social relations of production, meaning the relationship between man and man in the various types of economic activities, namely, industry, agriculture, trade, commerce as well as services. It represents the relationship between one worker and another, between the worker and a trade union, between one employer and another, between one employee and another, between one employer and his employers' organization, between the State or the community and the productive unit, between the state on the one hand and the employer and workers on the other. In a narrower sense however the term means the arrangements for resolving the conflict between the management and labour. In another sense it is defined to mean processes of control over work relations, which take into account the sources and consequences of the conflict. In his report to the International Labour Conference held in June 1985, the Director General, ILO, refers to the term Industrial relations as representing the institutions and procedures for determining conditions of employment and adjusting them to changing circumstances and for representing the interests of the parties concerned. They therefore provide key processes through which tensions between different interests are handled and resolved. For purpose of this talk we are going to use the term in its broad sense meaning the social relations of production.

The Industrial relations system is viewed as a part of a larger economic-political system; indeed, it is regarded as a subsystem. In this view the functions of a state in the field of industrial relations vary according to the nature of the society or the economic/ political system. The International Institute of Labour Studies has catalogued nine types of industrial relations systems from the peasant-lord to the socialist system in which intervention by the State ranges from nil to great. I would like to have a simpler classification dividing them into three groups feudal, capitalist or socialist. In a feudal society the State is a loose combination of more or less autonomous constituents; its functions are very much limited. In matters relating to the constituent units it is largely neutral. In a capitalist society also the functions of the state are limited but not so limited as in a feudal society. In a socialist society, however, the state is the major repository of power and authority. Its presence is felt in every walk of life. In developing societies like India, which have adopted the planning technique and the State has assumed responsibility for the socio-economic development of the society, the role of the state is taken to that of a Socialist State.

India has been declared to be a democratic socialist state. It is a developing society. It is therefore believed that the power of the Indian state is especially formidable. But the Indian society is not homogeneous. It possesses the characteristics of all types of societies, the feudal, the capitalist as well as the socialist. In economic terms it can be divided into four sectors – namely, the rural-agricultural and the unorganized sector, the private corporate sector, the public sector and the government sector. The role of the state therefore varies according to the sectors.

The rural and the unorganized sector display the characteristics of a feudal society where the relationship between the employer and the employee is that of a master and a servant. The landlords and other employers consider themselves to be autonomous and keep the workers in a state of bondage. Although the begar and other forms of forced labour was prohibited in the Constitution itself and the Bonded Labour Abolition Act was passed in 1976 the system of bonded labour is believed still to exist and there are widely varying estimates of the number of bonded labourers. Even if the conditions do not strictly conform to the legal definitions of bonded labour, it cannot be denied that they have the characteristics of forced labour. The Supreme Court has recently ruled that where a person is forced to work on wages, which are lower than minimum wages it constitutes, forced labour. The incidence of such forced labour is quite high where workers are forced to work at very low wages even below the minimum wages, where they are prescribed, out of economic necessity for want of better alternatives. This is especially so among agricultural workers, migrant workers, construction workers, child labour and other such vulnerable sections of labour. The State has a special role in relation to such labour where the workers are in bondage, they have to be identified, released from bondage and rehabilitated. Where the workers are employed on low wages and made to work and to live under unhygienic and unsafe conditions the state has to prescribe minimum wages and other amenities to be provided and see that these prescriptions are respected in practice. Several laws have been enacted with this object, namely, Minimum Wages Act, the Contract Labour Act, the Inter-State Migrant Workmen's Act, the Equal Remuneration Act, the Employment of Children Act etc. It is to be ensured that the provision of these laws is enforced. India has a very large workforce numbering about 450 million of which nearly ninety per cent is in this sector. The State has the responsibility of assuring this work force at least a subsistence wage and reasonably satisfactory conditions of work and living. This is a major task.

In a capitalist economy the relationship between the employers and the employees is contractual as that between the buyer and the seller in a market. The basic characteristic of this relationship is that it is essentially bilateral based on the principle of freedom of contract – freedom to hire and to fire on the one hand, to accept and to resign on the other. In such an economy the normal tendency would be to keep the Government out or to keep its role to the minimum. It is believed that the relations between employer and employees can best be regulated through collective bargaining and that left to themselves the parties can negotiate agreements and are therefore called market economy countries. However the faith in collective bargaining has gradually been dwindling and government regulation has been growing. For example, in the UK the century old tradition of non-intervention was thrown overboard and replaced by a detailed framework of legal rules during the decade 1965-75. This was because the overall performance of the British economy had deteriorated sharply and it was attributed to the manner in which Industrial relations had been conducted. Indeed the history of the entire labour legislation could be traced to the fact that the laissez-faire policy had led to severe exploitation of labour after industrial revolution. In a number of other European countries also collective bargaining is becoming an increasingly tripartite process.

In India, the Industrial relations have never been left entirely to the market forces even in the private corporate sector. Legislation to protect labour was started with the Factories Act as early as 1881. State Intervention in the settlement of industrial disputes was started with the Trade Disputes Act, 1929. Although the trade union organizations have been demanding and asserting the right to collective bargaining, the workers as well as the employers have been seeking government intervention at the slightest pretext whenever they see or anticipate trouble. And the Government has entered the industrial relations scene in a big way. Let us see how they have done so.

The major aspects of industrial relations concern wages, working conditions, social security, individual and collective grievances and disputes.

In the matter of wages, settlements by and large take place through collective bargaining. But it is not so in all cases. In the newspaper industry wages are fixed by the Government on the recommendations of statutory Wage Boards or tribunals. In the sugar industry a Central tripartite committee is involved in revision of wages from time to time. In the cement industry wages are revised on the recommendations of arbitrators appointed by the parties through the Government. In the textile and jute industries too, the State and the Central Governments help the parties concerned significantly in arriving at settlements. Intervention of the State is particularly noticeable in dealing with the question of bonus. There is a law, which seeks to regulate the payment of bonus based on profits, production or productivity with provisions for payment of a minimum bonus. Yet disputes arise in the settlement of which the Governments at various levels play a prominent part by way of informal arbitration.

As regards working conditions, these are generally regulated by law, namely, the Factories Act and the Mines Act, Beedi and Cigar Act, Shops and Establishments Act etc., which prescribe the hours of work, holidays, leave, the conditions of safety etc., to be maintained and the amenities to be provided at the workplace. These are minimum standards to which all industrial and commercial establishments are expected to conform. These standards are changed and improved upon from time to time. It is the function of the State to lay down these standards, maintain them and ensure that they are adhered to. The laws are enforced through a system of inspection and penalty provisions.

In India, we do not have social security in the sense as it is understood in the advanced countries of the west or the east. The ESIC however provides social insurance to a limited extent. EPF organization provides some kind of old age benefit. Both the schemes – the social insurance scheme and the EPF and the allied schemes are administered by the Central Government through tripartite bodies. The Workmen's Compensation Act, the Maternity Benefit Act and the Payment of Gratuity Act are all employers' liability laws. The Central and the State Governments enforce these laws.

As regards settlement of disputes and grievances, they are ordinarily expected to be settled bilaterally failing which the appropriate Government is approached for intervention. The I.D. Act is the principal instrument for Government's intervention in Labour disputes. It provides for settlement of disputes through conciliation and adjudication. It empowers the appropriate Governments to appoint conciliation officers and/or Boards of conciliation to mediate in and promote settlement of industrial disputes. It also empowers the appropriate government to refer disputes for adjudication by an industrial tribunal. The Act makes a distinction between disputes arising in public utility services and those in other industries and provides for compulsory conciliation and adjudication to resolve the former. Restrictions are placed as on strike/lockout in public utility services. Every Government has set up conciliation machinery, which intervenes, in all unresolved disputes and a large number of disputes are settled with the help of this machinery. In some cases however conciliation fails whereupon it is left to the Government to refer the dispute for adjudication or arbitration. A vast network of labour courts and industrial tribunals has been set up to handle such cases. Special Courts, Boards or Tribunals may also be set up for the purpose whenever considered necessary.

The law requires that if an employer intends to close down an establishment he should give notice of sixty days to the appropriate government. In cases where an establishment employs not less than one hundred workmen no workman may be laid off or retrenched without prior permission of the appropriate government. Closure of an establishment in which not less than one hundred workmen are employed also requires prior permission of Government. Where any money is due to workmen from an employer he may make an application to the appropriate government and if that government is satisfied that it is so due it shall issue a certificate to the Collector who shall proceed to recover the same in the same manner as arrears of land revenue. The law also requires that notices of strike or lockout in public utility services should be given to Government and the Government may under the Essential Services Maintenance Act (ESMA) prohibit such strikes/lockouts. Persons who violate the prohibition are liable to severe punishments.

There is a law, which seeks to regulate the conditions of service of workers. It is the Industrial Employment Standing Orders Act. Under this Act model standing orders have been framed by the Government. Every establishment is required to frame its own standing orders based on the model scheme, which are to be certified by the Government. In the absence of certified standing orders the model orders will be applicable.

There is a Registrar of Trade Unions in every State whose function is to register trade unions and to regulate their working in accordance with the law—Trade Unions Act. The Central as well as the State Governments also undertake the verification of the strength of the unions for purposes of recognition and representation in consultative or negotiating bodies.

The foregoing provisions are applicable to the public sector as much as to the private sector since the law does not distinguish between the two sectors. In practice however, differences do arise in the application of the law. For example, while conducting wage negotiations the management of the public sector is governed by the guidelines issued by the Bureau of Public Enterprises. The Railways, the major public enterprise, do not recognize the authority of the Central Industrial Relations Machinery to intervene in their dispute with their workers; they have consistently refused to participate in conciliation proceedings. The Ministry of Labour, which is the concerned ministry, is also not free to refer to adjudication all cases where conciliation has failed; the administrative ministry concerned is required to be consulted and that Ministry rarely concurs in such proposals. In the implementation of the awards of the courts and tribunals the public sector units have been rather tardy. In other words the public sector establishments generally expect to be treated differently. Since in these cases the state is itself the employer there is often a conflict within itself-between the state as the employer and the state as the conciliator or adjudicator– between the Administrative Ministry and the Labour Ministry. And there are similar conflicts in the State Governments too.

The Government sector is a class apart. Government servants are not allowed to form trade unions. They have no right to collective bargaining. Their salaries and allowances are determined on the recommendations of Pay Commissions, which are expert bodies – not representative bodies. Their conditions of service are fixed by rules framed by the Government. A joint Consultative Machinery has been set up for settlement of collective disputes. There are departmental agencies for dealing with individual grievances. Persons who are not satisfied by the agencies can take their grievances to High Courts – which are now replaced by Administrative Tribunals or the Supreme Court.

It may be seen from what has been described above that the State is all-pervasive. It has a variety of roles ranging from that of conciliator to that of administrator and arbiter.

Labour Administration is a branch of public administration. It has however certain distinctive characteristics. Firstly, it is tripartite in character. At the apex of these administrations the India Labour Conference a tripartite body with representative of the entire major central trade union organizations as well as employer's organizations and the Governments. This conference is expected to advise Government on all policy issues. It was however moribund for over 14 years. It has since been revived. There are similar consultative bodies at State level also. Tripartite Advisory Bodies have been set up for the administration of many of the labour laws. Administration of the ESI, the EPF and Workers' Education Scheme is entrusted to tripartite bodies. These bodies have a moderating influence on the exercise of the state power.

The major function of Labour Administration is to enforce the labour laws. There are over hundred labour laws many or all of which provide for registration, license, inspection and penalties. A number of inspection agencies have been created for enforcement of the various laws. Multiplicity of registrations, licenses, inspections and inspection agencies are known to have created a control – license raj with attendant abuses and difficulties for industrial and other establishments, especially the small ones. There is a demand for rationalization and simplification of the laws and the procedures.

There is a separate branch of the judiciary to deal with labour cases consisting of labour courts and industrial tribunals which are however subject to the respective High Courts. There is a proposal to set up Labour Appellate Tribunals to relieve the High Courts of the responsibility of hearing appeals. These courts do not however have jurisdiction over criminal cases, which have to go the regular criminal courts. Pendency of cases in the Courts is heavy notwithstanding the fact that the Industrial Disputes Act now specifies the period within which the cases are to be disposed of.

A few words now about the philosophy of State intervention. Historically the attempt in India has been to have a balance between collective bargaining and State intervention. The First Plan wanted the states to arm themselves with powers for intervention in labour disputes. At the same time it stressed that endeavor should be to encourage mutual settlement, collective bargaining and voluntary arbitration to the utmost extent, and thereby to reduce to the minimum occasion for its intervention in industrial disputes. The Second Plan emphasized mutual negotiation as the effective mode of settling disputes. The National Commission on Labour observed that the requirements of national policy make it imperative that state regulations will have to co-exist with collective bargaining. At the same time they felt that there was a case for shifting the emphasis in the direction of an increasing the scope for and reliance on collective bargaining. As I see it the current trend seems to be towards more of state intervention. There is a view among certain academicians that the Governments have a class bias against labour and they operate generally in favour of the employers. This is a matter of opinion. In my opinion industrial relations involves three classes of interest, those of the employers, workers and the public. The State represents the public interest. It remains neutral so long as the public interest is not affected. Very often however public interest overlaps those of workers and/or the employers and the state action appears to be partisan. Sometimes it becomes difficult to decide when private interests end and the public interest begin. Perception and motivation of individuals constituting the Government do influence State action. Personal equation also plays a part.

It should be noted that a Government in a country like ours consists of two levels: the political leadership and the bureaucracy. Much of state action is taken at the level of bureaucracy without even the knowledge of the political leadership. The number of cases going up to the political level are few and far between. By and large bureaucracy is neutral. It may even be indifferent. Indeed, a moot question is whether in the circumstances a bureaucratic form of State action is appropriate. It is interesting to note that neither the employers nor the workers are satisfied with the present arrangements and both have demanded the establishment of Industrial Relations Commissions to take over the functions of the Industrial Relations machinery of Government.

In this connection it is relevant to refer to the observations and recommendations of the National Commission on Labour. The Commission said: the evidence before us is strongly in support of reforming the industrial relations machinery so as to make it more effective and more acceptable. What is called for therefore is a formal arrangement which is independent in character expeditious in functioning and which is equipped to build up the necessary expertise. It would not be enough to secure some of these improvements through suitable modifications in the existing machinery. A more basic change is called for and this can be ensured only through the replacement of the existing machinery, which will be entirely independent of the administration. We therefore recommend the setting up of an Industrial Relations Commission at the national and state levels for settling interest disputes". The Commission had envisaged that the IRCs would combine in themselves both the conciliation and adjudication functions and that they should also be entrusted with the functions relating to recognition of representative unions for purpose of collective bargaining. These recommendations were reiterated by the National Labour Conference held in 1982. But for some reason the Governments are somewhat lukewarm about the recommendations and the decision is still pending.

Thus there are three questions concerning the role of the state in Industrial relations:

a) Whether the state has or should have a role in industrial relations or whether the parties should be left to themselves to sort out their affairs.
b) If there is a role what is the nature of that role and the extent of that role.
c) What should be the mechanism for performing the state role?

Industrial Relations in the Public Sector

In the matter of industrial relations the position of the Public sector is somewhat distinctive as compared to that in the private sector. In the public sector the State being the owner the relationship between the management and labour is that of a community as a whole vis a vis a section thereof. The State has the responsibility for the welfare of the community as a whole. In so far as the employees of the public sector are also part of the community the government is interested in promoting their welfare as much as that of the others. So long as one does not expect to be treated as a privileged person it could reasonably be left to the State to look after their interests as well. Trade unions or staff associations can however draw the attention of the Government to the legitimate aspirations of their members in order to ensure equity and fair play in their treatment.

It should be noted that the general well being of the community depends to a large extent on the socio-economic development of the country and that given the level of development the living standards one can attain cannot be much different from that of the others in the same egalitarian society. If the cake is small the portion each member of the family can get would also be small, unless one grabs a large chunk by depriving the others of their share. If the cake is large everyone will get a larger share. It would therefore be in the interest of all to produce a larger cake so that everyone may have a large share.

Trade unions are apt to agitate from time to time for increase in wages and other benefits. In doing so it is often not realized that there cannot be a wage increase unless there is an increase in productivity or profitability; for if there is no increase in productivity but an increase in wages is allowed the increase would have to be met of capital or reserves which would be harmful to the enterprise in the long run. If therefore we strive to increase productivity we can then reasonably expect an increase in wages too.

We are a democracy committed to the various types of freedom including Freedom of Association. But the concepts underlying such freedom are going through an evolutionary process. At the beginning there was great stress on the freedom of the individual and minimization of State interference in their endeavours. Today the stress is on self discipline, restraint and realization of one's responsibility for the consequences of one's action on others. In the field of industrial relations the emphasis is on the promotion of cooperative type of relationship in place of conflicting type of relationship. It is said that institutions of democracy should adapt themselves to the new age through a spirit of joint responsibility and participatory planning and action. This is the raison d'etre for workers participation in management. Promotion of workers' participation in management is therefore a major plank of labour policy of Government. The public sector can give a lead in this regard. Staff Associations can make significant contribution to such participation.

Emerging Trends in Industrial Relations

The most important trend noticeable unmistakably in the field of industrial relations is that the very nature of the relations between the employers and the employees is undergoing a change. Following the establishment of the International Labour Organization, Universal Declaration of Human Rights, adoption by the UN of International Convenants on Economic, Social and Cultural rights and the Philadelphia Declaration of the aims and objects of the ILO and the various Conventions and recommendations of the ILO, it has come to be accepted that labour cannot be treated as a commodity nor a worker be regarded as an inferior human being. The master-servant relationship which was prevalent in the past has given or is giving place to functional relationship where all persons are equal though they may perform different functions. It has come to be recognized that the workers have a vital interest in the working of an organization. Correspondingly therefore they should have a say in it. In dealing with labour related problems the rights, dignity and interests of the workers should be kept in view. There is therefore a growing emphasis on the rights of the workers to influence the decision making process. This trend is taking different forms. At one end, there is collective bargaining where all important decisions are subjected to negotiation. At the other hand there are arrangements under which labour replaces the private capitalist in the control of the industry. In between, there are work councils, joint councils of management, co-determination and self-management. The essential feature of all these arrangements is the recognition of the need for co-operation/collabouration between the employers and the employees. Even in a country like USA where labour and management play adversary roles it has been felt necessary to organize a labour management consultative group at the highest level to see how they can deal with national issues of common concern jointly by mutual discussions. The Supreme Court has recently ruled that the affected workers have a right to be consulted even on a proposal to wind up a company. The challenge that this trend poses is to provide institutional framework for a similar arrangement but suited to the culture of this country.

Another important development that has affected the nature of employer-employee relationship is the growth of the Public Sector. It should be obvious to anyone that the nature of relationship between the employer and the employees in the public sector is not the same as in the private sector because there is a fundamental difference in the very objectives of the two sectors. While maximization of profits is the primary objective of the private sector with necessary corollaries which need not be spelt out, the objective of the public sector is welfare of the people including labour which eliminates altogether any need for or intention of exploiting it. In the public sector the State is the owner as well as the employer. All those engaged in it, whether they be in the management cadre or among workers, are all employees. There is hardly any difference between management and labour. Thus there is a fundamental difference in nature of the problems between the private sector and the public sector and they call for a different approach and different institutional arrangements for settlement of labour related problems. The problem however is that they are being handled in much the same way as in the private sector and it is not yielding the desired result.

Incidental to the first point made is the development of social legislation. Laws have been enacted and more or them are being enacted at national and international levels to safeguard the rights of the workers and to protect/promote their interests. The ultimate objective of these laws is to provide social security to the workers. When I say social security I do not mean only protection against certain occupational risks but I use it in a broader sense meaning the protection of the social as well as the economic and cultural rights of the workers as envisaged in the Universal Declaration of Human Rights. The problem here is to bring forward necessary legislation covering all aspects of employer-employee relationship and more importantly to implement the laws which have been enacted. The Indian scene is characterized by piecemeal legislation, often overlapping and leaving several gaps. Attempts to bring forward comprehensive legislation in the past have not been successful for various reasons. We therefore necessarily had to go slow. It is therefore said that there is too much of legislation in this country. There are certainly too many laws but I cannot say that they are enough. We are yet to cover a much wider ground. There is also a general feeling that most of our laws suffer in implementation. Although we believe in Dharma, many of us have little respect for law and evasion of law has been turned into a fine art and it has become a profession. We need therefore a strong enforcement machinery which has never been adequate. Even the existing machinery is breaking down under pressure of work. Workers lack organization. They need to be educated. We have a long way to go in this area.

This brings us to another phenomenon of the Indian labour scene, i.e., multiplicity of trade unions. Freedom of Association is enshrined in our Constitution as a fundamental right and this right has been exercised with great zeal. We have a large number of trade unions conforming to different ideologies which come into conflict at certain levels. These conflicts have tended to weaken the labour movement. Divided as they are, the trade unions have not been able to put up a united front on issues of basic nature. Solidarity which is essential for the effectiveness of labour is unfortunately lacking in this country. This weakness manifests itself sometimes in violence and tends to discredit it. Consolidation of labour movement is therefore the prime need of the day. The labour leaders should put their heads together to bring about this consummation.

At Government level too there is need for a measure of co-ordination among different Governments belonging to different parties. Labour is a concurrent subject. Many of the laws enacted by Parliament are to be administered by the State Governments. There has therefore necessarily to be a proper understanding between the Central and State Governments.

Social Security and Industrial Relations in the Public Sector[1]

The subject of this paper is the interrelationship among three concepts, namely, industrial relations, social security and public sector.

Let us first define our terms.

Shegle has defined 'industrial relations' to mean[2] "the relationships between workers and employers, between workers organizations and employers organizations and between those respective organizations and authorities". It is concerned mainly with collective bargaining, settlement of grievances and disputes, communication, consultation and co-operation between employers and workers, the State authorities performing mediatory function between them.

The term 'public sector' is the collective expression for the economic organizations wholly owned or controlled by the State represented by Governments at the National, State or Local levels. It is to be distinguished from the private sector where the activities are carried out by organizations owned or controlled by private entrepreneurs.

The term 'social security' stands for[3] "public measures for protecting public from the economic distress, that is the absence of such measures would be cause of stoppage of earnings in sickness, unemployment invalidity or old age and death; for making available to the same public, medical care as needed; and for subsidizing families in bringing up young children". In other words, the term 'social security' represents the measures undertaken by the State to provide economic security to the individual. This has to be distinguished from security through private means such as savings or private insurance or through the employers. ILO Convention No.102 concerning Minimum Standards of Social Security envisages the following types of social security measures:

a) Medical care
b) Sickness benefit
c) Unemployment benefit
d) Old age benefit
e) Employment injury benefit
f) Family benefit
g) Maternity benefit
h) Invalidity benefit
i) Survivors benefit

Lately, Rehabilitation benefit is also included under Social Security. We have to consider in this paper the relevance of the social security systems to the industrial relations generally and industrial relations in the public sector, in particular.

Social security is usually provided in two forms, namely, Social Insurance and Social Assistance. In the former case, it is financed out of contributions from the employers and workers. In the latter case, it is financed entirely out of the exchequer.

There are several legislations in India designed to protect the workers against sickness and loss of earnings as a result of various contingencies. They are:

a) The Employees' State Insurance Act, 1948
b) The Employees' Provident Funds & Miscellaneous Provisions Act, 1952
c) The Workmen's Compensation Act, 1923
d) The Maternity Benefit Act, 1961
e) The Payment of Gratuity Act, 1972

The Employees' State Insurance Act provides for medical care, sickness benefit, disability benefit and dependants' benefit in the event of a worker meeting with an accident or death, contracting a disease in the course of employment, maternity benefit and funeral expenses. This is a contributory scheme. The employers as well as the workers contribute to the scheme at specified rates.

The Employees' Provident Funds and Miscellaneous Provisions Act provides for three schemes, namely, the Employees' Provident Fund Scheme, the Employees' Family Pension Scheme and the Employees' Deposit Linked Insurance Scheme. The Employees' Provident Fund Scheme is essentially a savings scheme but it provides a measure of income security during old age. The Family Pension Scheme is essentially a survivors benefit scheme; there is also an element of insurance benefit. In case the members survive till the age of retirement or withdraw from the scheme the scheme also provides for a retirement benefit and withdrawal benefit. (This scheme has since been replaced by a new scheme called the Employees' Pensions Scheme) The Employees Deposit Linked Insurance Scheme is also a survivors' benefit scheme under which the family members get an amount actual to the amount subject to the maximum. All these schemes are contributory.

The Workmen's Compensation Act provides for payment of compensation to the workers or their families in the event of their being disabled due to accidents or diseases contacted or in the event of their death in the course of and arising out of employment. The Maternity Benefit Act provides for payment of wages during maternity leave up to 12 weeks. The Payment of Gratuity Act provides for payment of gratuity as a pensionary benefit at the rate of 15 days wages for each completed year of service on a worker attaining superannuation, or on his retirement or resignation. In all these cases the liability for payment of the benefits rests exclusively with the employers concerned; there is provision for contribution by the workers or the Governments to these schemes.

It may be seen that the ESI Scheme introduced under the ESI Act is the only social security measure of the nature of social insurance in the true sense.

Collective bargaining and consultations with and between employers and workers or their organizations are the basic elements of industrial relations. In the case of social security established under law there is no scope for collective bargaining but consultation with the organizations of employers and workers is possible.

Ordinarily, wherever the system of tripartite consultations exists, social legislation represents the consensus reached by these consultations. It may be noted that India has ratified the Convention concerning tripartite consultation and there is an institutional framework for consultation with the employers and workers on all matters of labour policy including social security through Indian or National Tripartite Conferences, Industrial Committees and other such forums.

The ESI Act was passed in pursuance of a decision taken at the Indian Labour Conference held in 1942. Presently there are proposals for amendment of this Act and these proposals are also based on the recommendations of the tripartite committees, namely, ESIS Review Committee and High-powered Committee set up by the ESI Corporation itself and the Hoshing Committee. Such consultations ensure acceptance of the provisions of the law by the workers as well as the employers.

The law does not, however, make a distinction between the private sector and the public sector. But the law provides for grant of exemptions under certain circumstances. Most of the public sector establishments have sought and obtained exemptions from the provisions of this Act. The implication of the exemption is that the public sector establishments assume the liability for providing themselves the various types of benefits which are required to be provided under the ESI Act. In other words, in so far as the employees of the public sector are concerned, social security is replaced by employers' liability schemes.

One consequence of the grant of exemptions in these case is, that the types and standards of benefits to be provided have become negotiable and subject to collective bargaining. A further consequence is that the types and standards of benefits provided vary from establishment to establishment depending on the strength and wisdom of the negotiating parties.

For example, the wage agreement in the coal industry provides that for service beyond 30 years, gratuity shall be calculated at the rate of one month's wage last drawn for every completed year of service in excess of 30 years. The term 'wage' is defined to include basic wage, D.D.A., V.D.A., S.D.A., and underground allowance. The agreement in the Steel Industry also has the same provision that for service in excess of 30 years gratuity will be calculated at the rate of 30 days wages for each completed year of service. But in this case the term 'wage' means basic pay plus d.a. only. There is however an additional provision that for the purpose of computation of gratuity the requirement of 240 days will be for the first year of service only and not for subsequent years. No such provision exists in the agreement in the coal industry.

While many of the undertakings are able to provide better medical care through their own dispensaries and hospitals the other benefits admissible to the employees of the exempted public enterprises are not comparable to those they would be entitled to under the ESI Scheme. For example, public sector undertakings generally provide 10 to 15 days sick leave in a year on full pay (or 20 to 30 days on half pay), as against sickness benefit equal to about 50 per cent of pay upto 91 days in a year and extended sickness benefit admissible upto 124/309 days under the ESI Scheme; in case of death or disability the beneficiaries would be entitled to lump-sum compensation admissible under the Workmen's Compensation Act as against the pensionary benefits admissible under the ESI Scheme which would be more beneficial.

What are the advantages and disadvantages of employers liability scheme *vis-à-vis* social security?

Social security schemes are generally meant[4] "to mitigate social tensions and to contribute towards a less unequal distribution of income through the mechanism of spreading risks and the pooling of financial resources for the provision of medical care and cash benefits in the case of contingencies inherent in the process of industrialization".

One of the general principles of social security laid down in recommendation No.67 concerning income security adopted by the ILO is that "income security should be organized as far as possible on the basis of compulsory social insurance whereby insured persons fulfilling prescribed qualifications are entitled in consideration of the contribution they have paid to an insurance institution, to benefits payable at rates, and in contingencies, defined by law".

ILO Convention No. 102 concerning a minimum standard of social security also requires that "the cost of benefits provided in compliance with this Convention and the cost of administration of such benefits shall be borne collectively by way of insurance contributions or taxation or both in a manner which avoids hardship to persons of small means taking into account the economic situation of the member and of the classes of persons protected".

The philosophy underlying this concept of social insurance is that the protection of individual against various risks should be financed in such a way as to [5]"maintain in the mind of the person protected a fair return of the costs of the benefit he receives but at the same time invoke a wide application of principle of solidarity as between rich and poor, male and female, the working population, and those too young or too old to work, the robust and the delicate".

If the public sector enterprises keep away from social insurance scheme it will detract from those principles and defeat the main object of spreading of risks and pooling of resources; it will also add to inequality of incomes.

While some benefit such as sickness pay, can be negotiated at the enterprise level, certain types of benefits such as unemployment benefits, old age pension etc. have necessarily to be dealt with at the macro level. Although ESI Act does not at present provide for these latter types of benefits, the possibility of their being introduced at a later date cannot be ruled out. In that event the provision to grant of exemptions from the law would have to be reviewed.

It cannot be denied that in the short run employers' liability schemes will be more advantageous to the workers in as much as they can get the various types of benefits without making any contribution and the standards of benefits would also be higher than are normally admissible under a social security scheme. In the long run, however, it may be disadvantageous to the workers as well as the employers. For, in a social insurance scheme the risk is pooled and shared with other units whereas in an employers' liability scheme the entire risk is borne by the establishment itself. Cost of providing the various types of benefits to the workers would be greater under the employers' liability schemes than under the social security scheme. An employer may be able to bear the additional cost when the enterprise is working profitably but in times of financial difficulties the burden may become unbearable leading to defaults.

Convention No. 102 concerning minimum standards of social security requires that old age benefit, invalidity benefit and survivor's benefit should be in the nature of periodical payment. This will call for a network of organization. If each establishment were to create and maintain such an organization it would add to the administrative costs.

There are many cases where the establishments have gone into closure or liquidation without making provision for payment of workers' dues resulting in a large number of workers being deprived of the benefits under the various labour laws. Such a situation may not arise in the public sector where Government guarantee of the payments is implied. Even so prudent management would demand that the risk should be insured.

It may be noted that historically social insurance schemes came into being because of the inadequacy of the employers' liability method to provide the required degree of security to the workers. It would seem to be a retrograde step to revert to that method from social insurance.

The right of the worker to secure better benefits through collective bargaining is not denied but it can be exercised in a better way than by withdrawal from social security schemes. For example, if a public sector establishment has the capacity to bear the entire cost of providing economic security to the workers it can offer higher wages, or bonus or supplementary benefits not admissible under the social insurance law while continuing to contribute to social insurance so that the workers may also be assured of the minimum benefits under the social security law without being affected by the vicissitudes of business.

Employee Grievances

By the recent amendment of the Industrial Disputes Act Government has made it necessary for all establishments employing 50 or more persons to have a Grievances Settlement Authority. The manner in which industrial disputes connected with an individual workman may be referred to the Authority and the procedure to be followed for settlement of such disputes are to be prescribed by Government by rules. These rules however have not yet been framed and the amendment has not come into force.

Settlement of grievances of employees of an establishment is essentially a management problem and their solution is also to be found through the management process. As in any other field of management, management of employee grievances also has different aspects, namely, the legal or administrative framework within which the grievances are to be settled, methods and techniques of settlement and so forth. Again as in any other field of management, the management of employee grievances though it may be formalized to some extent has to be left largely to the ingenuity and the initiation of the managers. As it has been widely recognized management is more an art than a science and whatever form or technique has come into vogue represents only the quintessence of the experiences of the managers of the past. These formal arrangements should therefore not rule out fresh innovations, new experiences and development of better arrangements. Our constitution imposes an obligation on all of us to strive for excellence. There is no field where there is need and scope for achieving higher and higher degrees of excellence than in the field of management. This is as much true with respect to the management of human relations as to any other area of management. I would therefore like to stress more on the non-formal methods of settlement of grievances than on the formal methods which tend to become rather mechanical.

Employee Grievances and their settlement are the substance around which industrial relations are built up and the quality of this relationship depends to a large extent on the quality of the arrangements for giving expression to and settlement of the grievances.

There can be a variety of grievances on the part of the employees; some are collective in nature and most of them are individual grievances. The individual grievances unless satisfactorily resolved can snowball into collective grievances affecting the working of the whole organization.

The best way to redress grievances is to prevent them. This calls for considerable alertness and forethought on the part of the management while taking decisions affecting the workers. When the grievances do arise management should be quick enough to nip them in the bud. If the workers are allowed to nurture their grievances it will affect their relations and also the quality of life of the people in the organization.

There are certain general principles governing the examination and settlement of the grievances of workers. The basic principle is that any worker who has grounds for a grievance should have the right to submit such grievance without suffering any prejudice whatsoever as a result and to have such grievance examined pursuant to an appropriate procedure. With a view to minimizing the number of grievances the greatest attention should be given to the establishment and proper functioning of a sound personnel policy. Further the grievances should be settled as far s possible within the undertaking itself. As a general rule an attempt should be made to settle grievances directly between the worker affected and his immediate supervisor. Where such attempt fails the worker should be entitled to have his case considered at one or more higher steps. Grievance procedure should be such that there is a real possibility of achieving at each step a settlement of the dispute.

It should be noted that the quality of working life movement is to some extent concerned with the social organization of the production unit. The concept of occupational welfare has emerged to cope with the social problems arising in this organization. These problems arise from two sources: the work place and the home. There is accumulating evidence linking work stresses with accidents and psychosomatic and mental illnesses of employees. Stresses may include noise and toxic conditions as well as role overload, role conflict and role ambiguity. The activities of occupational welfare are addressed to these. If a deep enough study is made I am sure that many of the grievances of the workers can be traced to these problems. Some of them can also be traced to disturbances caused by domestic worries and problems.

Management literature recognizes different approaches to people working in the industry. There is the welfare approach, the personnel management approach, etc. The welfare approach smacks of paternalism but lately with the advent of the theories relating to quality of working life more and more attention is being given to this approach. This approach requires that management should give due attention to the problems of the people who work for the organization and help them to resolve those problems. This calls for basic sympathy and understanding on the part of the managers. The immediate boss is likely to be emotionally involved in the conflict with the worker; in that case, the next higher authority should be in a position to consider the problem with greater objectivity.

I had an occasion to visit an I.B.M. factory. As you all know IBM is a world wide organization. But it has generally been free from labour disputes. When we enquired of the secret of the success of this organization we were told that the organization had the most effective grievance settlement arrangement whereby anyone who had a grievance could walk to the boss or to his boss and represent his case, the grievance was given a patient hearing and every effort was made to resolve it without resorting to formal procedures. The Company had made it a policy not to allow individual grievances to become a running sore.

On the other hand I shall tell you how an Indian corporation has been dealing with individual grievances. A lady employed in an organization applied and was granted maternity leave. She was however asked to work till almost the confinement day because she was found to be indispensable for a special job she was doing. When she proceeded on leave she was told that the maternity leave would be without pay because there was no provision for maternity leave in the Company rules. She pointed out that she was covered by the Maternity Benefit Act and was entitled to maternity leave with pay. The management tried to argue that she was not covered by the M.B. Act. Later, reluctantly after intervention of the labour officer concerned the Company agreed to pay for a period of six weeks after the date of confinement. When she pointed out that she had foregone her right to leave before the date of confinement she was told that there was something like job satisfaction. You can imagine what kind of satisfaction the employee will have in working for such an organization. She has now resolved to take her pound of flesh.

This goes to prove, that in dealing with grievances of the employees one should not forget that they are human beings; they have their own perceptions and feelings. The grievances cannot be settled satisfactorily unless there is a proper appreciation of this fact. This cannot be done entirely by creating a machinery for settlement of the grievances; the machinery should be infused with the necessary spirit of sympathy and understanding if it has to have the necessary impact.[6]

Industrial Relations and Productivity[7]

The subject of the seminar "Management practices with special reference to industrial relations and Productivity" is a fascinating subject. It covers three inter-related elements, namely, productivity, industrial relations and management practices, all of which are of equal interest individually and more so collectively.

The country has embarked upon an adventure of planned development with major objectives of growth, modernization, self-reliance and social justice. Enormous resources in the form of money, men and materials have been/are being invested in the various socio-economic programme. Optimum utilization of these resources and improvement in productivity are the sine qua non of development.

Promotion of productivity consciousness through processes of dialogue, discussion, education and training is an essential aspect of productivity improvement.

It is well known that productivity is the result of combination of various factors, namely, efficiency of management, technological improvements and efficiency of labour. It is difficult to isolate any single factor as being entirely responsible for productivity or its movement. Each factor however plays a crucial part in this movement. While discussing productivity in the context of industrial relations and management practices relevant thereto, we cannot go into the entire gamut of productivity but confine ourselves to labour productivity.

There are again several factors, which affect labour productivity of which three important ones may be mentioned. Firstly, training—it should be obvious that a trained worker will work better than an untrained or inexperienced worker. Training and re-training are more necessary under the modern conditions of technological revolution. Training is therefore an indispensable factor for achieving the development objectives, in as much as it improves and protects human resources and at the same time contributes to the self-fulfillment of each individual and to the fulfillment of development needs. Secondly, the worker should have a congenial work environment. Modern thought on management lays great emphasis on the need to provide a proper work environment. It is recognized that bad working conditions are uneconomical and improvements often quite small can produce marked increase in productivity. It is rightly said, "Unhealthy and unhappy workers doing their jobs under conditions of physical or mental strain are inefficient producers unlike machines which are relatively indifferent to their surroundings". Proper ventilation, lighting, cleanliness, noise control and several precautions contribute significantly to labour productivity. Thirdly and most importantly, the workers would need proper motivation to give their best to the enterprise in which they are engaged.

There are many theories about what motivates a worker. There are also many management practices designed to motivate them. It may however be noted that a happy and congenial industrial relations atmosphere is basic to motivate the workers to their productivity.

The term "Industrial relations" stands for the system under which transactions take place between employers or their organizations on the one hand and workers and their organizations on the other; the governments playing a part of mediation between them. It governs the role and functions of the parties concerned, the methods by which the transactions are affected and the general climate, meaning the policy and legislative framework, the industrial and social structure, the traditions and cultures, within which they take place. A sound system of industrial relations consists of machinery and the procedure for collective bargaining, settlement of disputes and grievances, communications between workers and employers. Development of an integrated system of industrial relations is expected to ensure industrial peace, which is vital to achieve production and productivity at a high level. This depends upon the spirit, quality and strength of the cohesion and consensus that exist among the social partners.

The system of industrial relations varies from country to country and from enterprise to enterprise. There are a variety of practices relating to each element of the system. We cannot go into all of them within the short time available. I would however like to touch upon one of the practices to which Government of India attaches importance.

Recommendation No. 94 of the International Labour Organization adopted in 1952 requires that appropriate steps should be taken to promote consultation and co-operation between employers and workers at the level of the undertaking on matters of mutual concern not within the scope of collective bargaining machinery, or not normally dealt with by other machinery concerned with the determination of terms and conditions of employment. It is needles to emphasize the advance of co-operation between workers and employers. Stronger employee commitment to the goals of the organization and improved climate of industrial relations are the best insurance of productivity in business.

There are a variety of forms in which consultation takes place between employers and workers and the employers secure the co-operation of the workers. One of these goes by the name of "Workers Participation in Management". It makes for decentralization of authority involving more and more people in the process of decision making which in turn leads to sharing of responsibility, improvement in productivity and the quality of the working life.

The basic assumption underlying the concept of workers' participation is that the goals of an organization or enterprise are best achieved if there is identity of interests between management and workers. The general objective of a scheme of workers' participation is to secure the willing co-operation of the workers in the achievement of the goals of the organization. It seeks to make the workers better informed about the affairs of the organization and to consult them in finding solution to the problems so that they may realize that the achievement of the goals is as much in their own interest as in that of management and that there is no attempt to exploit them.

The traditional employer-employee relationship implies conflict of interest between "we" and "they" but it is not conducive to peace and harmony as it separates "us" from "them". The ideal form of organization is that in which all those engaged in an activity is brought together in relationship of partnership or co-operation. This calls for an institutional arrangement in which a worker can sit with the manager and consider the policies, programme and problems of the organization jointly. Such an arrangement will enable the workers to exercise the influence on the decision making process in the organization or enterprise in which they are employed.

This is a technique of management, which is still in an evolutionary stage in this country. There are certain impediments in its way. Success of this technique depends on the extent to which these impediments can be cleared.

The biggest impediment is the attitude of the employers and the workers towards one another. Trade union leaders are hesitant to share responsibility with management because of their mistrust of management especially when the management has to take unpleasant decisions affecting labour itself. Managers are equally hesitant to share the power of taking decisions with the representatives of labour. If the co-operative approach to management were to succeed both have to change their attitude. Management should recognize that decision-making is no longer its exclusive privilege and be prepared to enlist the rank and file in that process and associate the workers in the formulation of policies and solving problems. At the same time, union leaders should change their attitude realizing that by actively participating in the management of enterprises they can exercise greater influence on the policies and programmes of the organization on a continuing basis. Both the groups should realize that the adversarial approach cannot be relied on settlement of issues in a lasting manner.

Another major impediment in the way of co-operation between labour and management is the lack of information. The management is hesitant to make the information required by labour for intelligent participation in the decision making available to it for fear that it may take advantage of the information for raising demands or that it may pass the information on to competitors. Even where such information is made available it is doubtful if the representatives of labour will be able to make use of it.

These difficulties can be overcome by education and training. Both the managerial personnel as well as workers need to be educated on the value of co-operation and the methods of co-operative endeavour by which they can derive maximum mutual advantage.

There is another Recommendation of the I.L.O., No. 129, concerning communications between Management and Workers within the undertaking. This Recommendation requires that employers and their organizations as well as workers and their organizations should in their common interest recognize the importance of a climate of mutual understanding and confidence within undertakings that is favorable both to the efficiency of the undertaking and to the aspirations of the workers.

It goes on to say that this climate should be promoted by the rapid dissemination and exchange of information, as complete as possible, relating to the various aspects of the life of the undertaking and to the social conditions of the workers. With a view to the development of such a climate management should after consultation with workers' representatives adopt appropriate measures to apply an effective policy of communication with the workers and their representatives.

I need hardly say that implementation of this recommendation will go a long way to remove misunderstanding and mistrust and to bring about harmonious relationship between employers and workers which in turn will lead to better productivity.

NOTES

1. Paper presented at the International Seminar on Industrial Relations and Public Enterprise management in Third world Perspective.
2. "Negotiating Development" (p.1), by Johannas Schragle, published by ILO, Geneva.
3. "Introduction to Social Security" (p.15), published by ILO, Geneva.
4. "Social Aspects of Industrialization" (p.93), published by ILO, Geneva.
5. "Introduction to Social Security" (p.17), published by ILO, Geneva.
6. Valedictory address at the Seminar on Employee Grievances on April, 21, 1984.
7. Speech delivered at the All India Engineering Seminar on Dec. 12, 1983.

XI
Working Class Movement

The working class movement in India is of comparatively recent origin. It has acquired momentum only since Independence. As elsewhere, it has been an offshoot of the development of industries in the country.

The National Labour Commission has described the genesis of the organization of workers in the following words:

> "The setting up of large-scale industrial units created conditions of widespread use of machinery, establishment of new lines of productions, changes in working and living environments of workers, and concentration of industries in large towns, all of which introduced a new class of workers who were dependant on wages for their livelihood. They were at a disadvantage in an age when the doctrine of laissez faire held the field. In the absence of collective action, they had to be content with the wages which each of them could separately negotiate with the employer from a position of disadvantage. Workers had to join together at least to maintain, if not to improve, their bargaining power against the employer."

In a discussion on the future of the working class movement the first question that will have to be considered is whether the circumstances under which the unions came into being continue to subsist and whether the objectives of the organizations remain the same.

It is a well known fact that world is changing fast. The socio economic conditions obtaining in the country today are not the same as in the twenties or thirties.

We have now a democratic form of Government wedded to socialism. The most important change that has occurred since the beginning of the movement is that the doctrine of laissez faire no longer holds the field. There is certainly a private sector in the economy but the public sector has been growing and dominates the economic scene. The estimated employment in the public sector in 1978 for which figures are available was about 14 million as against 7 million in the private sector. Employment in the public sector has been growing from year to year and it is expected to grow further in the future.

The working class movement had its origins in the conflict between those who sell their labour and those who buy it, inherent in the capitalistic economy where a person employs another for his profit. In a Socialistic economy characterized by State enterprises where the State is the employer and the citizen the employee, there can be no such conflict; can there be a conflict between the whole and a part thereof? But there can be a conflict of interests between the community at large and an individual or a section of the community. A trade union organization is ordinarily meant for the protection and promotion of the interests of its members. But Government has the welfare of the whole community in view. It can happen that sometimes the interests of the workers may have to be subordinated to those of the people, the consumers. It seems therefore that the whole movement has to be reoriented to the changing conditions.

What is public sector? It is the sector in which the State has employed people for various types of economic activity. Many of the public sector enterprises are organized as companies; some are in the form of Corporations and others are societies. Whatever the form be the owner in all these cases is the State. Though each organization may have a General Body and a Board of Management, called by various names, members of these bodies are mostly appointees of Government and they derive their authority from the Government and their powers are limited. In the ultimate analysis the workers of public enterprises are employees of the State. The question therefore arises as to what is the role of an organization of workers vis-à-vis the management and the owners of a public enterprise. Would it be valid to extrapolate the functions of the workers organization in a private firm or industry to a Government Department or public enterprise? This brings us to the question as to what are the functions of a trade union and how relevant they are in the changing context. The National Labour Commission has listed the following:

(a) The primary function of a union is to promote and protect the interests of its members. It has to strive to better the terms and conditions of employment and generally to advance their economic and social interests so as to achieve an improved standard of living.

(b) Welfare activities like organizing mutual benefit societies, co-operatives, employment assistance, libraries, games, cultural programme, etc.
(c) Education of its members in all aspects of their working life, including improvement of their civic environments.

The Commission also added that while a union will function in the interests of its members, it should also accept community responsibilities. They observed "It is being widely suggested that unions should seek to harmonize the sectional interests with the larger interests of the community."

They suggested:

It is imperative that unions keep the well-being and progress of the community constantly before them even in the midst of their endeavours to help the working class. Unions have to adapt themselves to changing social needs, and rise above divisive forces of case, religion and language. Some important social responsibilities of trade unions appear to be in the field of:

(i) promotion of national integration;
(ii) generally influencing the socio economic policies of the community through active participation in their formulation at various levels;
(iii) instilling in their members a sense of responsibility towards industry and the community.

It seems to me that in the context of the changing socio-political and economic conditions of the country of the various social responsibility for promoting the interests of the community is acquiring greater importance than the responsibility for raising the standard of living of the workers.

Let us see what this means in specific and concrete terms.

The preamble to the Constitution of India says that the people of India have resolved to constitute India into a Sovereign Socialist Democratic Republic. It is therefore to be expected that in the foreseeable future a form of socialism will be established in India whereby the private sector will gradually yield place to the public sector and the public sector will increasingly dominate the economic scene. In such a situation there would hardly be any distinction between the management and workers, except in the area where private sector operates, and the trade union organizations would have to partake the responsibilities of management in certain respects. Their activities would have to be complementary to those of the State. They will undoubtedly continue to look after the interests of their members, but in the overall framework of the national plans and programme and not in isolation. There is at present a large unorganized sector mostly in private hands where there is need for improvement in the conditions of labour. It is likely that this area will continue to be in the private sector and the workers have to organize themselves to protect and promote their interests. This is the field where the trade unions will have to continue to function in the traditional manner.

Collective bargaining implies free play of market forces of supply and demand. In a planned economy the market forces will be under check. The scope for collective bargaining will be limited. The Sixth Five Year Plan says:

> "In a society dedicated to the ideals of social justice, it is doubtful if the wage rate can be left entirely to be determined by market forces of demand and supply."

Alternative means would therefore have to be evolved for fixing wages and other conditions of service especially in those activities which are vital to the needs of the people such as water supply, electricity, communications, etc. these may be in the form of wage Boards or Pay Commissions. The Plan document goes on to say:

> "The National wage policy should be based on a rational system of wages which inter alia provides for wage differentials justifiable mostly on economic criteria. It is in this context that certain guidelines have to be prescribed even while the primacy of collective bargaining is stressed."

Efforts are being made from time to time to evolve a wage policy or an income policy or wages, Income and Prices policy. When such a policy is evolved the wage fixing authorities will have to conform to the guidelines that may be issued in pursuance of the policy.

Although the trade unions' role in collective bargaining may diminish their constructive role in improving the quality of life of the workers will increase. The Plan says:

> "Serious efforts need to be made by trade unions to promote a spirit of greater involvement of workers if enterprises fulfill the norms of greater efficiency and also achieve excellence in their

> overall performance so as to be able to share the benefits of such improved functioning." "They should evince greater interest in welfare programme for their members such as education, including literacy, health and family planning, and recreational and cultural activities. They can also promote personal and environmental hygiene and promote a sense of thrift and savings."

The Prime Minister, Indira Gandhi in her inaugural address at the ICFTU World Conference said :

> "One of the principal responsibilities before enlightened trade union leadership is to kindle social consciousness and make workers aware of the problems of the less favoured sections within the working class."

Workers' participation in management has been an article of faith with the people in so far as it has been incorporated as a directive principle in the constitution. But the objectives of such participation would need to be defined. This being a political democracy it will need to be ensured that the system of industrial democracy that is built up will not overlap or conflict with the political institutions.

Many autonomous organizations have been created for implementation of certain programmes. There is a demand for greater autonomy for such organizations in reaching settlement with their workers. While they would certainly need to have a measure of autonomy to function effectively they cannot work totally independently of the Governments even though they may have their own resources and the Government so as not have to make any contributions thereto. They will have to remain within and confirm to national policies.

XII
Trade Unions[1]

Trade Unions in India

Organization is the source of strength to the workers and whatever gains workers have achieved so far are the products of their organizational endeavour. The comparative advantage organized labour has over the rural unorganized labour is obvious to anyone. Yet the extent of unionization of the labour force in India is rather limited. Not more than 3 per cent of the workers are said to be organized. The Government of India therefore attaches the greatest importance in its labour policy to the promotion of organization of workers particularly in the rural sector.

The Government of India has already ratified the ILO convention which enjoins that it shall be an object of the national policy concerning rural development to facilitate the establishment and growth of strong and independent organization of rural workers including agricultural labourers, artisans, share croppers, and small farmers so that they get their due share in the benefits of economic and social development. Organization of the rural poor needs to be sponsored by the workers themselves and voluntary organizations. Experienced members of trade unions should carry the message of the trade union movement to the unorganized labour force, educate them and help them to organize themselves. It is realized that it will take time for trade unions to make much headway in this effort and that the State machinery will have to facilitate the process. The Government of India is considering the measures to be taken in this regard. One of the measures in view is legislation to confer specific rights on the rural poor to set up unions, to safeguard their interest, registration of such unions, grant of immunity to office bearers and members of such unions from certain criminal and civil suits, creation of a machinery for settlement of disputes among the rural workers, training and education of the cadres. But these efforts of Government alone will not be enough; they have to be followed up by efforts of voluntary and trade union organizations.

The Trade Union movement in India has been marked by the proliferation of unions and inter-union and intra-union rivalry. This divisive element has affected the bargaining power and weakened the financial position of the trade unions. To overcome these weaknesses some people have taken to the path of violence bringing discredit to the whole movement. All well-meaning trade unionists should be concerned at this development. I would therefore appeal to all workers to avoid the temptations of multiplying the unions. The approach to trade unionism calls for a reorientation. It should be based on a value system of social obligations, mutual trust and fair practices in an atmosphere of goodwill and understanding. All Trade Unions must give serious thought to these matters in the interest of healthy growth of the movement.

Industrial harmony is indispensable for a country to make economic progress and trade unions have a vital interest in industrial peace. In the ultimate analysis the problem of industrial relations is essentially one of attitudes. Employers and Workers should recognize that while they are fully justified in safeguarding their respective rights and interests they must also bear in mind the larger interests of the community. The INTUC, befitting its status as the largest organization of workers, has displayed a remarkable spirit of constructive cooperation with management and has become a partner in the governance of this country. I commend this spirit to the other organizations as well.

An important element in the economic programme of this country is the scheme of workers' participation in management. Government believes that workers' participation in management should become an integral part of the industrial relations system to serve as an effective instrument of modern management. It should be made a vehicle of transforming the attitudes of both employers and workers for establishing a cooperative culture which may help in building a self confident and self reliant country with a stable industrial base. There is a very wide area of relationships in an enterprise outside the domain of collective bargaining where employers and workers can work jointly for the benefit of different interest groups and for the common interest of the enterprise as a whole. Such a system of consultative and joint decision making would ensure frictionless operation at various levels, provide job satisfaction, release the latent creative energy of workers, reduce their alienation and enhance the commitment of workers and management to the common ideal of better performance. Various measures have been tried in the past to promote workers' participation. Starting from the limited scheme of statutory workers' committees, voluntary arrangements were made in the form of joint management councils, scheme of worker directors, and voluntary schemes of workers' participation for manufacturing/mining industries and for commercial and service organization as essential ingredients of the 20 point programme. A new article 43A has been introduced in the Constitution under the Directive Principles of state Policy to secure the participation of workers in management in order to create better mutual understanding between labour and management and facilitate the adoption on both sides of an objective approach towards the problems of industry and the workers. But no scheme of participation of workers in management can succeed unless there is a recognition and acceptance of the mutual rights and obligations. Management is an art. It calls for education and training. The Central Board of Workers Education has been imparting some training to the workers in participative management. This needs to be greatly augmented and supplemented by the trade union organizations. One of the hurdles in the effective implementation of the scheme of workers' participation has been the problem of determining the representative character of the trade unions and selecting the workers to be associated in management. This issue has defied solution for long. The leaders of the major trade union organizations should sit together and come to an understanding in this regard.

It is essential for the workers to be properly educated if they have to play their role in the development of an enterprise as well as of the nation. Workers' education is a function of trade unions. For historical reasons this scheme is being administered through an autonomous organization created by Government. Till recently a government official used to be Chairman of this organization. He has since been replaced by a trade union leader who has been appointed as the Chairman. This is only symbolical of Government's desire that eventually trade union organizations should themselves take up the responsibility. They should gear themselves to this task.

Trade Unions have a vital and constructive role to play in improving the quality of life of the workers. They should evince greater interest in welfare programme for their members such as education, health, family planning, recreation and cultural activities. They can also promote environmental hygiene and promote a sense of thrift and savings.

Thus trade union movement has multiple functions and responsibilities. If it has to grow on healthy lines the rank and file should be aware of these. Conventions of this type will help to bring about such awareness.

Social Responsibility of Trade Unions

Since the Madras Labour Union was founded some sixty years ago trade union movement has acquired such a status and importance in the economic life of the country that it can be said without fear of contradictions that the economic development of the country, nay, the very sustenance of the country, has come to be dependant upon trade union action. Production is the crying need of the hour. It calls for industrial peace and trade unions hold the key to it. A great social responsibility therefore rests on the trade unions and their leaders. They are expected to conduct themselves in such a manner that while they strive to promote the interests of their members the interests of the community at large do not suffer.

Inaugurating a Seminar on Social Responsibilities of Trade Unions, in 1966, the then Home Minister, and one time Labour Minister, had said that the labour movement is essentially meant for its members and it has to protect their interests. " But even in the pursuit of those interests success has to be measured not merely in terms of the material gains secured or the extent or redress obtained with regard to day to day grievances. The degree to which the workers have been helped to develop their moral and social consciousness has also to be an important criterion....The worker may be a poor man but he has to be equal to anyone else as an honorable truth loving and socially conscious person. The worker's complaints and demands have to be fair reasonable and well founded and the advocacy on their behalf must have no element of exaggeration." This advice is as much relevant today as it was then. All of us who are interested in the healthy growth of the trade union movement should reflect on it and try to follow it howsoever difficult it may be.

The employees of some of the public sector enterprises in Bangalore were recently on strike for seventy seven days demanding revision of wages on the ground that there had been a revision in another enterprise somewhere else. Although the strike has ended, one wonders whether it was really essential for them to have gone on strike.

You all know public enterprises provide the essential goods and services for defence and development of the country. They do not work so much for profit as they do it for service. They function altogether on a basis different from that of industrial units in the private sector. There can be no question of exploitation of labour in these enterprises. On the other hand, Government has provided an example in establishing and maintaining high standards of safety and welfare or workers in these enterprises. Their wage levels are by no means low. The employees of some the enterprises are enjoying the highest rates of wages in the country. Yet some workers had chosen to go on strike to press their demand.

This experience raises certain issues which we should consider. The first question is whether there can be uniformity in wages between different units of the same industry or between different industries in the same or different regions. India is a vast country with diverse conditions of life. The economic conditions of the industry also vary. How right is it to demand a rise in one's rates of wages because there has been a wage rise in another unit?

Labour is a factor of production. Wages have to be paid out of the value of the product. Wage increases should therefore have some relation to increase in productivity or one will be eating into one's own capital which is the surest way to bankruptcy and unemployment. But are all demands related to productivity; if not what is the justification for the wage increase demanded and how can it be met without endangering the future of the industry? What is the justification for leap frogging mechanism built into wage agreements?

It has been customary for the trade unions to demand that determination of wages should be left to collective bargaining and that State regulation should be limited to protecting the weaker sections of labour from being exploited. But can wage rates be left entirely to be determined by market forces of demand and supply especially in essential services? Can water supply, electricity, communications and other services provide the vital necessities of the common man be exposed to dangers of strike? Can the workers of such establishments be locked out? Is it not necessary to apply a voluntary restraint on the workers' right to strike in such cases and other means devised for safeguarding the interests of workers?

There can always be differences on any issue but given the goodwill all differences can be resolved by mutual discussions failing which by adjudication or arbitration. Strike should be the last resort; it should not be resorted to unless all other possibilities of resolving the disputes are exhausted. Human relations are a delicate mechanism. They call for infinite patience and an effort to understand the other's point of view. They cannot be forced or they break. Once the relations are severed, rebuilding the same relations takes much time. It is by cooperation and not by confrontation that one can achieve something. Cooperation should be fostered and confrontation avoided.

The trade union movement is at present characterized by multiplicity of unions and inter-union rivalry. This has tended to weaken the movement because of which many unions are resorting to coercion and violence. These methods are self defeating and should be eschewed. The leaders of all organizations who have the interests of the country and the movement at heart should sit together and forge unity. From unity comes strength, power and confidence.

Freedom of Association and Trade Union Rights[2]

Freedom of Association is a basic human right. It is one of the cardinal principles on which the ILO is founded. It is also a fundamental right guaranteed to the citizens of India under the Constitution. According to the Universal Declaration of Human Rights everyone has the right to form and to join trade unions for the protection of his interests. Convention No.87 of the ILO provides that workers and employers without distinction whatsoever shall have the right to establish and subject only to the rules of the organization concerned, to join organizations of their choosing without previous authorization. The Constitution of India lays down that all citizens shall have the right to form associations and unions.

The International Labour Organization has set up a Committee on Freedom of Association to deal with complaints of infringement of Freedom of Association. The Committee has dealt with more than 800 cases since it was set up in 1951 and taken decisions covering the various aspects of Freedom of Association and Trade Union rights. These decisions have tended to become a charter of workers' rights. These comprise the Rights of Workers generally and Rights of Trade Unions in particular. Some of these rights are in the nature of basic human rights and the others are derived there from. A few major decisions of the Committee are enumerated below:

The Freedom of Association must be guaranteed without discrimination of any kind on the basis of occupation, sex, color race, beliefs, nationality, political opinion, etc., not only to workers in the private sector of the economy but also to civil servants and employees of public services in general. The denial of the right of publicly employed workers with the result that their associations do not enjoy the same advantages and privileges as do trade unions involves discrimination in the case of government employed workers and their organizations.

Where there is more than one organization the workers have the right to join any organization of their choosing; they also have the right to form new organizations should they deem it necessary notwithstanding the fact that there already exist one or more organizations in the field.

While unification of the trade union movement is desirable it should not be brought about by compulsion; trade unions should be encouraged to join together voluntarily. A situation in which an individual is denied any possibility of choice between organizations by reason of the fact that legislation permits the existence of only one organization in the sphere in which he is employed—one union in one industry—is contrary to the principles of Freedom of Association. A provision authorizing the refusal of an application for registration of a union on the ground that there is already another union or that the other unions are sufficiently representative contravenes the principle.

The organizations which, by virtue of their strength are recognized as the most representative for purpose of collective bargaining or for nomination to national or international tripartite bodies should not be given any privilege which gives them an unfair advantage over the others. Further the procedure for certification of unions as exclusive bargaining agents should be subject to appropriate safeguards against abuse, namely:

(a) Certification should be made by an independent body (such as Industrial Relations commission establishment of which was recommended by a National Commission on Labour and the National Tripartite Conference held in 1982).
(b) The representative organization should be chosen by a majority of the employees of the unit concerned;
(c) The organizations, which fail to secure a sufficiently larger number of votes, should have the right to ask for a new election after a stipulated period.

A legislative provision stipulating a minimum number of members for registration of a union would offend the principle of Freedom of Association if that number were too high. (The proposals contained in the Trade Unions Amendment Bill should be considered in this light). The committee on Freedom of Association has expressed the view that a minimum number of 20 may not be excessively high but a number of 50 would be.

The principle of freedom of association implies that the workers should not be required to obtain previous authorization to form a union or to the constitution or rules of the organization.

This is however without prejudice to the authority of the state to frame rules to regulate the normal working of industrial organizations. The committee has suggested that it would be desirable to provide that the registration is done by an agency independent of the local authorities and that the decisions of such an agency should be subject to a right of appeal to the Courts. In the view of the Committee normal control of the activities of trade unions should be affected by judicial authorities.

Convention No.87 concerning Freedom of Association lays down that workers' organizations shall have the right to draw up their constitutions and rules, to elect their representatives in full freedom, to organize their administration and activities and to formulate their programme. The Committee has clarified that workers' organizations should have the right to draw up their constitutions and rules, to organize their activities and to formulate their programme, that the public authorities should refrain from any interference which would restrict this right or impede the lawful exercise thereof, and that the law of the land should not be such as to impair or be so applied as to impair, the effective enjoyment of the right. The Committee has also clarified that any legislative provisions which lays down that trade union leaders must belong to the occupation in which the organization functions would not be in conformity with the right of the workers to elect their representative freely (in this connection the proposal to reduce the percentage of office bearers of a union drawn from outside the organization contained in the Trade Union Amendment Bill presently before the Parliament is relevant). The Committee has also expressed the view that no person may be debarred from holding office in a trade union on grounds of his/her political opinions or activities.

The Committee has pointed out that convictions on account of offences the nature of which is not such as to be prejudicial to the proper exercise of official trade unions functions, should not constitute grounds for disqualification for trade union office.

Freedom of Association implies not only the right for workers to form freely associations of their own choosing but also the right to pursue lawful activities in defence of their occupational interests. In every democratic trade union movement the annual congress of members is the supreme trade union authority which determines the regulations governing the administration and activities of trade unions and which lays down their programme. This right should be unhindered by interference by any public authority.

The committee has however advised that in order that trade unions may be sheltered from political vicissitudes and avoid being dependent on public authorities it would be desirable if they limit the field of their activities without prejudice to the freedom of opinion of their members to the occupational and trade union fields. The fundamental and permanent mission of the trade union movement is the economic and social advancement of the workers. When therefore the trade unions decide to establish relations with a political party or to undertake constitutional political action as a means towards the advancement of their economic and social objectives such political relations or actions should not be of such a nature as to compromise the continuance of the trade union movement or its social or economic functions irrespective of political changes in the country. Government should not therefore attempt to transform the trade union movement into an instrument for the pursuance of political aims nor should they attempt to interfere with the normal functions of a trade union movement because of its freely established relationship with a political party. It should be possible for the Government without prohibiting in general terms political activities of occupational organizations to entrust to the judicial authorities concerned the task of repressing abuses which might be committed by organizations losing sight of their basic objectives.

The right of workers to set up the organizations of their own choice and of the freedom of such organizations to draft their own statutes and internal regulations and to organize their own management and activities presuppose financial independence. Financial independence implies that workers' organizations should not be financed in such a way as to allow the public authorities to enjoy discretionary powers over them. But it is open to the Government to take measures to prevent abuses in and to protect the members of a trade union against mismanagement of funds by means of audit through an independent and qualified auditor or otherwise subject to the control of a judicial authority. The principle of freedom of association does not prevent the control of the trade union action if it is violative of law. But this control should be exercised by a judicial authority.

Any legal or other provisions involving interference by the public authorities in the various stages of the electrical process would be incompatible with the right to hold free election.

The dissolution or even suspension of the legal personality of a union is contrary to the generally accepted principle of freedom of association. If however dissolution or suspension of a union is considered necessary in a state of emergency there should be a judicial safeguard against abuse of that power.

It is generally accepted principle that no person should be prejudiced in his employment by reason of his trade union membership or activities. One of the fundamental principles of freedom of association is that workers should enjoy adequate protection against all acts of anti-union discrimination in respect of their employment such as dismissal, demotion, transfer or other prejudicial measures and that this protection is particularly desirable in the case of trade union officials because in order to be able to perform their trade union duties in full independence, they must have the guarantee that they will not be prejudiced on account of the mandate which they hold from their trade unions. This does not however imply that the fact a person holds a trade union office confers on him immunity against dismissal irrespective of the circumstances. Complaints against anti-union practices should be examined by a national machinery which in addition to being speedy, should not only be impartial but also be seen to be as such by the parties concerned who should participate in the procedure in appropriate and constructive manners.

The right to bargain collectively in full freedom of all wage earners, not covered by the guarantees embodied in statutory conditions applicable to public officials, is a fundamental trade union right. Collective agreements constitute the most certain method for the determination on an equitable basis of wages and conditions of employment in private industry. Both employers and trade unions should bargain in good faith making every effort to come to an agreement, particularly when unions are not allowed to have recourse to strike action in the public service or in essential services.

Convention No. 98 which mainly concerns collective bargaining permits the exclusion of public servants engaged in the administration of the state from its purview. A distinction should however be drawn between civil servants employed in government ministries and departments on the one hand and other persons employed by the Government in public undertakings or by independent corporations.

While the public authorities have the right to decide whether they will negotiate at the regional or national level on their side, the workers whether negotiating at the regional or national level, should be entitled to choose as they wish the organization, which shall represent them in the negotiations. Direct negotiation between the undertaking and its employees by passing representative organizations where these exist, would be detrimental to the principle that negotiations between employers and organizations of workers should be encouraged and promoted.

If the state establishes machinery for the representation of the occupational interests of a whole category of workers, this representation should normally lie with the organizations, which have the largest membership in the category concerned.

The fact that a trade union organization is debarred from membership of joint committees does not necessarily imply infringement of the trade union rights of that organization. But for this, two conditions must be met: first, that the reason for which a union is debarred from participation in a joint committee must lie in its non-representative character, determined by objective criteria; second, that in spite of such non-participation the other rights which it enjoys and the activities it can undertake in other fields must enable it effectively to further and defend the interests of its members.

Employers should recognize organizations that are representative of workers in a particular industry for the purpose of collective bargaining. The competent authorities should in all cases have the power to proceed to an objective verification of any claim by a union that it represents the majority of the workers in an undertaking, provided that such a claim appears to be plausible. If the union concerned is found to be the majority union, the authorities should take appropriate conciliatory measures with a view to obtaining the employers' recognition of that union for collective bargaining purposes. If a union acquires majority in the course of a collective agreement concluded by another union and it requests the cancellation of that agreement, the authorities, notwithstanding the agreement, should make appropriate representations to the employer regarding the recognition of this union.

The requirement of prior approval by a government authority to make an agreement valid is contrary to the whole system of voluntary negotiation. Where intervention by the public authorities is essentially for the purpose of ensuring that the negotiating parties subordinate their interests to the national economic policy pursued by the government, whether they agree with that policy or not, it would not be compatible with the generally accepted principles that workers' and employers' organizations should enjoy the right freely to organize their activities and to formulate their programme that the public authorities should refrain from any interference which would restrict this right or impede the lawful exercise thereof and that the law of the land should not be such as to impair or be so applied as to impair the enjoyment of such right. Ways could however be found of persuading the parties to collective bargaining to have regard voluntarily in their negotiation to consideration relating to the economic or social policy of the government and the safeguarding of general interest. But to achieve this it is necessary first of all that the objectives to be recognized as being in the general interest should have been widely discussed by all parties on a national scale through a consultative body.

If as part of its stabilization policy, a government considers that wage rates cannot be settled through collective bargaining such a restriction should be imposed as an exceptional measures and only to the extent that is necessary without exceeding a reasonable period and it should be accompanied by adequate safeguards to protect workers' living standards.

The right to strike by workers and their organizations is generally recognized as a legitimate means of defending their occupational interests. Where strikes are prohibited or subject to restriction there should be adequate guarantees to safeguard the interests of the workers thus deprived of an essential means of defending their occupational interests through impartial and speedy conciliation and arbitration proceedings in which the parties concerned can take part at every stage.

Strikes of a purely political nature directed against the policy of government and are not in furtherance of a trade dispute and strikes decided systematically long before negotiation taking place do not fall within the scope of the principles of freedom of association.

Recognition of the principle of freedom of association in the case of public officials does not necessarily imply the right to strike. Civil servants enjoying statutory terms and conditions are in the majority of countries denied the right to strike as a normal condition in the legislation governing their employment. The right to strike can be restricted or even prohibited in the civil service or in essential services because a strike there could cause serious hardship to the national community. But it would not be appropriate for all publicly owned undertakings to be treated on the same basis for limiting the right to strike. A distinction has to be made between those undertakings which are genuinely essential because their interruption may cause public hardship and those, which are not essential according to this criterion.

Whenever strikes in essential services or in the civil service are forbidden or subject to restriction should be accompanied by adequate impartial and speedy conciliation and arbitration procedures in which the parties can take part at every sage and in which the awards are binding in all cases on both parties; these awards, once they have been made, should be fully and promptly implemented.

A genuinely free and independent trade union movement can develop only under a regime, which guarantees fundamental human rights. Freedom of assembly for trade union purposes constitutes one of the fundamental elements of trade union rights. The right of members of trade unions to meet in their own premises for the discussion of trade union matters constitutes a fundamental trade union right. Workers have the right to hold congresses without previous authorization. The presence of any official representing the police or any other authority at such meetings may have an effect on the deliberations and therefore might constitute interference.

The right to organize public meetings is an important element in trade union rights. The right to hold meetings does not release the organization from the obligation to comply with the reasonable formalities for the use of public premises. Trade Unions should respect legal provisions, which are intended to ensure the maintenance of public order.

The right to express opinions through the press or otherwise is one of the essential elements of trade union rights. The full exercise of trade union rights calls for a free flow of information, opinions and ideas. Trade Union organizations, when issuing their publications should however have regard in the interests of the development of the trade union movement to the principles enunciated by the ILO at its 35th session. It is only in so far as trade union organizations do not allow their occupational demands to assume a clearly political aspect that they can legitimately claim that there should be no interference in their activities.

The right to protection of trade union property is one of the civil liberties, which is essential for the normal exercise of trade unions right. If trade union premises are used as a refuge by persons committing outrages or as an assembly point by a political organization the trade unions concerned cannot claim immunity against the entry of the authorities into the premises.

The preventive detention of trade unionists on the ground that breaches of the law may take place in connection with a strike involves a serious danger of infringement of trade union rights. Detention of trade union officials even for reasons of internal security may constitute a grave interference with trade union rights unless attended by appropriate judicial safeguards.

Critique of the Resolution Concerning Trade Union Rights

Freedom of Association is undoubtedly one of the fundamental principles on which ILO is founded. Indeed it is one of the fundamental rights embodied in the Indian Constitution. We have the greatest respect for the supervisory mechanism set up by the ILO, particularly, the Committee on Freedom of Association and we have honoured and have been honouring the requests for information made by the Committee; the complaints against India regarding violation of the Freedom of Association and Trade Union Rights have by and large been settled amicably.

It has been our experience that the complaints procedure which is in vogue takes advantage of by some organisations representing or supported by political parties, in opposition to the party in power to embarrass the Government and to malign it. We feel that there should be some safeguards against it.

According to our constitution the Freedom of Association is subject to reasonable restrictions being imposed in the interest of sovereignty and integrity of the nation. In other words sovereignty and integrity are more supreme. No individual or body of individuals can act in a manner prejudicial to the sovereignty and integrity of the nation. What constitutes a prejudice to the sovereignty and integrity of a nation is for the national Parliament and the national judiciary to judge. It will be difficult for an outside agency to appreciate adequately the situation obtaining in a country on the basis of a complaint or a written reply thereto. One should have a feel of the milieu in which incidents occur to understand them in proper perspective.

The Preamble to the Constitution of the ILO says that universal and lasting peace can be established only if it is based on social justice. According to our Constitution it is an obligation of the State to work for Social Justice. Improvement in the living standards of the poorest groups of society and reduction in inequalities in asset distribution is one of the objectives of our plans. It has however been our experience that sometimes when sectional interests seek to dominate the interests of the community, programmes designed to achieve social justice may come into conflict with certain other ideals. Those who have are able to get more while those who do not have continue to be denied even their basic needs. The State is therefore sometimes in a dilemma to decide as to what should have precedence, social justice or the other freedoms of man. The Philadelphia Declaration is unambiguous in this regard. It says that all national and international policies and measures should be judged in the light of the fundamental objective of social justice and accepted only so far as they may be held to promote and not hinder the achievement of that objective. We therefore feel that when complaints are received about violation of the Freedom of Association and trade union rights it would be necessary to keep this basic premise in view in judging Government action.

It should be noted that in a developing country like ours the number of organized workers represent a small percentage of the total workforce bulk of which is unorganized. They remain unorganized not because of lack of freedom to organize themselves but for other socio economic reasons, the basic one being unemployment and poverty. In such a situation while it should be the endeavour of all concerned to help and encourage the workers to organize themselves, pending such organization, the State has the responsibility to ensure that they are not exploited and that they get their due share of the fruits of development. How can this be done except by means of a regulatory mechanism contributing to a reduction in inequalities of income and wealth involving some restrictions on the freedom of the comparatively more privileged sections of the people from getting away with larger slices of the national cake by free and licentious exercise of their rights? It is normally to be expected that the organized work force accept such restrictions voluntarily; if it does not should the State watch helplessly the failure of its policy?

We feel that over emphasis on rights can be harmful; there should be equal emphasis on the duties of a citizen as well. We believe in dharma, the right conduct on the part of everyone. We feel too that sectional interests should be subordinated to those of the community.

We believe too that the members of trade unions are not above law. They have no immunity against action under a law for which they may become liable, not as trade union members, but as citizens of the State. If for example, some persons assault the chairman of the Corporation as it happened in one case of complaint to the ILO are they to be exonerated solely because they are members of a union?

Besides, what are the trade union rights. For example, in an establishment where there are many unions – there are twenty to thirty in some of our public sector establishment such as electricity boards - and the management has entered into agreement with the largest or majority union. Can the minority unions who are not party to the agreement have the freedom to disrupt the working of the organization holding the industry or economy to ransom by use of force, violence, coercion or duress? We have a case where the management of the Railway system, representing the very life line of the country, had entered into an agreement with the recognized majority union representing about 1.3 million workers; a small minority union with the strength of about 100,000 workers representing a category of workers in a strategic position tried to bring the whole system to a standstill to press its own demands affecting the movement of food grains to drought affected areas and the much needed raw materials to basic industries vital to the whole economy. How do you expect the government to deal with such a situation. Let the economy grind to a halt or negotiate with the minority union under mining the position of the majority union and encourage more exaggerated demands from the other dissenting union?

There is a practice in our country known as *Gherao* which means surrounding a man, the manager or other key official of an organization and not letting him move for hours and days altogether, even to answer calls of nature, without food or sleep and wearing him out psychologically so that he may sign agreements on the dotted line under duress which he is not able later to implement. Is that a basic human right? If not, when we assert the primacy of trade union rights as basic human rights should they not be codified and a code of conduct prescribed for trade unions?

Role of Trade Unions in Public Enterprises

India has been declared in its Constitution to be a Sovereign Socialist Democratic Republic. The word 'Socialist' was added recently, consciously and deliberately with a view to take the country in the socialist path as distinguished from the capitalist path. It is the characteristic feature of Socialist State that the means of production are owned or controlled by the State; in other words economic activity will largely be in the Public Sector. As it is, the Public Sector in India, in terms of employment, is larger than the private sector if we exclude agriculture and it is growing. It should be expected to grow further until it acquires the commanding heights of the economy.

A public enterprise is a unit in the Public Sector. It may be a company, a corporation, a society or a departmental undertaking; whatever its form be, its nature is the same. It is wholly or largely owned or controlled by Government, set up to provide goods and service needed by the people. Their basic objective is service and welfare of the people. Although they are also expected to yield a return on the investments, profit is not their motive. This is the basic difference between the private and the public sector. Even if they make a profit it goes to augment the resources of the State and not to a private coffer and the resources would be available for the development of the country and welfare of the people.

It is necessary to note these facts because they are highly relevant to the considerations of the role of trade unions in the Public Enterprises but before we take up this issue it is also necessary to note the nature and purpose of a trade union.

A trade union is an organization of workers formed with the object of serving the needs of its members. As the National Commission of Labour stated the primary function of a union is to promote and protect the interests of its members. It has to strive to better the terms and conditions of employment and generally to advance their economic and social interests so as to achieve for them a rising standard of living. It undertakes welfare activities by organizing co-operatives, mutual benefit societies, employment assistance, libraries, games, cultural programme, etc.

It is also expected to provide education to its members in all aspects of their working life including improvement of their civic environments. But the trade unions in India, at present, are mainly engaged in securing better terms of employment to its members. This is because of historical reasons.

The working class movement had its origins in the conflict between those who sell their labour and those buy it, inherent in the capitalist economy where a person employs another for his profit. The capitalist employer has the money power. To match this the workers needed to be organized so as to protect themselves against exploitation. The National Commission on Labour has described the genesis of the movement in the following words :

> The setting up of large scale industrial units created conditions of widespread use of machinery, establishment of new lines of production, change in working and living environment of workers, and concentration of industries in large towns, all of which introduced a new class of workers who were dependant on wages for their livelihood. They were at a disadvantage in an age when the doctrine of laissez-faire held the field. In the absence of collective action, they had to be content with the wages which each of them could separately negotiate with the employer from a position of disadvantage Workers had to join together at least to maintain, if not to improve, their bargaining power against the employer.

In a public enterprise these conditions do not obtain and there can be no question of exploitation of labour. Government is as much interested in the welfare of the workers as of other people. Indeed it is the policy of Government to protect the workers from exploitation wherever they are liable to be exploited. Several laws have been enacted for the purpose. It should therefore be obvious that the role of a trade union organization in a public enterprise is materially different from that of a private undertaking and it may not be correct to apply the same kind of trade union action as may be necessary and valid in the private sector. The working class movement in its relation with the public sector would seem to call for a complete reorientation. This would be more obvious if we examine closely some of the concepts prevalent in the relationship between employers and workers, otherwise known as industrial relations.

Let us take collective bargaining. What is collective bargaining? It is the means by which the price of labour is determined by negotiation between the employer and a group of workers or between a group of employers and a group of workers. The basic assumption of collective bargaining is that labour can withdraw its service if it does not get the price it demands or that the employer can close down his business if he cannot afford to pay the price demanded. It implies free play of the market forces based on free mobility of labour and capital, characteristic of a competitive capitalist economy in which the price of labour as well as capital is determined by application of the principle of what the traffic can bear. This principle is not applicable in the case of the Public Sector for the following reasons.

Firstly, who is the employer in a State enterprise? Is it the management? No. in a public enterprise there is hardly any difference between a manager and a worker. Both are employees of the State. In the ultimate analysis the employer in a public enterprise is the State which means the people. Can there be a bargain between the people and the workers? Are they two different categories?

By all tokens, a planned economy is a regulated economy where the pattern of investment, employment and the prices to be paid are all predetermined in furtherance of the socio-economic objectives of the nation. In such an economy the free exercise of the right to strike and lockout can cause heavy damage to the economy, defence and life of the community as a whole. There has necessarily to be a restraint in the use of these weapons. In other words, there has to be a limitation on the application of the principle of collective bargaining.

But it should also be realized that in a socialist economy the levers of power are largely in the hands of the bureaucracy which can often be unthinking and mechanistic and its control can stifle the aspirations of the people. There has therefore to be an alternative to collective bargaining for safeguarding the interests of the workers. It can be a Wage Commission, a Tribunal or an arbitral body. There can be bargaining in these bodies too. The employers and workers are often represented in them or before them. The trade unions have a vital role to play in the working of such bodies. They can put the case of the workers before them and fight for it. But the fighting will be under controlled conditions so that it may not harm the interests of the people.

Let us now take another concept – Workers' participation in management. As already stated, in a State enterprise there is hardly any difference between the management and the workers. The managers as well as workers are employees. They belong to the same class. They are co-partners in running a business for the State; they are the common trustees of the interests of the community viewed in this light the concept of workers' participation in management acquires a different meaning. It means that the managers and workers have to work as a team and there has to be a mutual consultation at all levels and on all aspects of the business. It is not only a question of sharing responsibility. They have to assume joint responsibility.

In the circumstances it seems to me that while the trade unions in the Public enterprises have to continue to work for promoting the interests of their members they have a greater social responsibility. It is imperative that the unions should keep the well-being and progress of the community constantly before them even in the midst of their endeavours to help the working class. They have to adapt themselves to the changing social needs and rise above the divisional forces of class consciousness. It may be necessary sometimes to subordinate their own sectional interests to the interests of the community.

NOTES

1. Speech delivered at the 10th Conference of Maharashtra INTUC.

XIII
Workers' Participation in Management

Workers Participation in Management – The Concept

The basic assumption underlying the concept of Workers Participation is that the goals of an organisation or enterprise are best achieved if there is identity of interests between management and workers. The general objectives of a scheme of workers' participation is to secure the willing cooperation of the workers in the achievement of the goals of the organization it seeks to make the workers better informed about the affairs of the organization and to consult them in finding solutions to the problems so that they may realize that the achievement of the goals is as much in their interest as in that of management and that there is no attempt to exploit them.

Institutional structures and procedures are no doubt necessary for maintenance of harmonious industrial relations but they cannot bring about harmony in a state of mutual suspicion and lack of confidence. It is therefore more important that there should be a change in the attitudes.Both the employers as well as the workers should learn to consider themselves as partners in the business and to look upon each other with greater trust and faith. Concerted efforts should be made by both the parties to avoid confrontation and to promote cooperation.

The traditional employer-employee relationship implies conflict of interest between "we" and "they" but it is not conducive to peace and harmony as it separates "us" from "them". The ideal form of organization is that in which all those engaged in an activity are brought together in relationship of partnership or cooperation. This calls for an institutional arrangement in which a worker can sit with the manager and consider the policies programme and problems of the organization jointly. Such an arrangement will enable the workers to exercise an influence on the decision making process in the organization or enterprise in which they are employed.

There is a general trend all over the world towards industrial democracy resulting in the participation of workers in the decision making process which was till recently regarded as the sole prerogative of management. Workers participation in management has become one of the key issues in the field of industrial relations. In the past the employers used to oppose it vehemently and the trade unions were also somewhat lukewarm. The situation is fast changing. Although the employers continue to oppose the scheme they have tended to take a more positive view and the workers have started supporting it. Management experts have come to look upon it as one means of organizational development. Indeed, workers participation in management has become an element in the political philosophy of a nation and it is said that advanced systems of participation correspond to a choice of society implying a significant change in power relationship within an undertaking as well as in the economy itself. Several countries including India have therefore incorporated the principle of worker participation in their Constitutions and have been promoting it in various ways.

Changing Concept

Traditionally workers participation was concerned mainly with welfare amenities, personnel matters, etc. During the last decade the concept was extended to financial and other general management problems. In recent times there is greater emphasis on safety and health.

In the past, safety legislation did not give workers any say in safety matters. For example, the Factories Act in India, which is mainly concerned with safety and health at the work place in the factories, makes no provision for workers participation in that regard. There is a feeling that protection of health and safety of the workers is the responsibility of the employer and that it is a technical matter which should be dealt with by experts. Opinion is changing. It has come to be realized that protective measure cannot be devised without the cooperation of the workers and that the workers are aware of the hazards of work and can make positive contribution to their prevention. There is therefore a growing tendency to set up joint safety committees. The status of the committee varies from country to country but its importance is growing. In France every undertaking over a particular size is required to establish health and safety committees which would be responsible for improving the conditions of health and safety and reducing the incidents of accidents and occupational diseases. The committee includes representatives of workers. The Health and Safety Commission, which has overall responsibility for occupational health, and safety policy at the national level is a tripartite body. It has set up several advisory committees, which are also tripartite. At the industry level most of the public sector establishments have set up bipartite safety committees. At the shop level there is provision for the appointment of trade union representatives to deal with occupational health and safety. This is a special feature obtaining in that country. In the Soviet Union Trade unions have powers of inspection and supervision over the implementation of safety regulations.

Dimensions of Workers Participation in Management

The question of workers participation in management has three clear dimensions, namely, the levels, forms and functions. In an enterprise there can be workers participation at different levels, namely, the shop floor, plant level and the corporate level. In some organizations there are more levels. For example, Steel Authority of India Ltd. Has introduced workers participation in five levels-the national level, the corporate level, plant level, the zonal level and the shop level.

Workers participation takes different forms such as collective bargaining, works councils, participation in the Boards of Directors, etc. Lately several participatory bodies outside the formal management structure have come into being, such as, Safety Committees, Grievance Committees, etc. There are about ten to twelve such committees in each of the plants under SAIL. Rourkela Plant has canteen committee, works committee, general and departmental safety committees, central grievance committee, zonal grievance committee, central production committee, departmental production committee, joint implementation committee and township and amenities committee. Durgapur has additionally a hospital committee and a sports committee. Bhilai has an environmental hygiene committee, a merit rating review committee and an education committee. In other industrialized countries such special bodies have been set up for dealing with matters relating to safety and health, training, question of redundancies and collective dismissals.

Growth of Participative Management in India

In India workers participation in management is one of the Directive Principles of State Policy embodied in the Constitution. It is also a basic ingredient of the economic policy of the ruling party at the Centre. The economic resolution adopted by the Indian National Congress at its plenary session held in Calcutta required that the new industrial culture in the public sector should be based on participative management; the workers must feel that they are not mere wage earners but also have a place in management. Several schemes have therefore been introduced from time to time to give effect to this policy.

The Industrial Disputes Act provided, for the first time, for limited participation of elected representatives of workers in bipartite work committees, which aimed at promoting measures for securing and preserving amity and good relations between employer and workmen. Following the Industrial Policy Resolution of 1956 and Second Plan recommendations a scheme of Joint Management Councils was introduced in 1958. In 1970 the Nationalized Banks Scheme provided for the appointment of one director from among the employees of the nationalized banks. In 1971, a scheme of inducting representatives of workmen as directors in the boards of management of public sector undertakings was introduced in a few selected enterprises. Then followed the two voluntary schemes, workers participation in industry at shop floor and plant level and workers participation in commercial and service organizations having large-scale public dealings. Recently Government have notified a new scheme of workers participation in the management of central public sector undertakings. The scheme is compulsory for all public undertakings. It was required to be implemented within one year of the notification that is by December 1984.

Experiences

Many public sector establishments already have workers participation in management in one form or the other. It has been reported that out of the 192 central public sector undertakings 124 have implemented the voluntary schemes in the same form as notified or in a modified form. Many of the undertakings have claimed success for their schemes. These schemes however need to be evaluated.

The discussion on the subject of workers participation focuses more attention on the form and other procedural matters than on the substance of the scheme, which lies in fostering the spirit of cooperation between workers and the management. The similarity or differences in the form of different schemes are therefore not quite significant. What is more important is whether the scheme is designed to secure cooperation between the workers and the management and whether in fact it has enabled them to work together in a spirit of cooperation.

The National Textile Corporation has reported that the experimental scheme it has introduced in a few mills has to a large extent resulted in better understanding between the management and the workers and that the workers feel more involved in the affairs of the mills, and their suspicion of the management has been removed to a significant degree. It has also been reported that the reports of the periodical meetings of the bipartite management committee show overall improvement, financial gains as a result of energy saving, rationalization of mills, optimum utilization of capacity and consequent increase in production.

SAIL has reported that the bipartite bodies at all levels are functioning satisfactorily and that they have yielded good results in toning up productivity and discipline and that they have gone a long way in fostering participating and cooperative culture paving the way for amicable solution to all common problems. As a result of successful functioning of all the forums no major industrial relations problems has occurred in the company for long.

BHEL has reported that the Joint Committee it has set up at the corporate level can take legitimate satisfaction on its achievements during its life of one decade. It is said that considering the size and composition of the Joint Committee its achievements are unique and unparalleled. It goes on to say that with each settlement on issues of mutual concern the status of the Joint committee has enhanced and the Committee enjoys the confidence and respect of both sides resulting in a declaration by the labour side that nothing would be done by way of agitation, etc. which would impair the effectiveness of the Committee with a matching response from the management side in sharing details on matters which are traditionally considered management prorogation. This happy situation has come about by the recognition on both sides that whatever intrinsic prerogatives they enjoy they should be subordinated to the common objective of the growth and prosperity of the organizations and its members. The positive approach of developing the company coupled with eagerness to ensure justice to the employees through negotiations, avoiding frustrating technical trivialities have been largely responsible for the success of the Committee.

If these reports are true, there can be no better endorsement of the scheme for workers participation in management.

Struggle for Power

There are however certain findings of the studies carried out by various agencies, which need to be noted and carefully considered. Firstly, it is observed that there are at present several schemes of workers' participation in management operating concurrently; they are the works committees, joint management committees, the schemes introduced in 1975 and 1977 and the scheme introduced in 1983. It is necessary to ensure that these schemes do not overlap and that if one scheme is working satisfactorily it should be allowed to continue notwithstanding the fact that a new scheme has been introduced.

The Gandhi Labour Institute, Ahmedabad on a study of the Joint Management Councils in Gujarat observed, inter alia, that in terms of practice, conformity to prescribed statutory norms was evident in the regularity of holding meetings, etc. but in terms of performance the study revealed that the councils pay more attention to workers petty grievances such as toilet, urinals, cleanliness of the canteen, cycle-stand, etc. than to the more substantive issues like production and productivity.

It has also been reported by the Gandhi Labour Institute that there is a general complaint from the workers representatives that they have no 'power' or authority to compel the management to implement the decisions taken in the JMC meetings. They are aggrieved by the fact that majority of the problems discussed in the meetings remain unresolved. On the other hand, the representatives of management complain that the problems discussed in the JMC meetings are generally outside the scope of the JMC and they also feel that workers give undue importance to the 'power' factor than to arrive at mutually agreeable solutions.

According to the Gandhi Labour Institute, another factor, which perturbed the workers representatives, was managements' denial of information regarding the financial affairs of the undertakings. The management's answer to this was that the workers representatives were not in a position to understand the balance sheet. Quite a few managers also expressed the view that in matters of production and finance managerial personnel should exercise final authority. It is obvious that for successful implementation of the scheme of workers participation this kind of prejudice should be shed. This calls for education.

This was also the finding of a survey carried out by the National Productivity Council which observed that the unions tend to use the participative fora for eliciting better welfare facilities. It has therefore been suggested that the agenda placed before the participatory fora should be carefully drawn up and scrutinized so that 'interest' related issues such as wages and bonus are not raised in the meeting. Surfacing interest related problems tends to jeopardize the role of collective bargaining and restricts the jurisdiction of workers representatives. More stress needs to be given on inclusion of production related problems in the agenda and petty grievances should be resolved at supervisory levels instead of bringing them in the councils. It has also been observed that there is generally lack of interest in the schemes of participation on the part of either party-the management or the workers-especially the management but wherever the management has taken interest and posed problems relating to work and production it has benefited from these.

The National Productivity Council has observed a tendency on the part of the workers to expand the area of discussion to get a leverage of power.

Education and Training

The Gandhi Labour Institute has suggested that as an important means to improve the functioning of JMC, the significance of orientation and training of the concerned members needs to be stressed. The training aspect has an added significance because much of the problems, doubts, confusion and misunderstanding between the two partners that have arisen out of lack of proper awareness, knowledge, understanding and functions of the JMC in an enterprise.

An expert committee, which studied workers participation in management of certain public undertakings, observed that the process of workers participation in management has been interpreted differently by different managements. Some have interpreted it as a means of effective communication resulting in information sharing; others as a consultative process ending in joint decision and collective implementation of such decisions. There are still others who do not take it seriously but adopt some schemes simply to satisfy the Government rules and directives. The impact accordingly varies. The committee has therefore highlighted the need for and contribution of powerful intervention by way of training in the actual implementation of any participatory scheme.

Thus the key to the success of the scheme of workers participation in management lies in education. This calls for two kinds of education. Firstly, the workers as well as the managerial personnel need to be educated about the value of cooperation between management and workers through successful implementation of the schemes of workers participation in management. Secondly, the workers need to be trained in the principles and practices of management and the specific functions of the various participatory fora so that they may be able to take part in the decision making process effectively.

As most of the public enterprises have already introduced workers participation in one or the other form and the remaining ones are also required to introduce them before long all the institutions engaged in worker education should gear themselves up to provide this education to all those who have been elected or nominated to the participatory fora or likely to be elected/nominated. This is a major challenge facing these institutions.

There is also need for monitoring of the working of the schemes of participation and for intervention by the Department of Labour for removal of difficulties when problems arise in the implementation of the schemes. The Gandhi Labour Institute has suggested that the officials of the Labour Department should attend the meetings of the participatory bodies and guide them when necessary. This pre-supposes that the officials of the Labour Depart themselves are well trained or experienced in the scheme.

Issues relating to Workers Participation in Management

The problem of workers' participation in management is multi-dimensional. In discussing the subject several questions arise for which we have to find an answer. First what are the activities of the management in which workers can participate. Traditionally workers' participation in management is thought of in the context of an industrial unit. Even within this limited area, questions arise as to whether the workers should participate at the floor level, factory level and/or corporate level. Conceptually however the concept can be extended to every activity where there is management -worker relationship. In the recent Asian Regional Conference of the International Labour Organization, participation of rural workers in rural development through their own freely chosen organization was stressed. It was said that the rural workers must have the opportunity to fully participate in the planning and implementation of the development activity as opposed to merely being mobilised for it. In a resolution on workers' education it was urged that all possible steps should be taken to encourage programmes designed to promote the full involvement of workers in the formulation of policies which will effect substantial social and economic progress. In a meeting which the Trade Union leaders had with the Prime Minister a demand was made that workers should be associated in the formulation of national plans and policies. This brings to the force the question as to how industrial democracy is to be reconciled and co-ordinated with political democracy. Workers represent a class. Their interests may conceivably be in conflict with that of the 'people' at large. In whatever arrangement we make for workers' participation there should be no conflict between the workers on the one hand and the people on the other.

The second question is the reason for workers' participation in management. What is the need for it? What is its raison d' etre? Whatever schemes we undertake the objective should be clear.

The general objective of workers' participation would be to secure the willing co-operation of the workers in the achievement of the goals of the organization. It seeks to make the workers better informed about the affairs of the organization and to consult them in finding solution to the problems so that they may realize that the achievement of the goals is as much in their interests as in that of the management and that there is no attempt to exploit them. It should however be understood that management is a complex affair; it cannot be viewed as functioning in the interest of the management only or the workers only. Management has a variety of responsibilities; personnel management and welfare of workers being only one of them.

The extent of participation of workers in management therefore varies according to the nature of the organization and the willingness of the workers to share the responsibility of management. In a cooperative form of organization where the workers are also the owners and managers there is total commonality of interest and full participation is possible. In an entrepreneurial form of organization however the interest of the workers may not entirely be identical with that of the entrepreneur. The entrepreneur takes risks and expects a reward for it. The workers may however not be willing to share the risks. They would be more interested in job and income security. In such a case full participation may not be possible. In the case of a Government Organization on the other hand there is hardly any difference between the management and the workers; in a sense they are all employees of Government and they are jointly and severally responsible for achievement of the goal set before them by Government. In such cases the interest of the community would be supreme. The interests of the management as well as the workers have to be subordinated to it.

The next question is what should be the form of participation, whether it should be statutory or non-statutory, formal or non-formal. We have at present non-statutory schemes or workers' participation. They do not seem to be working well. Suggestions have therefore been made to make them statutory. We have also statutory works committees under the Factories Act. It is doubtful if they are functioning any better.

It should therefore be realized that the form is not important. If there is willingness on both sides the scheme can succeed in any form. Co-operation is an act of will. It cannot be forced. We should therefore work towards the general acceptance of this system. It calls for education of the members of the management as well as the workers.

One of the most vexed questions relating to workers' participation is in regard to the selection of the representatives of the workers, whether they should be selected through secret ballot or whether the recognized union should be authorized to nominate the persons. There has been no unanimity among the Trade Unions leaders on this subject. Whatever decision is taken may be against one section of opinion or the other. The scheme cannot succeed unless the representatives of workers can speak with authority for all or the majority of workers.

The basic assumption underlying the concept of workers' participation is that the goals of an organization and enterprise are best achieved if there is identity of interests between the management and the workers. This calls for recognition of the fact that an organization cannot grow under conditions of adversary relationship between management and workers. The master-servant relationship or the employer-employee relationship implies conflict of interests between "we" and "They" and it is not conducive to peace and harmony as it separates "us" from "Them". The ideal form of organization is that in which all those engaged in an activity, in whatever capacity, are brought together in a relationship of partnership or cooperation. This calls for structural as well as attitudinal changes in industrial organizations. A formal or institutional frame-work in which the workers can sit together with the managerial personnel and consider the policies, programme and problems of the organization jointly should be evolved. But that is not enough. It is more important to inculcate among the managerial personnel as well as the workers a spirit of cooperation. The participants in an enterprise, managers as well as workers, should be educated in the principles and practice of participatory management so that it may be worked in the true spirit.

Before we proceed further we should also note that workers' participation in management is part of the Directive Principles of State Policy and it is also a basic ingredient of the economic policy of the ruling party. The economic resolution adopted by the Indian National Congress at its plenary session held in Calcutta requires that the new industrial culture in the Public Sector should be based on participative management. The workers must feel that they are not mere wage earners but also have a place in management. Both the workers and management must realize that the public sector is a national asset and that it has a great responsibility in maximizing production. The structure of Public Sector management should be such as will enthuse the patriotic working class to respond to the responsible tasks of increasing productivity, reduction in costs and technological change with a social awareness it has inherited from the days of the freedom struggle.

Workers' participation in management is therefore not to be viewed as a mere cliché. It has a loftier purpose of enlisting the wholehearted support of the working class in the national developmental effort.

The Public Enterprises are therefore expected to implement the scheme in the true spirit and to make it a success. The notification issued by Government should be treated as a direction which leaves no option. There is however room for flexibility as to the manner in which it is to be implemented.

It is obvious that since the public undertakings differ largely in size, form of organization, etc., there cannot be a single model of workers' participation for all of them. It may be necessary to evolve separate models for each undertaking or group of undertakings.

Since the scheme is meant for workers' participation in management, it follows that the workers should be consulted as to how they would like to be associated in the management process. The first step therefore is to take the workers or workers organizations of each undertaking to confidence and invite their suggestions. It is understood that many of the undertakings which have not implemented the earlier schemes could not do so because the unions were not cooperative. Reasons for non-cooperation by the union in a scheme which is intended to give them more power and authority need to be ascertained.

The scheme announced by the Ministry of Labour is in broad terms. Several details have been left to be decided in consultation with the representatives of labour. Firstly the scheme is applicable to all Central Public Sector undertakings except those which are given exemption. The question of granting exemption to any undertaking has not arisen so for. In the event of a request being made it will have to be considered according to some fixed criteria.

The scheme will be operated at the shop floor and the plant level in all public undertakings. Participation at the Board level will be introduced in a few undertakings to begin with selectively. Each Ministry/Department concerned with Public Enterprises is expected to prepare a list of undertakings in which Board level participation should be implemented. The Ministry/Department would naturally be guided by the views of the undertakings themselves in this regard.

The scheme envisages workers' participation at three levels, the shop level, the plant level and the Corporate level. But the scheme does not specify the number of persons to be in the participatory bodies at each level. Both the workers and the management will get equal representation at the shop floor and the plant levels. Each party will have a representation of five to ten members depending on the size of the workforce. The exact number is to be arrived at by the management in consultation with the trade union leaders in the undertaking.

The representation of workers at the shop floor and plant levels would cover different categories of workers. Managerial personnel would be excluded but supervisory categories would be included. The distribution of seats as between workers and supervisory personnel has been left to be decided by the respective organizations in consultation with the concerned leaders of the employees.

It is also left to the management to decide through consensus in consultation with the trade union leaders the mode of representation of workers at the various levels at which the scheme is to be implemented. This is perhaps the most crucial point of the whole scheme. It is recognized that if no consensus is reached on this vital issues it would not be possible to implement the scheme.

There are also a few incidental but important issues on which a view has to be taken: (a) whether the participatory bodies will be consultative bodies or decision-making bodies. In other words whether the decisions of the bodies will be advisory or mandatory. In the latter case what will be the powers of these bodies; (b) will the participants be accountable for the decisions to which they would be party and be held responsible for the consequences of their decisions; (c) whether the workers nominated to the various participatory bodies function in their individual capacity or as representatives of the workers at large or the trade unions. If they are to function in a representative capacity how will they ascertain the wishes and views of the bodies whom they represent on the various matters which come up for consideration in the participatory force.

A comparatively more fundamental issue is whether, management being a specialized function requiring a measure of expertise, the workers participating in the participatory fora would be able to function effectively.

From the foregoing recital it might appear that a large number of issues have been left to be decided by the enterprises themselves. It is indeed so. It is not because that Government could not decide them but they have been deliberately left to be resolved in consultation with the workers' representatives instead of being imposed by Government. The following suggestions are however for consideration

Workers' participation in management means workers participation in the decision-making process. It is based on the assumption that decision-making is not the prerogative of the managers and that the power of taking decisions should be shared with the workers. In other words, the participatory fora are meant to be decision-making bodies and not merely consultative bodies. In 1969, President Keenath Kaunda of Zambia, calling for workers participation in management through works councils is reported to have said:

> "The purpose of the workers/councils will be to provide machinery within the undertaking for the participation of the workers in the management decisions. In certain clearly defined areas which have been traditionally regarded as so-called management prerogatives decisions will only be taken with the participation of the works councils"

The Zambian Industrial Relations Act of 1971 specifies the powers of the workers councils which vary according to the nature of issues and are classified into three categories, namely:

(a) Those issues over which the councils have a veto power,
(b) Those over which the councils must be consulted by management and,
(c) Those about which the councils must be informed.

If the participatory fora are regarded as decision making bodies they cannot be unduly large. The number of workers to be nominated to such bodies can be determined with reference to the number of workers involved. For example, at the plant level, there could be one representative for every 500 or 1000 workers. The number of seats to be allotted to the supervisors could be in the same proportion as the number of supervisors in the organization bears to the vital number of workers.

As regards the mode of representation, the following alternatives are possible: they may be nominated by he recognized trade unions; they may be elected by secret ballot, a third alternative would be a combination of both, e.g., at the shop level election for two-thirds of the seats through secret ballot which may be open to all workers, the remaining seats being filled by nominations by the recognized unions. At the plant level half the seats may be filled by selection and the remaining by nominations by the recognized unions. It should be noted that the Committee on Workers' Participation in Management and Equity had recommended that the representatives at the participative fora should be elected through secret ballot. It may also be noted that in majority of the countries workers on participatory fora are elected through secret ballot but in some there is a combination of election and nomination for specified number of seats.

Since the Central Trade Union organizations are divided on the mode of representation of workers the only way to resolve this conflict would appear to be to have a combination of election as well as nomination; the relative strength of the two groups being decided with reference to the relative strength of the Central Trade Union Organizations in the relevant enterprises. For example, where there is a single union belonging to the INTUC all the seats may be filled by nomination by the union. The ratio of seats to be filled by election and nominations could be infinitely varied.

The Committee on Workers Participation had considered it desirable that the representatives should as far as possible be from amongst the workers employed in the shop or the plant but it had suggested that it would be advantageous to provide inter-linkages in the representation amongst the various fora such a linkage among he participatory for a seems essential.

The Scheme is silent about the number of representatives to be put in the Board. There is therefore greater room for flexibility in this area. To begin with perhaps two or three seats may be reserved for the representatives of workers in the Board.

In this connection a question may arise how the workers are to be given representation in companies having more than one plant. There could be two alternatives: to allot one seat for each plant- this may make the Board unwieldy-, or to rotate the seats among the plants.

The scheme also requires that management and trade union leaders should ensure that there is adequate representation for women in the participative fora where women workers constitute ten per cent or more of the total workforce. This objective can perhaps be served by prescribing a minimum number of seats to be given to representatives of women workers – who should necessarily be women and proportional representation in excess of the minimum.

The Scheme does not specify the term of the participatory bodies. The earlier schemes had provided that the councils once formed would function for two years. Same term could be fixed under the new scheme as well.

The scheme is also silent about who would preside over the participatory fora and who would service them. The scheme introduced in 1975 had provided that the Chief Executive of the Unit should be the

Chairman of the Joint Council and that there should be a Vice-Chairman nominated by the worker-members. It also provided that the Joint Council should appoint one of the members of the Council as its secretary and necessary facilities for the efficient discharge of the functions of the Secretary should be provided within the premises of the undertaking. It envisaged that at the Shop Council the Chairman would be the nominee or the management and the worker members could elect a Vice-Chairman.

Whether the workers are elected or nominated to the participatory bodies there can be no doubt that they represent the workers in general or the trade unions which have nominated them; they cannot therefore function totally autonomously as individuals although they ought to have some authority to exercise their judgment when decisions are to be taken in a hurry. There should therefore be some arrangement for briefing the representatives on matters to be taken up at or to be considered in the various fora. In cases where they are nominated by the trade unions the executive committee of the trade unions may do so. In other cases, it might be necessary to have separate consultative bodies of workers to back up their representatives on the participatory fora.

On the all important question as to how the workers will be able to function in a managerial capacity it is obvious that they need to be trained. I foresee that there may have to be two types of programme; one for publicizing and popularizing the scheme of participation and the second for providing the worker leaders some rudimentary education in management. The first type of programme can be organized by the Central Board of Workers' Education or other institutions specializing in workers' education. It may be necessary to have at least one such programme in each public undertaking during the current year. The second type of programme will have to be organized by institutions specializing in management education. It may be necessary to design a special short term course for this purpose. Just as there are financial management courses for non-financial executives, there could be general management courses for non-executives or labour representatives. Institutes of Management, Management Development Institutes and Universities may be involved in designing and conducting such courses.

The next question to be considered is how often the fora should meet. This is a matter which each forum has to decide for itself. But it could perhaps be provided that each forum should meet at least once in three months. The Shop Level committees can meet more often. The earlier schemes had provided that the Shop Councils should meet once a month and Joint Council once a quarter.

XIV
Wages and Incomes Policy: The Indian Experience

What is Wage Policy?

Wage Policy is understood to mean legislative or administrative action "calculated to affect the level or structure of wages or both, for the purpose of attaining specific objectives of social and economic policy." It implies that the wage rates and the wage structure are regulated by law and/or administered by a state authority.

The ILO Asian Regional Conference held in New Delhi during October 1947, adopted a resolution concerning wage policy and family budget inquiries. According to this resolution "collective agreements between employers and workers are normally the most satisfactory means for the adjustment of wages". The governments have, therefore, been exhorted to assist by all means in their power, the conclusion of such agreements. It is recognized, however, that for various reasons including the comparative lack of organization among the employers and to a greater extent among workers, governments have had to take an active part in the fixing and enforcement of wages. Thus wages policy, according to this resolution, lies in promotion of collective agreements, failing which, fixation and enforcement of wages by government action.

There is little for a government to do in cases where wage agreements are reached by collective bargaining which implies settlement of the issues relating to wages through the free play of the market forces of supply and demand. There are however few countries which have left the wage determination entirely to market forces. Even a country like the USA has had to intervene and to regulate the wages occasionally in times of emergency. But a wages policy is more relevant in the context of a planned economy, more so, in the case of a developing country. In India it has always been an essential element of national development plans.

What are the circumstances which warrant Government action in the field of wages? Government may have to regulate wages in the following circumstances :

(a) Free collective bargaining requires that the two sides, the employers and the workers, are well organized and matched in strength; when they are not, one side takes advantage of the other's weakness. The strength or weakness may not be entirely financial or organizational; it could be strategic. In such a situation, Government may have to intervene to protect the weaker side from exploitation.

(b) Collective bargaining implies that there are only two sides to the bargain; it ignores the third party, namely, the consumer or general public. The employer and the worker may agree between themselves to share the gains of productivity at the expense of the consumer, Government may have to intervene to protect the interests of the consumers.

(c) In a planned economy national development may require that the resources available or generated should be deployed or redeployed in a particular manner necessitating the imposition of austerity and cut-back on the distribution of income in the form of dividends or wages.

(d) In an economy dominated by the public sector since demands and expectations of its employers can only be met by raising resources from the public in one form or the other Government would have to strike a balance between the interests of the workers *vis-à-vis* those of the community at large.

It should thus be obvious that the scope of collective bargaining is rather limited in the unorganized sector, the public sector and the sector in which goods and services essential for the life of the community are produced; correspondingly, the State authorities have a role to play in these areas. Wage policy is therefore concerned mainly with the determination of levels and structure of wages in the areas where the scope for collective bargaining is limited.

Objectives of Wage Policy

What could be the objectives of wage policy? Wage policy is often identified with a policy of wage freeze. But it is wrong to do so. There is no doubt that in the developed countries wage policy has often taken the form of wage control. In the developing countries however wage policy has a more positive role to play. The Third ILO/Asian Regional Conference held in Tokyo in September 1953, considered that it should be the common objective of governments, employers and workers to establish wages at the highest possible level which the economic condition of each country permits and that in future such wages should aim to provide the worker with a fair share of the increased prosperity of the country as a whole resulting from economic development.

In 1966, the Government of India had set up a National Commission on Labour. The Commission in its report, submitted in 1969, analyzed the issues involved in the formulation of a wage policy and concluded, *inter alia,* that the main aim of the wage policy was to bring wages in conformity with the expectations of the working class and, at the same time, to maximize wage employment.

In 1973, the Government of India set up a Committee of Wage Policy. The Committee dealt with the problem of evolving a wage policy for the organized sector of the economy leaving out the Government Sector. The Committee was of the view that the appropriate objectives of a wage policy might, *inter alia,* be:

(a) to ensure minimum wages not lower than the poverty line;
(b) to ensure the workers get a due share in the fruits of growth;
(c) to eliminate or to rationalize wage differentials,
(d) to compensate the workers for the rise in the cost of living; and
(e) to eliminate malpractices in payment of wages, etc.

The Sixth Five-Year Plan enunciated the objectives of wage policy in the following words:

> "The determination of the size and level of wages is linked with the problems of evolving and sustaining a wages structure which while based on accepted notions of fair remuneration of labour takes into account the relevant consideration of economic efficiency and incentive. In a society dedicated to the ideals of social justice, it is doubtful if the wage rate can be left entirely to be determined by the market forces of demand and supply. The accepted purpose of policy is to narrow down the existing inequalities and to eliminate malpractices in regard to wage rate and wage payment.
>
> On the other hand the commitments to the principles of freedom

of association and collective bargaining would require that state regulation should be minimized and it should be limited to ensuring that the weaker sections of labour are not exploited. The tasks of policy here are to lay down criteria for fixation and revision of minimum wages and to evolve wage structure without impinging on the freedom of the parties to negotiate wage agreements."

In the light of these pronouncements the main objects of wage policy in developing countries may be summarized as follows:-

i) to raise the levels of wages where they are unduly low consistent with the needs of economic development;
ii) to obtain for the workers a fair share of the fruits of development;
iii) to protect the real wages from falling under inflationary conditions; and
iv) to protect the wages against malpractices in payment.

Incomes Policy

Wage policy is often distinguished from incomes policy though sometimes, the term 'incomes policy' is used in the sense of being inclusive of wage policy.

The term 'wages' means payment for hired labour; the term 'income' represents the income of the self employed, the income from property, profits earned from trade, business or industry.

There are several classes of hired labour; some are paid very low wages, some are paid very high wages; the others fall between these extremes in various grades. It is said that the earnings of the upper grade employees in an organization are not a pure category at all. "They contain, besides remunerations for labour, elements which are analogous to rent, and quasi-rent, not infrequently, monopoly surpluses also."

In evolving a wage policy one should be clear whether it is concerned with the wages of hired labour only or whether it covers the other incomes also.

This brings us to another problem: whether a wage policy can be evolved independently of the income policy; in other words, whether income other than wages should also be regulated while regulating the wages. Trade union organizations have opposed the concept of a wage policy under the apprehension that it seeks to control the wages while the other incomes remain unchecked. Attempts have therefore been made in

India to evolve an integrated wages, income and prices policy. Such a policy is conceived as an antidote to inflation, its main object being "to ensure that wage increases and increase in other incomes do not outstrip the growth in real national product".

In 1964, the Government of India had appointed a Steering Group to study the problems in the field of income policy. This Steering group had specified the essential objectives of an Incomes and Prices Policy as including "the generation from domestic incomes savings necessary for ensuring non-inflationary financing of investments, the adjustment of domestic demands in such a manner as to minimize the pressure on balance of payments and the narrowing of the disparities in real incomes as between sections of the community through more effective arrangements for distribution of the national product". The conclusions of the Steering Group and the guidelines for a wages and incomes policy drawn up by it are given in Annexure-I.

In October, 1977 the Government of India set up a Study Group to prepare a draft policy on wages, Incomes and Prices. The Study Group submitted its report in May, 1978. The Study Group observed: "Income Policy, as generally understood in the western countries in which they have been tried out or practiced in varying degrees, has usually concentrated on the short-term regulation of income increase as one of the main methods of controlling inflation. As wages constitute the bulk of incomes, income policy in those countries has tended to be equated, in the ordinary man's view with restraint on wage increases in order to prevent inflations," incomes policy has relevance only in the sense of "a consciously integrated set of economic policies designed to increase national income through appropriate economic development, and to bring about a more equitable distribution of the national income but in ways consistent with continued growth". In this sense the scope of an income policy becomes very broad. According to the Study Group "the basic objectives of an integrated income and price policy cannot be different from those nationally adopted for planning economic and social development."

The need for a policy expressed in such broad terms may be undeniable but in a country like India wedded to a social policy of raising the standard of living of the people, a distinctive wage policy which has the object of raising the levels of wages where they are unduly low seems to be more urgent. The Sixth Five-Year Plan of India recognizes this when it says that in India, "the main attention has still to be towards providing employment and also minimum levels of wages so that bulk of the population comes above the poverty line," and that, "the level of minimum wages should be raised in such a manner that soon the concept of a need-based minimum wage becomes a reality."

How to Evolve a Wage Policy?

A policy evolved by an expert sitting in an ivory tower is likely to be suspect as to its motives. This is what happened to the Wages, Incomes and Prices Policy evolved by the Study Group referred to above; it was rejected by the trade union organizations primarily for the reason that they were not associated with it. It is, therefore, desirable that there should be an effective participation of the people concerned in the formulation of policy, as a policy can be implemented only if the public accept it.

There is a persistent demand for a statement on wage policy in India. It has been decided to finalize the statement only after full consultation at a national tripartite conference.

Wage policy cannot also be evolved in isolation of the broad economic issues. Rise in wages, being largely consumption-oriented, may affect employment by reducing the savings available for investment which is the crying need of the hour in most developing countries. It may also affect exports by raising the costs of the exportable commodities. It may under certain conditions lead to inflation. On the other hand, a rise in the wage levels may give an impetus to indigenous production of consumer goods. The wage policy needs, therefore, to be well balanced and co-ordinated with the industrial, fiscal, monetary, import and export policies. It follows, therefore, that in the formulation of a wage policy the persons responsible for policy in other related fields should also be associated. In India, the Planning Commission, the Department of Economic Affairs of the Ministry of Finance and the other Ministries concerned are invariably consulted before formulation of such policies; the State Labour Departments are also consulted.

Elements of Wage Policy

Let us now consider the principal elements of a wage policy.

According to the National Wage Policy Commission of Ceylon (1961), a national wage policy must have two essential components, namely, (i) the principles or rules of wage determination, and (ii) the procedures and machinery for the application of such rules or principles.

According to the Sixth Five-year Plan the issues and problems of the wage policy relate to the elements like need-based minimum wage, protection of the real wages through compensation for rise in the cost of living, incentives for increase in productivity, allowances for hazards of occupations, wage differentials for skills, responsibilities and other justifiable reasons, essential fringe benefits, bonus and other ex-gratia payments, social security arrangements like medical care, provident fund, gratuity, family pension, etc.

The major elements of wage policy can be grouped under the following heads:

(a) Principles of wage determination with reference to (i) Minimum wages; and (ii) Fair Wages
(b) Revision or adjustment of wages due to (i) increase in cost of living, and (ii) increase in productivity
(c) Other components of a wage structure such as Bonus
(d) Wage differentials
(e) Machinery for fixation and revision of wages and allowances.

Principles of Wage Determination

It will be recognized that the most important element of the policy is to determine the quantum of wage to be paid for a particular work done. There are several theories of wages which explain how the levels of wages and changes therein are determined. The classical economists believed in the subsistence theory; John Stuart Mill advanced the wages fund theory. Presently, the marginal productivity theory seems to hold the field. The practical situation is however complex and does not conform strictly to any of the theories, though each of these may have some relevance to the formulation of a wage policy.

In a developing economy, where a large majority of workers is living below the poverty line the major plank of the wage policy would necessarily have to be such as would ensure payment of at least the subsistence level of wage to all workers. At the same time the quantum of wages paid cannot be totally unrelated to productivity and the availability of resources. Wages cannot be paid out of capital for long; if they are, and the capital is eaten up, the unit may have to close down leading to the workers being thrown out of employment. Increase in wages have, therefore, to come out of increase in levels of production. Larger the value of production per worker, the larger could be his share. The value added by production should be the broad limit for increase in wages. Any payment in excess of this will result in erosion of the capital at the micro level and inflation at the macro level.

In India wages are determined in various ways, namely, (i) under the

Minimum Wages Act, 1948, (ii) through adjudication by Industrial Tribunals under the Industrial Disputes Act, (iii) through the mechanism of Wage Boards, or (iv) by collective bargaining. Wage policy is mainly concerned with the first three methods of wage determination. The general principles evolved for determination of wages by these means are analysed below. Before proceeding to this analysis it may be noted that according to the National Commission on Labour the determination of wages implies evolving and sustaining a wage structure which permits, (i) a fair remuneration to labour; (ii) a fair return to capital, and (iii) strengthening incentives to efficiency. These can be said to be the basic principles of wage determination.

Minimum Wages

(a) *Concept :* The major objective of wage policy being to raise the levels of wages, where they are unduly low, fixing of minimum wages becomes the primary task of the policy.

The Asian Advisory Committee of the ILO at its meeting held in 1950 agreed that the immediate need in Asia was for a minimum wage structure which would secure a reasonable living standard from which should emerge, as the economy developed, proper living standards, including a fair share of labour through rising productivity.

Convention No. 131 of the ILO concerning Minimum Wages Fixing requires that each member of the ILO should establish a system of minimum wages which covers all groups of wage earners whose terms of employment are such that coverage would be appropriate."

The wage policy should, therefore, aim at securing minimum wages to all workers within a reasonable period of time.

(b) *Minimum Wages Act, 1948:* India is one of the pioneers in enacting a law for Minimum Wages. The Constitution of India directs the State to endeavour to secure by suitable legislation or economic organizations or in any other way a living wage to all workers. Even before the Constitution was adopted in 1950, the Central Legislature has passed the Minimum Wages Act, 1948. The passing of this Act is considered to be a landmark in the history of labour legislation in the country, perhaps in the whole of Asia. It recognized that wages cannot be left to be determined entirely by market forces which idea has dominated the thinking in India since then. The object underlying the enactment was to prevent exploitation of labour through the payment of unduly low wages.

The Act applied initially to 13 employments including employment in agriculture and it permitted the appropriate Governments to make additions to the list of employments covered by the Act. There are at present over 200 employments in the schedule of the Act.

The Conference of Labour Ministers in India held in July, 1980, recommended *inter alia* that it should be the endeavour of appropriate Governments to prescribe in accordance with the law minimum wages for as many employments as possible by making additions to the schedule to the Minimum Wages Act from time to time. The next Conference held in August, 1981 recommended coverage of practically all the employments not included in the Schedule by prescribing a general minimum wage in respect of such employments.

The Act makes it obligatory on the appropriate Government to fix minimum wages in respect of employments specified in the schedule to it. It provides that, so far as agricultural employments are concerned, the rates of wages might be fixed for the whole State or part thereof. The Act also provides that the minimum wages might be fixed differently for different scheduled employments, different classes of work in the same scheduled employment, adults, adolescents, children and apprentices, and for different localities. Again the rates of wages might be fixed by the hour, by the day, by the month, or by such other larger wage period as may be prescribed. The wages may consist of a basic rate and special allowance adjustable according to the variation in the cost of living index, a basic rate and the cash value of essential commodities supplied free or at concessional rates or be an all-inclusive rate. The Act also provides that in cases of employments for which minimum wages are fixed the appropriate Government may fix the number of hours of work which shall constitute a normal working day providing for a day of rest in every period of seven days and for payment of overtime allowance for work on the day of rest.

(c) *Level of Minimum Wages:* The term minimum wages is not defined. In India four different concepts of minimum wages are prevalent, namely, bare subsistence wage, minimum wage under the Minimum Wages Act, the living wage and the need-based minimum wage.

The Supreme Court of India has explained the distinction between bare subsistence wage and statutory minimum wage as follows: "The former is a wage which would be sufficient to cover the basic physical needs of a worker and his family, that is a rate which has got to be paid to the worker irrespective of the capacity of the industry to pay; if an industry is unable to pay its workmen at least a bare minimum wage it has no right to exist." The statutory minimum wage according to the Court "may be higher than the bare subsistence wage providing for some measure of education, medical requirements and amenities".

In 1948, the Government of India had appointed a Committee to determine the principles on which fair wages should be determined and to suggest the lines on which those principles should be applied. According to this Committee living wage represents a standard of living which provides not merely for bare physical subsistence but also for the maintenance of health and decency, a measure of frugal comfort including education for the children, protection against ill-health, requirements of social needs and some insurance against the more important misfortunes.

The 15th session of the Indian Labour Conference held in July 1957, recommended that minimum wages should be need-based and suggested the following norms for computing it:

(i) The standard working class family should be taken to consist of three consumption units for one earner; the earnings of women, children and adolescents should be disregarded.

(ii) Minimum food requirements should be calculated on the basis of a net intake of 2700 calories for an average Indian adult of moderate activity.

(iii) Clothing requirements should be estimated at a per capita consumption of 18 yards per annum or 72 yards per family.

(iv) In respect of housing the minimum rent charged by Government for houses provided under the subsidized industrial housing scheme for low income groups should be taken into account.

(v) Fuel, lighting and other miscellaneous items of expenditure should constitute 20 per cent of the total minimum wages.

The Committee on Wage Policy set up by the Government of India in 1973 recommended that minimum wages should not be less than the poverty line in the interest of health and efficiency of workers. The Conference of Labour Ministers held in July 1980, also made a similar recommendation. This was reiterated in the subsequent Conference held in August 1981.

Convention No. 131 of the ILO lays down that as far as possible the following facts should be taken into account in determining the level of minimum wages:

(a) the needs of workers and their families, the general level of wages in the country, the cost of living, social security benefits and the relative living standards of other social groups; and

(b) economic factors including the requirements of economic development, levels of productivity and the desirability of attaining and maintaining a high level of employment.

Considering the variety of concepts in vogue it should be obvious that in evolving a wage policy, so far as minimum wages are concerned, the policy-maker has to decide the level at which the minimum wages are to be fixed. This level will vary according to the economic conditions of a country. The demand for payment to all workers need-based wage as recommended by the 15th Indian Labour Conference has been voiced from time to time but it has not been considered feasible so far. The Second Central Pay Commission which went into the question observed that a minimum wage hitched above the level of *per capita* income and intended for very wide application is beyond the country's capacity and that in ignoring the vital need for savings and investment such a wage gives no thought to the future. The majority of the wage boards set up by the Government of India for various industries have also expressed the view that the need-based minimum wage according to the norms laid down by the ILO are beyond the capacity of the respective industries to pay, that it would unduly affect the relativity of wages among the industries in the same region and that it would be extravagant at the cost of the consumer on whom the burden of increased wages would fall.

There could however be no doubt that "at any level of the national income there should be a certain level of minimum wages which the society can afford" and it should be the endeavour of the

Government to determine that level and assure minimum wages to all workers of that level. It would also perhaps be agreed all-round that no minimum wage can in any case be lower than the subsistence wage sufficient to cover the bare physical needs of a workers and his family.

(c) *Criteria for Fixation of Minimum Wages:* The following four criteria are usually followed in fixing the minimum wages :

(a) the needs of workers;

(b) comparable wages;

(c) capacity to pay; and

(d) the requirements of economic development.

As stated above the Supreme Court has held that the bare minimum wage has to be paid irrespective of the capacity of the industry to pay. The National Commission on Labour has expressed the view that the minimum wages should be paid irrespective of the capacity to pay. A similar view has been held by the Committee on Fair Wages in respect of the minimum wages as defined by it. The Supreme Court has however held that any wage above the subsistence wage postulates the capacity of the industry to pay and that no fixation of pay which ignores this essential factor of the capacity of industry to pay could ever by supported.

The conclusion that emerges from this analysis is that capacity to pay is an important criterion except at the lowest level of wages which have to be paid in any case to enable the workers to meet their basic needs. The basic needs of a workers also vary according to the food habits and climatic conditions. These will, therefore, have to be assessed separately area-wise or State-wise. In view however of the difficulties of ascertaining the needs of the workers objectively, the general practice in India has however been to fix the minimum wages with reference to the general level of wages prevailing in the area, or comparable industry or employments. Thus the minimum wages vary from employment to employment, region to region and sometimes even within the same region and it has not been possible to evolve a uniform set of principles for fixing or revision the minimum wages. In this connection, the National Commission on Labour says:

> "Prescribing some rigid criteria in regard to minimum wage fixation is therefore, neither feasible nor desirable. It will necessarily have to be flexible. We are further of the opinion

> that laying down a rigid cash equivalent of the content of a statutory minimum wage whose coverage is essentially transitional under conditions of development would not serve any useful purpose."

Yet, the search for a set of criteria which brings about a greater measure of uniformity and rationality into the fixation of minimum wages is continuing.

(e) *National Minimum Wage:* In this connection it is relevant to mention that the question whether there could be a national minimum wage has been debated for long in this country. The National Commission on Labour had concluded that a uniform national wage in the sense of a uniform monetary remuneration for the country as a whole is neither feasible nor desirable. On the other hand, the Study Group of Wages, Income and Prices considered that the real minimum wage can only be the absolute national minimum irrespective of sectors, regions or States below which no employment would be permitted. The Labour Ministers' Conference held in July 1980, however, decided that national minimum wage is not practicable.

(f) *Genera minimum wage vs. Employment-wise minimum wage:* This brings us to another related issue. The Minimum Wages Act envisages fixation of minimum wages by the appropriate Government employment-wise. The employments to which the Act applies are listed in the Schedule to the Act. A question has arisen as to the rationale of fixing minimum wages on the basis of employment/industry. The practice in other countries in this respect has not been uniform. Some countries have a national minimum wage with regional differentials; others have a system of fixing different minimum wages industry-wise. In a third group of countries the two systems are combined. Fixation of wages industry or employment-wise would be necessary if the capacity to pay is to be taken into account as the capacity of each industry would be different. If minimum wages are to be paid irrespective of the capacity to pay it may be possible to fix general minimum wage on a territorial basis with reference to the basic needs of the workers which may not vary widely in an area or State. The Labour Ministers' Conference held in August, 1981, had therefore, recommended that a system of general minimum wage should be introduced in respect of those employments which are not included in the Schedule to the Act.

Fair Wages

In India, the concept of minimum wages is applied mainly in relation to the employment in the unorganized sector, the so-called sweated industries. These are fixed as explained in the foregoing paragraphs under the Minimum Wages Act.

So far as employments in the organized sector are concerned, wages are fixed generally by collective bargaining, failing which through adjudication by Industrial Tribunals; in some cases they are also fixed by Wage Boards, Pay Commissions and other similar bodies. These bodies follow the principles of fair wages as enunciated by the Committee on Fair Wages, which are set out in annexure-II. The pronouncements of the Supreme Court of India in this regard are given in annexure-III. The basic principle of fair wages is that they should be related to the fair load of work on the one hand and the capacity to pay on the other.

These principles recognize that there cannot be one uniform level of wages for an industry as a whole. Distinction has to be made among the various units of an industry according to their capacity to pay and also according to the region depending upon the cost of living of the area. Capacity to pay varies from unit to unit, industry to industry and region to region. The Committee on Fair Wages has therefore recommended that for ascertaining the capacity to pay the circumstances of the particular industry in specified region should be taken into account. The Supreme Court has also ruled that the principle of industry-cum-region has to be applied to ascertain the capacity to pay.

It is one of the important functions of the wage fixing machinery to determine the capacity to pay before recommending wage rates. In India, many tribunals have recommended determination of the capacity of the industry to pay with reference to the gross profits or gross revenue. The Tribunals for Working Journalists and non-Journalists Newspaper Employees have recommended classification of newspaper establishments on the basis of gross revenue including receipts from all sources; the scales of pay and allowances recommended by the Tribunals vary according to the classification of establishments.

Revision of Wages

Wage rates once fixed cannot remain static for long. They will have to be adjusted from time to time for variation in the cost of living and for improvement in economic conditions. The resolution on wages adopted in 1953 by the Third Asian Regional Conference, therefore, requires that the wages should be subject to review when necessary or at regular intervals. The Minimum Wages Act, 1948, requires that the appropriate Government should revise the wages at least once in every three years and that if as a result of adverse price situation wage rates require adjustment within three years the local authority should make such adjustment. The Labour Ministers' Conference held in July, 1980, recommended that the minimum wages should be reviewed and if necessary revised once at least every two years or on the rise of every 50 points in the consumer price index. The Labour Ministers' conference held in august, 1981, has further recommended that a mechanism should be devised to link the minimum wage to the consumer price index numbers, to the extent possible, so that they can be revised periodically without delay.

There is however no regular periodicity for revision of wages in the organized sector except as provided in the wage agreements. What are the criteria for revision of wages? This is indeed a vexed question. There could be three reasons for revision of wages:

(a) to protect the wages against inflation
(b) to raise the minimum wages so as to approach progressively the need-based level
(c) to share with labour the gains of productivity.

(i) **Cost of living allowances:** The Minimum Wages Act envisages that the minimum wages fixed or revised under the Act may consist of a basic rate and the allowance to be adjusted to the variation in the cost of living index number applicable to such workers or an all-inclusive rate as the case may be. Where a cost of living allowance is given separately, this allowance only will have to be varied according to the variation in the cost of living index. A few States have already attached a dearness allowance to the minimum wages which is adjusted periodically. It has been decided that the others should also follow suit to the extent possible.

There is no uniformity in the D.A. formula adopted by the various governments. In evolving a formula consideration has to be given to the rate of neutralization, periodicity of adjustment and the basis of adjustment. The Supreme Court has ruled that except in the case of the lowest class of manual labourers it is impolitic and unwise to neutralize the entire rise in the cost of living by dearness allowances.

The higher categories of industrial employees cannot claim to be reimbursed to the full extent of the rise in the cost of living, and it is just that they should receive dearness allowance on a graduated diminishing scale based upon the scale of their basic wages. The National Commission on Labour recommended that the basic wages in all cases should be adjusted to a common base year, that dearness allowance should be linked to changes in the index over such a base year, that neutralization should be allowed at the rate of 95 per cent in non-scheduled employments, that capacity to pay is irrelevant for payment of dearness allowance at the minimum level, that a five point slab with reference to the consumer price index would be appropriate for adjustment of dearness allowance. The Study Group on Wages, Incomes and Prices recommended that future D.A. increase should be linked to cost of living on a per point basis and that the periodicity of revision should be quarterly. In practice, however, the arrangements for payment of dearness allowance vary considerably with reference to the linkage base, mechanism of linkage, degree of linkage, periodicity of revision and the degree of neutralization both inter-sectorally as well as intra-sectorally.

The Resolution concerning Wage Policy adopted by the Preparatory Asian Regional Conference held in 1947 required that the cost of living allowance should be measured by index numbers built and periodically revised on the basis of family budget enquiries. The Conference was of the view that the only effective method of judging the standard of living of workers was by means of family budget inquiries designed to ascertain their income and expenditure and the goods and services which they secured. The Conference therefore recommended the desirability of instituting at regular intervals family budget enquiries in association with nutrition experts and representatives of workers' and employers' organizations. In India, such family living surveys are conducted once in ten years and a new series of index numbers are started after each survey.

(ii) **Control of Prices:** In this connection it is relevant to mention the observations of the National Commission on Labour that the existing system of neutralization of a rise in the cost of living either through D.A. or periodic wage adjustment cannot fully safeguard against a fall in real wages. The Commission also observed that increases in money wages had not been associated with a rise in real wages, nor had real wage increases been commensurate with improvements in productivity. The Commission had, therefore, recommended that policies that hold down living costs should form an integrated part of wage policy.

(iii) **Sharing in the fruits of development:** The National Commission on Labour recommended that wage policy should aim at progressive increase in real wages. In India, a large section of the people is living below the poverty line. It is one of the priority objectives of the Sixth Five-Year Plan to raise them above the poverty line. This calls for additional employment and also improvement in the level of wages. But both are related to the development process. There can neither be additional employment nor increase in real wage unless there is economic growth. The Five-Year Plans therefore, emphasize that improvement in wage levels can only be made through increased productivity. The Third Five-Year Plan said :

"Neither the exercise of their organized strength in industrial conflicts nor laws nor the intervention of the state can help the workers much in realizing their aspirations. Their gains can arise only out of the strength and dynamism of the economy, the only enduring basis of which is a rising level of productivity."

The problem here is how to measure productivity and how to relate increase in wages to increase in productivity.

The ILO has observed that wage increases should be related to the rate of growth of labour productivity in the economy as a whole rather than to the rate of growth of labour productivity in particular industries for the single reason that:

"The scope of increased productivity is vastly greater in some branches of production than in others and the extent to which productivity increases in different industries over a period of time often bears little or no relation to the relative efforts and sacrifice made by workers in them....If wages in each separate industry were to increase in proportion to increases in productivity in that industry relative wage in different industries would soon be badly out of alignment and the result would be highly inequitable."

The productivity of an economy is usually expressed in terms of the rate of growth of the gross national product which is estimated for each plan. Distribution of this increase in the gross national product involves, firstly, its allocation between investment and consumption, between public consumption and private consumption, and between private consumption of the workers in the unorganized sector and those in the organized sector. If the real wages of the workers of the unorganized sector have to be improved it is obvious that they should be given a weightage in the distribution of the net G.N.P. by imposing, if necessary, some restrictions on the consumption of the comparatively more affluent.

This is however the theoretical position. In actual practice since wages are fixed and wage settlements take place separately for each industry such a macro approach does not seem to have much relevance.

(iv) **Bonus:** Profit-sharing by means of bonus or similar payments is one way of raising the income of workers. In India, the Payment of Bonus Act provides for payment of bonus on the basis of profits, production or productivity. A significant feature of this Act, however, is that it provides for payment of minimum bonus at the rate of 8.33 per cent of the wages annually irrespective of whether the organization has an allocable surplus or not. Simultaneously, a practice has developed of paying bonus on the basis of productivity to the employees of certain service organizations which do not work for profit. In this context, there has been a protracted debate as to the true nature of bonus. The representatives of the workers have been demanding payment of bonus as a deferred wage while the representatives of the employers have been advocating the philosophy that there should be no question of payment of bonus by an enterprise unless it earns profit. The Government of India had setup a Commission to evolve the principles of payment of bonus. Later, a Committee was set up to review the practices. But the debate has not ended. The Payment of Bonus Act has prescribed a formula for the determination of the amount of bonus payable in any accounting year. According to the formula the payment is subject to a maximum of 20 per cent of wages. Workers have suggested deletion of this provision. It has however been retained in the Act for the reason that unless there is a limit on the payment of bonus there would be very wide disparity in the wage levels among different industries, some of which are able to pay bonus at very high rates while the others may not be able to pay.

In practice, however, several establishments have been paying bonus under the pressure of the trade unions in excess of the maximum prescribed in the Act in the form of *ex-gratia* payment.

Wage Differentials

Wage rates differ from industry to industry and from grade to grade within an industry or establishment. The problem of policy in this regard is how to rationalize the differentials. As the capacity to pay varies according to the industry and the basic needs of the workers vary according to their way of life in different parts of the country, differences in wage rates cannot altogether be eliminated. But they could be minimized. In certain industries where there are wide disparities in wage levels the industries have shown a tendency to migrate to other areas. Even at the level of minimum wages, apprehensions are expressed that because of the disparities in the wage rates in certain industries, such as handloom, beedi, cashew, etc., common to more than one state, there is flight of capital from one State to another resulting in unemployment in the former. Demands are, therefore, often made for fixation of wages in such cases on a regional basis. This is however, opposed by some on the ground of State autonomy. The Study Group on Wage, Income and Prices observed that :

> "the determination of a homogenous national wage structure is very difficult. We are not beginning with a clean slate and the burden of history is with us. Disparities, anomalies and irrationalities exist and have come to be regarded as 'rights'. Further, there is no reasonable method of determining what should be the absolute level of wage for each category of workers and what is aright differential between one category or workers and another."

The Study Group recommended the appointment of a National Pay commission for harmonization of the wage rates among the Central and State governments, appointment of a pay committee for standardization of the scales of pay and allowances in the public sector and certain other guidelines for collective bargaining in the other sectors. The study group also made some recommendations for narrowing the differentials between the lowest and the highest levels of incomes.

The differentials within the industry are more pronounced. This is because of the existence of several grades involving duties and responsibilities varying in kind and importance. If these differentials are to be rationalized it would be necessary to classify the jobs and to conduct their evaluation on a scientific basis. One of the reasons for wide differences in wages and salary scales at different levels is that the supply of talent at higher levels is scarce and therefore they carry scarcity price. A.K. Das Gupta in his book, *Theory of Wage Policy* says :

> "..the scarcity of supply of specialized service is very often contrived. The class structure in the society, the system of education, stipulation of job requirements in various fields, values imputed to the various jobs – all these tend towards the perpetuation of monopoly at higher levels."

He further says that:

> "wage differences in wages and salary scales at different levels are a mark of social backwardness. It is in the nature of social progress that it should be marked over time by an increasing scarcity of unskilled labour and a decreasing scarcity in specialized talent in the market. And if these tendencies are to be reflected in the structure of wages and salaries, wage policy has to be accompanied by supporting measures in the field of education, in particular, and in regard to property relations in general. The aim of policy must be steadily to rub off the distinctions between 'wage' and 'salary' – to create conditions so that while the former move beyond subsistence, the later sheds its excrescences."

In some countries wage rates may also differ according to sex and age. In India, the Equal Remuneration Act passed in 1976 requires that there should be no discrimination in the matter of wages on grounds of sex. It envisages that no employer shall pay to any worker employed by him at rates less favourable than those at which remuneration is paid by him to the workers of the opposite sex and that where the remunerations, payable to men and women workers for the same work or similar work are different on the ground of sex the higher or the highest of such rate shall be paid to all workers.

The Minimum Wages Act provides that different minimum wages may be fixed for adults, adolescents, children and apprentices. In the case of employments for which the Government of India is the appropriate Government, minimum wages payable to persons below the age of 18 years are fixed at 80 per cent of the wages payable to adults. Some of the states have prescribed that adolescents should be paid 80 per cent and children should be paid 50 to 60 per cent of the wages payable to the adults.

Association of Workers and Employers in Wage Determination

The Resolution concerning Wage Policy referred to above requires the Governments of Asian countries to formulate appropriate legislative and administrative measures to set up Wage Boards on which workers and employers will be equally represented, with such members of independent persons as may be considered desirable to fix wages and allowances. ILO Convention No. 26 concerning the creation of Minimum Wages Fixing Machinery requires consultations with the representatives of workers and employers in deciding on the nature and form of the wage-fixing machinery and that they should be associated in the operation of the machinery. There is similar provision in ILO Convention No. 99 concerning Minimum Wage Fixing Machinery in Agriculture.

In India, several Wage Boards were set up in the past on a voluntary basis but the experience with such Boards was not encouraging; in course of time, the practice, therefore, was stopped. At present, there are no Wage Boards at the national level except the one for newspaper employees. There are however certain proposals for setting up Wage Boards for sugar and construction industries. The Labour Ministers' Conference held in 1982 decided that the Central Government should bring forward a legislation for setting up Wage Boards on a statutory basis. Some proposals in this regard were approved by the Conference held in August 1981.

In so far as minimum wages are concerned, the Minimum Wages Act provides for the constitution of Minimum Wages Advisory Boards on a tripartite basis. Minimum Wages cannot be fixed in any case except on the recommendations of these Boards.

In the case of Government employees, fixation and revision of salaries and allowances are done on the recommendations of a Pay Commission or Pay committee which includes representatives of Government as well as the staff with certain independent members. A Committee which reviews the working of the Life Insurance Corporation has recommended recently similar commissions for regulating the salaries and allowances of the personnel employed by Public enterprises.

Protection of Wages

Convention No. 95 concerning protection of wages aims at the prevention of unfair practices in regard to the payment of wages by the prohibition of unauthorized deductions, abolition of abuses concerned with payments in kind, regulation of works stores, periodicity, time and place of payment, treatment of wages as privileged debt and the exemptions from attachment of a part of wages necessary for the maintenance of the workers and his family. In India, statutory provision for protection of wages has been made under the payment of Wages Act, 1936. The scope of this Act is however limited. The possibility of extending its scope is considered from time to time. How to make it applicable to all workers, particularly those in the rural and unorganized sector is another problem confronting the policy makers.

Enforcement of Wages

The resolution concerning wages adopted at the Third Asian Regional Conference requires that the wages fixed by a tripartite machinery should be statutorily enforced with the sanction of penalties sufficiently severe to deter non-observance and that in order to make statutory wage regulation effective there should be an authority in each country fully empowered by law and adequately staffed and equipped, to carry out the responsibility for the enforcement of statutory wage provisions. Convention No. 26 concerning Minimum Wage Fixing Machinery and Convention No. 99 concerning Minimum Wage Fixing Machinery in Agriculture provide that each member who ratifies the convention shall take necessary measures by way of a system of supervision and sanctions to ensure that the employers and workers concerned are informed of the minimum rates of wages in force and that wages are not paid at less than these rates in cases where they are applicable.

Convention No. 131 concerning Minimum Wage Fixing requires that appropriate measures such as adequate inspection reinforced by other necessary measures shall be taken to ensure effective application of all provisions relating to minimum wages.

In India, the Minimum Wages Act requires that ever employer should exhibit in the prescribed manner notices containing prescribed particulars relating to wages and that the appropriate Government might providé for the issue of wage slips of wage books to employees employed in any scheduled employment. The Act also provides for appointment of inspectors with authority to enter any premises where workers are employed for the purpose of examination of any record and to examine any person. Any employer who pays to any employee less than the minimum rates of wages fixed for that employees' class of work or otherwise contravenes the provisions of the Act is punishable with fine and also imprisonment.

Each Government has a Labour Commissioner with an organization of Labour Enforcement Officers and Inspectors whose function it is to inspect the premises of the employers and to prosecute those who violate the law. In cases of non-payment or short payment of wages, these officers receive claims and decide the same after giving due hearing. In some States, the status of Labour Inspector has been given to a wide range of government officials active in rural areas such as Village Development Officers, Revenue Officers, Welfare Officers, and others. Some State governments have also set up tripartite implementation committees at the block and district levels to supervise the implementation of the Act. Review of the laws on minimum wages is one of the 20-point programme of the government of India. Implementation of the Act is therefore given much attention and reviewed at various levels from time to time.

It is difficult to say if this enforcement machinery is quite effective. Several surveys have been carried out to verify the impact of the Act with varied results. One survey showed that nearly 70 per cent of the workers covered, were getting more than the prescribed wages while 5 percent were getting less. Another survey showed that the agricultural workers in one State were getting even during the agricultural season substantially less than the prescribed wages working much longer than the prescribed hours and that during off season wages paid were less than 50 per cent of the prescribed wages.

All the governments have felt the need for strengthening the enforcement machinery. The Sixth Five-Year Plan makes provision for it.

In a country like India with a vast population no official machinery would be adequate for strict enforcement of all labour laws. Many laws would need to be self-enforcing. This can be done if the workers are educated. Gerald Starr in his book, *Minimum Wage Fixing,* published by the ILO says that :

> "a significant proportion of all violations occur because of a lack of awareness by employers and workers of their rights and responsibilities rather than a deliberate intention to flout the law. Information campaigns directed at promoting self-enforcement are likely to be especially cost-effective where, as in most developing countries, trade union organizations and the inspection programme together cover only a limited proportion of the establishments subject to minimum wage laws".

It is observed that the penalties for violation of the laws prescribed in the Act are not deterrent enough. proposals are therefore under consideration for making them more stringent. There are also proposals to set up special courts for labour laws to as to overcome the congestion in the courts and consequent delays in dispensing justice.

In some States like Maharashtra and Orissa public works projects are undertaken in the rural areas wherever the wage levels fall below the minimum rates in an effort to raise wages by providing alternative job opportunities.

With a view to educate the workers as to their rights under the various laws, the government of India has sponsored a Workers' Education Programme. Although workers' education is the normal function of trade unions the Government has taken the initiative in this regard as it helps self-enforcement of the laws. This programme is however administered through a tripartite body of which the Chairman is at present a trade union leader.

In the cases of wages of the workers in the organized sector the Industrial Disputes Act lays down the procedure for settlement of disputes and enforcement of wage agreements. Non-implementation of a settlement is liable to penal action. Where any money is due to a workman from an employer under a settlement or award the workman concerned may approach the appropriate Government and the appropriate Government shall, if it is satisfied that any money is due, issue a certificate to the Collector to recover it as an arrear of land revenue. If there is a dispute on the subject it may be referred to a Tribunal for decision.

Elements of Incomes Policy

Incomes policy as distinguished from wage policy consists of regulation of salaries of higher executives and other non-wage incomes. The idea underlying this policy generally is not to stop the earning of high incomes as such but to prevent conspicuous consumption which according to the Study Group on Wages, Incomes and Prices tend to distort the consumption pattern and consequently the investment pattern diverting the resources to non-priority sectors at the same time creating bottlenecks in vital industries apart from creating social tensions.

The major instrument of regulation of such incomes is personal taxation. The Government of India has also adopted certain direct measures to regulate them.

Income of the Self-employed

There has been no attempt to regulate these incomes except through taxation measures.

Prices and Dividend

Control on dividends is exercised in two ways:

(a) by controlling prices of essential commodities so as to prevent extortionate profits; and
(b) by imposing a ceiling on the amount of profits to be distributed as profit.

Price control is exercised in respect of about 38 commodities apart from agricultural products.

In the case of agricultural products the objective of price policy is to lend support to the efforts to increase overall agricultural production and to induce changes in the cropping pattern corresponding to the perspective levels of demand. What is sought to be done in the case of agricultural prices is generally to fix a minimum or a floor price below which the prices may not fall. There is however nothing to prevent a farmer from obtaining a higher price.

Fixation of the prices in respect of industrial products involves assessment of the cost and determination of a fair return on the capital. The rate of return is determined with reference to the net worth (after tax) as per guidelines issued by the Bureau of Industrial Costs and Prices which vary according to industries depending upon such factors as risk, priority, growth prospects, need for internal generation of funds, degree of obsolescence of capital stock and capital structure. The rate of return allowed limits the amount of dividend that may be declared.

In certain circumstances, a ceiling may be imposed on the percentage of dividend to be declared as an anti-inflationary measure. This was done during the 1970's when ceiling of 12 per cent was fixed for distribution of dividends.

ANNEXURE I

The conclusions of the Steering Group and the guidelines for a wages and incomes policy drawn up by it

(i) Administratively, the scope for regulation of wages is limited to areas of organized industry and economic activity where modern processes of production are used. The problem of wage regulation in agriculture is basically different from the one in industry.

(ii) As a general rule, we should aim at regulating movements in money incomes so as to keep incomes in step with trends in rational productivity moderated to some extent by the need to maintain a growth of consumption slower than productivity.

(iii) In measuring productivity it is necessary to take into account both the long-term and short-period trends, a five years' moving average of the rate of change of productivity in the economy would be a good general guide for regulating changes in money wages.

(iv) The trends in productivity are to be considered as outer limits for wage and income adjustments, so as to prevent increases in wages and incomes from generating inflationary pressure. In actual implementation, however the productivity criterion should be so operated that the entire gains in productivity are not absorbed by immediate increases in consumption. A suitable modification of the productivity criterion would be to allow an increase in wage rates at some combination of the trend rate of growth of productivity and consumption in the economy, both based on five years' moving averages, so as to provide the necessary margin for growth of savings and capital formation in the economy.

(v) Productivity would be rising at varying rates in different sectors. Employees in those sectors where productivity rises faster than the national average may have a claim to get increases in wages somewhat higher than the national average increases in productivity, especially where this is warranted by the contribution of labour to productivity. Correspondingly, wages in other sectors where productivity rises less than the national average would have to rise at rates somewhat lower than national average. The best general rule, however, is to regulate increase in wages and money incomes in different sectors and industries at a rate which not only takes account largely of the growth of productivity in the economy as a whole, but to some extent also of productivity in the sector or industry concerned.

(vi) Productivity-linked wage schemes should in general be such as will enable a part of the benefit of rise in productivity to accrue to the community in the form of lower prices of the products concerned.

(vii) In operational terms, in determining the income levels of various functional groups a variety of other factors such as the basic minimum or need to social amelioration, cost of living increases and incentive wages for the promotion of economic efficiency have to be given due weightage along with the trend in productivity.

(viii) Positive production and price policies are necessary to make an incomes policy effective, because rising prices of essential consumption goods depress real incomes directly and have the indirect effect of accentuating the degree of income inequality. This implies that there should be a closer relationship established between incomes policy and production and investment and price policies.

ANNEXURE II

Principle of Fair wages as enunciated by the Committee on Fair Wages.

1. The living wage represents a standard of living which provides not merely for a bare physical subsistence but for the maintenance of health and decency, a measure of frugal comfort and some insurance against the more important misfortunes.
2. The 'minimum wage' must provide not merely for the bare sustenance of life but for the preservation of the efficiency of the worker by providing for some measure of education, medical requirements and amenities.
3. While, the lower limit of the 'fair wage' must obviously be the minimum wage, the upper limit is set by the capacity of industry to pay. between theses two limits the actual wage will depend on:
   (i) the productivity of labour;
   (ii) the prevailing rates of wages;
   (iii) the level of the national income and its distribution; and
   (iv) the place of the industry in the economy of the country.
4. The wage-fixing machinery should relate a faire wage to a fair load of work and in case of a doubt whether the existing workload is reasonable or not, proper time and motion studies should be instituted on a scientific basis.
5. While rates of wages fixed as a result of proper collective bargaining will bear a close approximation, for he present, to fair wages, the same cannot be said of prevailing wages resulting from unequal bargaining. Due allowance should therefore, be made for any depression of wages caused by unequal bargaining.
6. For ascertaining the "capacity of industry to pay", the capacity of a particular industry in a specified region should be taken into account. This, in turn, can be ascertained by taking a fair cross-section of the industry in the region.
7. As regards the measure of the capacity to pay, the level of wages should be so fixed as to enable industry to maintain production with efficiency. The fair wages fixed should not be out of line with wages in other industries as to cause movement of labour and consequent industrial unrest.
8. It is not possible to assign any definite weight to any of the factors that should be taken into account in calculating fair wages.

9. Where a benefit granted by an employer goes directly to reduce the expenses of a worker on items of expenditure which are to be taken into account for the calculation of the fair wage, it must be taken into account for calculating the fair wage payable.
10. The standard family should be taken as one requiring three consumption units and providing one wage-earner.
11. In the initial stages, in view of administrative and other difficulties, provision need be made for the fixation of fair wages of only categories upto the supervisory level.
12. The appropriate Government should be authorized to appoint wage boards for such industries as it considers necessary from time to time.
13. Fair wages should be determined on an industry-cum-region basis.
14. A number of factors should be taken into account in fixing wage differentials.
15. Where employment is on piece-rates or where the work done by men and women is demonstrably identical, no differentiation should be made between men and women workers regarding the wages payable. Where, however, women are employed on work exclusively done by them or where they are admittedly less efficient than men, the fair wages of women workers should be calculated on the basis of a smaller standard family than in the case of man. The exact size of the family should be decided by the Central Co-ordinating Authority.
16. Basic wages should be fixed in respect of a living index number of 160 to 175, treating the cost of living index number of 1939 as 100.
17. For the lowest categories of wage earners the target should obviously be compensation to the extent of 100 per cent of the increase in the cost of living. For categories above the lowest, a lower rate of compensation is justifiable but he amount of compensation should be on salary scales of slabs.
18. There should be progressive improvement in the fair wage, but such improvement will depend on improvement in the economic conditions of the country and of the industry concerned.
19. In each province a Provincial Wages Board should be set up. Regional Boards for each industry taken up for wage regulation should also be set up according to requirements.
20. A Central Appellate Board should be set up.

ANNEXURE III

Principles of Wage fixation as enunciated by the Supreme Court

In *Kamani Metals & Alloys Ltd. Vs. Their Workmen (1967),* the court observed:

"Fixation of a wage-structure is always a delicate task because balance has to be struck between the demands of social justice which requires that the workmen should receive their proper share of the national income which they help to produce with a view to improving their standard of living, and the depletion which every increase in wages makes in the profits as this tends to divert capital from industry into other channels thought to be more profitable. The task is not rendered any the easier because conditions vary from region to region, industry to industry and establishment to establishment. To cope with these differences certain principles on which wages are fixed have been stated from time to time by the Court. Broadly speaking, the first principle is that there is a minimum wage which, in any event, must be paid, irrespective of the extent of profits, the financial condition of the establishment or the availability of workmen of lower wages. This minimum wage is independent of the kind of industry and applies to all alike big or small. It sets the lowest limit below which wages cannot be allowed to sink in all humanity. The second principle is that wages must be fair, that is to say, sufficiently high to provide a standard family with food, shelter, clothing, medical care and education of children appropriate to the workman but not at a rate exceeding his wage earning capacity in the class of establishment to which he belongs. A fair wage is thus related to the earning capacity and the work load. It must, however, be realized that 'far wage' is not 'living wage' by which is meant a wage which is sufficient to provide not only the essentials above mentioned but a fair measure of frugal comfort with an ability to provide for old age and evil days. Fair wage lies between the minimum wage, which must be paid in any event, and the living wage, which is the goal."

In *Hydro Engineers (Pvt.) Ltd. Vs. Their Workmen (1969)* the court stated :

"It is thus clear that the concept of minimum wages does take in the factor of the prevailing cost of essential commodities wherever such minimum wage is to be fixed. The idea of fixing such wage in the light of cost of living at a particular juncture of time and of neutralizing the rising prices of essential commodities by linking up sales of minimum wages with the cost of living index cannot, therefore, be said to be alien to the concept of a minimum wage."

In *M/s. Unichem Laboatorires Ltd. Vs. Their Workmen (1972),* the court observed :

"In the fixation of wages and dearness allowance the legal position is well established that it has to be done on an industry-cum-region basis having due regard to the financial capacity of the unit under consideration..........Industrial adjudication should always take into account, when revising the wage structure and granting dearness allowance, the problem of the additional burden to be imposed on the employer and ascertain whether the employer can reasonably be called upon to bear such burden...............One of the principles to be adopted in fixing wages and dearness allowance is that the Tribunals should take into account the wage scale and dearness allowance prevailing in comparable concerns carrying on the same industry in the region."

In *Woolcombers of India Ltd. Vs. Woolcombers Workers' Union and* another, the court observed :

".........it is now well settled that basic wage and dearness allowance should be determined in the light of the industry-cum-region formula, and the financial condition of an employer. For fixing basic wages and dearness allowance industrial adjudication sometimes leans on the industry part of the industry-cum-region formula, and he financial condition of am employer. For fixing basic wages and dearness allowance industrial adjudication sometimes leans on the industry part of the industry-cum-region formula and at other times on the region part of that formula. The industry part of the formula becomes relevant when the business carried on by the employer before industrial adjudication is also carried on by several other concerns in the region in which the employer is working...........The region part of the industry-cum-region formula requires that comparable concerns should nearly be similar to the line of business carried on by the employer before industrial adjudication."

ANNEXURE IV

Guidelines issued by the Government of India under the Companies Act, 1956, for regulation of managerial remuneration.

(i) The maximum remuneration payable to managing whole-time or part-time paid Directors, Managers from one or more companies put together, subject to the statutory limits has been fixed as under:

(a) The salary inclusive of dearness allowance and all other fixed allowance should not exceed ₹ 60,000 per annum; for Bombay this ceiling will be ₹ 62,700 per annum:

(b) A commission on net profits upto one per cent of the net profits may be allowed in addition to the salary as an incentive for efficient and sound management, but this should be at least 20 per cent of salary subject to an overall ceiling that salary plus commission would not exceed ₹ 72,000 per annum (bonus will be treated as part of commission):

(c) Where a company proposed to pay remuneration in the form of commission on net profits alone, this shall be subject to a maximum of limit of ₹ 72,000 per annum; and

(d) Henceforward, prerequisites will be restricted to an amount equivalent to the annual salary subject to a maximum of ₹ 60,000 per annum to be reckoned on the basis of actual expenditure or liability incurred by the company as provided under explanation to section 198 of the Companies Act, 1956. There would, however, be separate non-interchangeable ceilings for expenditure on pensionary benefits, medical treatment and housing. Within this overall limit, the perquisites that may be allowed by the company will be as under :

(e) Company's contribution towards Provident Fund :-
Not exceeding 10 per cent of salary as laid down in the Income tax Rules, 1962.

(ii) Company's contribution toward Pension/Super-annuation Fund
Such contribution together with the contribution towards Provident Fund shall not exceed 25 per cent of the salary as laid down in Income Tax rules, 1962.

(iii) Gratuity :

Payable in accordance with an approved fund and which does not exceed one-half months salary for each completed year of series subject to a non-inter changeable ceiling of ₹30,000 or 20 months salary whichever is less.

(iv) Medical benefits for self and family :
Reimbursement of expenses actually incurred the total cost of which shall not exceed of 1 month's salary in a year or 3 month's salary in a block of three years.

(v) Leave travel concession.

(vi) Housing including furniture, fixtures, appliances, gas and electricity :

(A) The expenditure by companies on hiring unfurnished accommodation for their managerial personnel will be subject to the following ceilings :

(a) Bombay : 35 per cent of salary over and above 10 per cent payable by the managerial personnel themselves.

(b) Delhi : 30 per cent of salary over and above 10 per cent payable by the managerial personnel themselves

(c) Calcutta and : 25 per cent of salary over and above 10 per cent
Madras payable by the managerial personnel themselves.

(d) Other Places : 20 per cent of salary over and above 10 per cent payable by the managerial personnel themselves.

(B) The expenditure incurred by the companies on gas, electricity water and furnishings will be valued as per the Income tax Rules, 1962. This will, however, be a ceiling of 10 per cent of salary of the Managerial Personnel.

(C) Wherever companies do not provide accommodation to a managerial personnel, House Rent Allowance may be paid and this would be in accordance with 'A' above. In case of company's own house, managerial personnel will pay 10 per cent of salary as in the case of Government and public sector. (Reimbursement of wages of servant or servants at company's expense are not permissible).

(vii) Free use of company's care with driver :
The monetary value of the perquisite will be evaluated as per rule 3 of the Income Tax Rules, 1962. Not more than one car

will be allowed to a Managing/Wholetime Director/Manager for both official and personal use.

(viii) Personal accident insurance

(ix) However, not more than one telephone will be provided at the residence of the managerial personnel and personal long distance calls have to be logged and paid for by the managerial personnel concerned.

(x) Fees of clubs, subject to a maximum of two clubs. Admission and Life Membership fees to clubs will not be allowed.

REFERENCES

1. *Wages – A Workers' Education Manual,* International Labour Office, Geneva.
2. *Problems of Wage Policy in Asian Countries,* International Labour Office, Geneva.
3. *Minimum Wage Fixing and Economic Development,* International Labour Office, Geneva.
4. *Gerald Starr, Minimum Wage Fixing – An international Review of Practices and Problems,* International Labour Office.
5. *Wage Policy Issues in Economic Development,* ed. By A.D.Smith, MacMillan.
6. K.N.Subramanian, *Wage in India,* Tata McGraw-Hill Publishing Co. Ltd.
7. *Report of the National Commission on Labour,* Government of India Publication.
8. *Report of the Study Group on Wages Incomes and Prices,* May 1978; Government of India Publication.
9. A.K.Dasgupta; *Theory of Wage Policy,* Oxford University Press.
10. *Report of the Committee on Fair Wages,* Government of India Publication.
11. *Sixth Five-Year Plan,* Government of India Publication.
12. *Report on a Framework for Incomes and Price Policy,* Reserve Bank on India.
13. Minimum Wages Act, 1948.
14. Payment of Wages Act, 1936.

XV
Workers Education

Workers Education - The Concept

Workers Education is the key element in the development of the Trade Union Movement and it is essential for its success. It is the aim of Workers Education to help the workers to organize themselves and to run the organizations.

Organization is the essence of life. By organization diverse forces are integrated and life is infused into the body. Lack of organization results in disintegration and decay.

Trade unions are the organizations of workers. Through such organizations the workers acquire a new body, a new life much more strong and forceful than an individual can be. In the absence of such organizations the workers remain weak and tend to be exploited. Witness the difference in strength between organized labour and the rural workers who are not organized. One of the measures contemplated for the uplift of the rural unorganized labour is to help them to organize themselves. Their education is the first step in that direction.

By education, the workers become aware of their status and how they can improve it. They are awakened from a sense of resignation to what Gods have willed for them to the realization of what they can achieve by human effort. Their ambition is kindled and they become conscious of their rights and their might. They develop confidence that they can do better and are prompted to strive for their betterment. Education helps them to realize that there is greater strength in unity

There is no end to education. The learning to live is a continual process. After an organization is formed one ought to know once role in the organization. The role may not remain the same; one plays different roles at different times.

The World is in a state of flux. Change is the order of the day. One has to adjust oneself to the change, that occur in one's environment. The workers organizations also have to change according to the changing times. It means that the members of the organizations have to learn new things and re-orient themselves from time to time.

We, in this country, have a total workforce of about over 400 million all of whom need education in one form or the other. One organization like the Central Board of Workers' Education (CBWE) cannot reach them all. This activity has necessarily to be de-centralized. While the CBWE can function as the nodal organizations, trade unions and other voluntary organizations have to function more actively in the field. We expect that ultimately the trade unions will take-over the entire programme.

In order to encourage the trade unions to develop their own Workers Education programme, the CBWE gives grants-in-aid to the extent of 90 per cent of the expenditure incurred by them in running the classes. Many unions have availed of this facility.

There is a large mass of unorganized labour in this country. The Central Board for Workers Education wishes to give greater attention to the education of these people in future. This can be done only if the responsibility for Workers Education in the organized sector is shared by the trade unions. For this purpose, trade unions should develop their own resources and the necessary infrastructure with such assistance as may be necessary from the Board, giving appropriate priority for running the workers education programme with in their plan-of-action.

The CBWE has lately expanded its programme to include Population Education, Functional literacy, Productivity Education, Workers Participation in Management etc. It is now proposed to widen the programme further to provide a forum for a campaign against the social evils like dowry, casteism, communalism and also for educating the workers in the functioning of democratic institutions etc.

Scope of Workers Education

The Asian Regional Conference of the International Labour Organization held in Manila passed a resolution concerning Workers' Education. This resolution *inter alia* calls for

(a) encouragement of the workers' education programme designed to promote the full involvement of workers in the formulation of policies which will affect substantial social and economic progress;

(b) expansion of workers' education activities for rural workers' organizations especially those designed to promote participation by the membership and the training of educators/organizers;

(c) promotion of activities to meet particular needs such as those of women and young workers; and

(d) promotion of the development of teaching and audio-visual aids for workers' education with special emphasis on country-specific materials.

While considering a technical item on Rural Workers, the Conference again stressed the importance of rural workers' education in the context of the need to develop effective self-reliant organizations of rural workers. The Conference observed:

> "Freedom to organize does not guarantee the development of effective organizations because it generally needs to be supplemented by educational activity to assist the members and their elected leaders to acquire the technical know-how for the successful running of the organization. It is necessary as part of educated activities to ensure that the ordinary members understand and are able to exercise their individual rights and responsibilities; that they know how to participate within their organizations and thus enable it to effectively defend and further their interests".

We have voted for these decisions and we have the responsibility to implement the same.

Whenever the Trade Union leaders meet the Prime Minister a plea is made for workers' participation in the formulation of national policies. But workers cannot actually participate in policy formulation unless they are able to understand the policy proposals and appreciate the significance thereof.

Participation by proxy through political leaders will not be the same thing as direct participation. If, therefore, workers have to participate effectively in the national affairs they have to be properly educated. The ultimate goal of the scheme of workers' education can be deemed to be achieved only when the workers are enabled to do so. It calls for a systematic programme response to the needs of the workers collectively and individually.

The need for extending he scheme of workers' education to cover the rural workers is well recognized. This need has been felt for long. It is only through their education and organization that they can derive the full benefit of the welfare legislation and other measures that are initiated by Government. It will however be difficult for any organization of this kind to reach the rural workers directly. They have to be approached through educators and organizers. I understand that the Central Board of Workers' Education has drawn up a scheme for training the educators/ organizers.

The International Labour Organization has called for promotion of activities to meet particular needs such as those of women and children. We have a large number of child workers. It is not easy to eliminate child labour at this stage of development of the country. We can only hope to make some arrangements for their education and health so that the children who have necessarily to work do not suffer from retarded development. The kind of education that the child workers need would be different from that of adult workers though some adults too need basic education. They cannot attend formal schools and colleges. They should be taught within their work environment. This can only be cone through a scheme of workers' education which may be specially designed for the purpose.

Central Board of Workers' Education should have separate scheme for young workers designed to develop the full potential of those workers who are deprived of formal education but have talent so as to channelize it to the advantage of the nation.

There is also a need for a special programme for women. The Asian Regional Conference observed:

> "Rural women constitute the most dis-advantaged sections of the rural society. They generally occupy low productivity, low income occupations and are grossly over worked. They are discriminated against in terms of access to education, health and training facilities. There is a need to awaken the consciousness of men to women's problems". There is greater need to awaken the consciousness of women themselves to their lot and how it can be bettered.

This brings us to the question of adult education. At the instance of the Ministry of Education the Central Board of Workers Education has been selected as an agency for the National Adult Education Programme. According to a programme approved sometime back the Board should have set up about 2500 adult literary centers by the beginning of this year. I believe that this target has not been achieved. I feel that the Board should make up the deficit.

I consider that population education is an important element in workers' education. It should in my opinion be built into the regular syllabus. The International Labour Organization has envinced keen interest in this and has offered financial assistance for promoting population education among the workers in this country. We have an International Labour Organization project for this purpose. I suggest that the Board make full use of that project.

There is an equal need for promoting productivity education. It is necessary to inculcate among the workers the concept of productivity – the need for adding value – that we cannot live on our capital and that we have to generate incremental value; larger that value, the greater will be the prosperity.

Workers education tends to place much emphasis the rights of workers. I feel that there should be equal emphasis on the duties of the workers The Constitution of India originally had only a set of fundamental rights. Later a set of fundamental duties was added. Of these, I consider that the duty enshrined in Clause (i) of Article 5(A) is the most important. This Article enjoins upon every citizen "to strive towards excellence in all spheres of individual and collective activity so that the nation constantly rise to higher levels of endeavour and achievement". We should all work for excellence in whatever walk of life. Workers' Education scheme should aim at excellence and for excellence.

Workers Education in the Rural Sector

The problems of education of rural workers has to be considered in the context of the obstacles and constraints under which they live. The social and economic structures in the rural areas are such that they militate against their organization. It calls for considerable time and effort before we can make any head way. First, an awareness should be created among them concerning their economic, social and cultural environment and then they have to be motivated to organize themselves. But these efforts will not succeed unless the feelings, problems, views, attitudes and aspirations of the peasants are fully understood. The would be educators have to identify themselves with peasants. The rural workers suffer from a sense of isolation. They feel that they have no control over natural phenomena, prices of produce, land owners, Governments and Law Enforcement Officers and they frequently are not aware of their legal and social rights. The sense of helplessness should be overcome. It calls for much patience to make the workers appreciate that, through organization, they can achieve those essential changes which they cannot bring about as individuals and to convince them that organization can help them to attain their rights. Their confidence should be won by recognizing their immediate and latent needs and helping to meet those needs. It is only then that the process of education becomes effective.

In the early stages the work will be slow and the achievements will be small but once a sound basis is established the going will be easier.

It is needless to say that consistent with the change in the field of activity the methods of operation have also to change. To be meaningful the methods and techniques of workers' education should aim not only at enhancing the effectiveness of the workers organization and its ability to promote and defend workers' interests but also at equipping individual members of the organization with the understanding, knowledge and technical skills required better to meet the wide range of social, economic, cultural and rural problems they face on a daily basis. I am not myself an educationist but I believe that the best educational methods are those which stimulate inter-active learning and promote full collective and individual participation in the learning experience. The cultural heritage and existing folklore should be creatively used in developing appropriate teaching aids and techniques. While the lecture method has some merits the other methods including group discussion, exchange of experiences, study circles, role play and skits should be adopted. Audio Visual aids such as slides, films, radio and television should be used along with more traditional teaching aids such as the blackboard, etc. The method to be used will vary according to the situation. The educators should, therefore, be innovative. I understand that the Indian Institute of Workers' Education which is part of the Central Board is responsible for training the education officers. This Institute should in my opinion evolve new methods and aids for workers' education according to the changing needs.

In dealing with the problems of Workers' Education we are apt to concentrate on the organizations and methods aspect than on the substantive aspect of the content of education. I consider that the syllabi and the course content are more important for it is through these that the objectives of workers' education are translated into concrete form and the true worth of education is realized.

Schemes of this kind need to be evaluated from time to time. The CBWE has set up a committee to look into the working of the programme. The Review Committee has done a signal service in bringing to light the impressions the Scheme has created among the workers and employers. It would appear from the report of the Committee that although the Central Board has done pioneering work in the field and a large number of workers have been trained its achievements in the fulfilment of its objectives has not been very perceptible; in other words the impact of the scheme has not been felt significantly enough. Similar reviews should be done periodically, not necessarily by an out-side agency. The Board itself and each of you in your respective areas of operation should elicit public opinion instead of working in isolation. You should have much closer association with the State Government agencies, Labour Institutes, Trade Union Organizations and Organizations of employers. Institutional arrangement should be made for such associations. You may like to discuss the modalities of such arrangements.

Integration of the Institutional Set up

There are several organizations, some of which are autonomous, under the Ministry of Labour engaged in workers education. There is a general feeling that their activities overlap. I understand that this question was discussed in the past but no definitive conclusions were reached and no concrete step has been taken to reorganize the work of the organizations. Some time back the then Chairman of the CBWE in one of his addresses made a pointed reference to the fact that there was duplication of efforts in the field of workers' education and suggested some measures for rationalization and integration of the organizations concerned and their activities so as to pool the resources available and to make better use of the same. Several meeting were held to consider these suggestions but it does not seem that there been any change in the arrangements

In this connection it may be mentioned when the Chief Technical Adviser of the Asian Regional Project for Labour Administration of the ILOvisited India some years back a suggestion was mooted that an Asian Labour Institute could be established in India to serve the needs of the whole region in the matter of training and Research. Before an Asian Institute can be constituted it seems necessary to have a counterpart Indian Institute to function as an umbrella for diverse activities under a unified/co-ordinated direction. We may also consider what form such an institute should take and whether a new body should be created for the purpose or an existing one can be converted into an institution of national importance.

Education in Participative Management

We should first be clear what we mean when we talk of 'Participative in Management'.

As I understand it, the term 'Participative Management' is the opposite of autocratic management, that is, management by the will of the manager. It means a cooperative endeavour where everyone engaged in it works for the achievement of a common goal. It implies that there would be an identity of the goals of the relevant activity and a joint effort to achieve these goals. In such an endeavour each person has a role to play and there will be no distinction between the manager and the managed. It helps to remove class consciousness and class conflict; it brings about a harmonization of the interests of all concerned. This is a new philosophy which, if properly understood and implemented, can provide an effective alternative to the economic systems which breed conflicts and strife.

The term 'management' covers a broad spectrum of functional roles. We may conceive of management of an economy, industry or service. We can conceive of management at shop level, plant level, corporate level or at the industry level. We may also talk of management of production, marketing, personnel or finance. Whatever the concept may be, the object of participative management is the same, namely, sharing of the responsibility, information and full involvement of workers in the processes leading to decision-making in the management of an activity. For example, the Planning Commission before it finalized the Sixth Five Year Plan, had discussions with the leaders of Trade Unions as well as Employers' organizations with a view, firstly, to ascertain their views on the Plan objectives, assumptions and the strategies proposed to be adopted, and secondly, to secure their cooperation in the implementation of the Plans. However, Sound a Plan may be on paper, it is of no consequence unless it is implemented properly and the implementation of the plan depends to a large extent on its acceptance by the people, their willing involvement and active participation in it. The plan therefore lays stress on public participation; participation of workers on the basis of equality with the managers in the management of an activity is a kind of participation which the planners look for.

There may be differences of opinion as to the best form or method of participation; undoubtedly there are. There may be practical difficulties in giving shape to the idea. For example, a question has arisen as to how the representatives of workers should be selected. But I feel that if the idea is accepted, means can be found; forms and procedures can be evolved to suit each situation.

The basic issue is to secure acceptance of the principle. This can only be done through a process of education. This should be given not only to the workers but also to the managerial personnel. We have introduced some schemes of workers' participation in management in this country. But I am sorry to say that they have not made much headway. It is because there is a good deal of misunderstanding as to the nature and purpose of workers' participation. Both employers as well as workers and trade unions seem to have some reservations about them and their wholehearted support is not forthcoming. It is therefore necessary and urgent that both the parties should be educated so as to remove their apprehensions, misconceptions and inhibitions about the schemes of workers participation in management. In this setting, I welcome initiative taken by the Central Board of Workers' Education to educate the workers and managers together on this most vital reform which the economic organization of the country needs.

Methods, Techniques and Tools of Workers Education

Workers Education in India has made great progress during the last fifty years thanks to the pioneering role played by the Central Board of Workers Education. There is however no information about the total number of workers benefited by the programme. There is however no doubt that considering the total number of workers in the country there is vast scope for extension of workers education; it has also to grow in different directions. Extension of the scheme physically and coverage in numbers are the least part of the problem. The more important part of it is to ensure that it will have the desired impact.

Volumes have been written about the impact of workers education in India. The general impression however is that the impact has been marginal; in the absence of a scientific evaluation of the scheme it is difficult to verify the correctness of the impression. There can however be no difference of opinion that there is need and scope for improvement.

While the extension of workers education depends on the physical and financial arrangements improvement in the quality of education depends on the soft-ware development of appropriate methods, techniques and tools of education. If workers education has to have the desired impact we should give as much, if not, greater attention to the soft-ware development as to the physical arrangements. I am not certain that it has been given due attention.

The Board consists mostly of representatives of trade union organizations, employers organizations and Secretariat officials and general administrators. Barring the sole representative of the University Grants Commission, there are no educationists in the Board. The technical aspects of education is therefore left largely to the official functionaries of the Board. It is desirable that if the Board has to give high level direction to the functionaries a few experts in the field of education should be inducted into it either as members or as advisers.

In developing the soft-ware the first thing that needs to be done is to design the appropriate types of courses keeping in view the needs of the target groups. The Board has developed a few standard types of courses namely, the course for education officers, the course for worker-teachers and the courses for grass-root workers. There seems to be need for designing more diversified courses at different levels. In this connection it may be relevant to point out that in the United Kingdom the Workers Education Scheme provides for courses for union representatives in four stages, which are called Induction Courses, Basic Introductory Course, Further Training course and the Advanced Course. The introductory course is meant for newly elected shop stewards, staff representatives and safety representatives, etc. It describes the job of shop stewards, their inherent responsibilities as well as the facilities available. It includes issues on trade union organization, collective bargaining and the improvements in wages and conditions, etc. The central aim of this course is to help participants become more effective as union work place representatives. It develops organizational skills such as talking to members and interviewing them, chairing meetings, reporting the proceedings, preparing plans for negotiation and negotiating with management. Training is also imparted in writing notes, reports and letters, filing and retrieving information, etc. The next course provides in-depth training in relevant subjects and skills. At the third stage training is imparted in work study, job evaluation and such other subjects. The Advanced Course is meant for persons serving on company boards.

Consequent on the introduction by Government of mandatory scheme of workers participation in management at various levels it seems necessary that the CBWE should also design courses to enable the representatives of workers to function effectively in the participatory bodies at various levels.

The courses conducted by the CBWE are clearly of two kinds: the education officers' courses and the workers-teachers courses whereby the candidates are trained to be teachers. The unit level classes are the real educational courses. The first two types of courses are intended to equip the teachers adequately so that they may be able to conduct the last type of classes effectively. The syllabi of these two types of courses will therefore have to be different and greater attention will have to be given in the former type of course to methods, techniques and tools of education than to the themes of education. While in the last type of courses the educational themes are all-important.

The workers education syllabi were recently reviewed by a committee set up by government. I was a member of the committee. Although the committee did give some consideration to the inclusion of methods of education in the syllabi for the education officers course and the worker-teacher courses, in retrospect, it seems to me that considering that there are essentially training schemes, methods, techniques and tools have perhaps not been given adequate attention in the syllabi for these courses. It may be worthwhile to have these syllabi scrutinized by a team of educational experts. It may also be worthwhile to request the ILO to make the services of a few experts available to the Board for the purpose. I would propose that the Board consider these suggestions.

I have been using in this speech three different expressions, namely, methods, techniques and tools. I am sure that I do not have to explain to this audience the difference in the meaning of these expressions. Method is defined as a combination of techniques; a technique is the procedure adopted for education such as lecture or discussion. Tools are the devices such as blackboards, charts, posters, etc. The educator should know and be well versed in all the techniques of education and should be able to design and use the necessary tools. The actual method, meaning the technique or techniques and tools he may use depends upon the situation and the educator should be able to choose the method appropriate to a situation. No one technique or method may be suitable in all circumstances and it may be necessary to vary them as the circumstances warrant. The educator should be able to do so.

The traditional method of education is the lecture method. This is now considered to be the most ineffective method and it has therefore given place to other new methods. There was an Asian Regional Seminar on New Methods and Techniques in Workers Education in March 1973 in Quezon city, Phillippines. This Seminar recognized inter alia that :

> Traditional teaching methods may fail to achieve the purpose of education which is to enable a person to express thoughts and develop abilities whereas new methods and techniques provide an inbuilt system of effective communication. In the traditional instructor-student situation, it is assumed, that one person, the instructor has knowledge and that it is his task and responsibility to transmit it to the student. The instructor will thus lecture, explain and ask questions. The student will listen, take notes and eventually reply. In the new methods which are based upon psychological and sociological studies of the communication and the learning processes there is a constant exchange of

information and reactions between the participants themselves. In this method, known as the Labouratory Method, it is assumed that the knowledge will be discovered by the student operating in a group. The task of the instructor is to create situations wherein the student experiments with his ideas, gains experience and draws his own conclusions. Group dynamics motivates the participants for in-depth study and creative thinking, and encourages full participation wherein the ideas, experience and knowledge of the participants are utilized in problem solving. Group dynamics enhances behaviourial changes which given self-confidence and development of leadership qualities. While group dynamics is a sophisticated method of teaching it can be a functional and effective method of workers education.

The National Labour Institute has tried group dynamics with great success in conducting its rural labour camps with the result that they are looked upon as a model.

I believe that the officers of the CBWE have also been using this method but my impression is that it needs to be perfected. The education officers who train the workers-teachers in the methods of education are themselves trained in the Institute of Workers Education where they undergo the education officers course. This course is of six months duration. In my conviction that this is too short a period. Teachers training for primary and secondary schools takes much longer time. By the same token the education officers of the CBWE as well as the worker teachers need to be given more intensive training in teaching methods. It may be worthwhile if the education officers are given opportunity for further training in established labour colleges such as those existing in Scandinavian Countries with a view to reinforce their skills in new methods and techniques based on group dynamics.

Index